AVID

READER

PRESS

ALSO BY GILLIAN TETT

Saving the Sun

Fool's Gold

The Silo Effect

ANTHRO-VISION

A NEW WAY TO SEE IN BUSINESS AND LIFE

GILLIAN TETT

AVID READER PRESS

NEW YORK LONDON TORONTO SYDNEY NEW DELHI

AVID READER PRESS
An Imprint of Simon & Schuster, Inc.
1230 Avenue of the Americas
New York, NY 10020

First Avid Reader Press hardcover edition June 2021

AVID READER PRESS and colophon are trademarks of Simon & Schuster, Inc.

For information about special discounts for bulk purchases, please contact Simon & Schuster Special Sales at 1-866-506-1949 or business@simonandschuster.com.

The Simon & Schuster Speakers Bureau can bring authors to your live event. For more information or to book an event, contact the Simon & Schuster Speakers Bureau at 1-866-248-3049 or visit our website at www.simonspeakers.com.

Interior design by Ruth Lee-Mui

Manufactured in the United States of America

3 5 7 9 10 8 6 4 2

Library of Congress Cataloging-in-Publication Data has been applied for.

ISBN 978-1-9821-4096-0
ISBN 978-1-9821-4098-4 (ebook)

Dedicated to the memory of

Ruth Winifred Tett and

Katherine Ruth Gilly (Tett),

who both took joy from the "familiar,"

but were always curious about "strange"

"The least questioned assumptions are often the most questionable."

—PAUL BROCA

"Research is formalized curiosity. It is poking and prying with a purpose."

—ZORA NEALE HURSTON[1]

CONTENTS

PREFACE

THE OTHER "AI"

(OR ANTHROPOLOGY INTELLIGENCE)

"The last thing a fish would ever notice would be water."

—Ralph Linton[1]

I sat in a drab Soviet hotel room in May 1992. Gunfire rattled the windows. Across the room, on a bed with a nasty brown blanket, sat Marcus Warren, a British journalist. We had been trapped in the hotel for hours, as battles raged on the streets outside in Dushanbe, the capital city of Tajikistan. We had no idea how many had died.

"What did you do in Tajikistan before?" Marcus asked me, as we nervously listened to the fighting. Until a year earlier this mountainous country, bordering Afghanistan, had seemed a permanent and peaceful part of the Soviet Union. But in August 1991 the Soviet regime had collapsed. That dissolution had propelled the country to independence and sparked a civil war. Marcus and I were there as reporters, respectively for the *Daily Telegraph* and the *Financial Times*.

But my background was weird. Before I joined the *Financial Times*, I had been based in Tajikistan doing research for a PhD in anthropology, that oft ignored (and sometimes derided) branch of the social sciences that studies culture and society. Like generations of earlier anthropologists, I had engaged in fieldwork, which meant immersing myself in a high mountain village a three-hour bus ride from Dushanbe. I lived with a family. The aim was to be an "insider-outsider," to observe the Soviet villagers at close quarters and study their "culture" in the sense of their rituals, values, social patterns, and semiotic codes. I explored questions such as: What did they trust? How did they define a family? What did "Islam" mean? How did they feel about Communism? What defined economic value? How did they organize their space? In short: *What did it mean to be human in Soviet Tajikistan?*

"So what exactly did you study? Marcus asked.

"Marriage rituals," I replied.

"Marriage rituals!" Marcus exploded, hoarse from exhaustion. "What the hell is the point of *that*?" His question masked a bigger one: Why would anyone go to a mountainous country that seemed weird to Westerners and immerse herself in an alien culture to study it? I understood his reaction. As I later admitted in my doctoral thesis: "With people dying outside on the streets of Dushanbe, studying marriage rituals did sound exotic—if not irrelevant."[2]

This book has a simple aim: to answer Marcus's question—and show that the ideas emanating from a discipline that many people think (wrongly) studies only the "exotic" are vital for the modern world. The reason is that anthropology is an intellectual framework that enables you to see around corners, spot what is hidden in plain sight, gain empathy for others, and fresh insight on problems. This framework is needed more than ever now as we grapple with climate change, pandemics, racism, social media run amok, artificial intelligence, financial turmoil, and political conflict. I know this from my own career: as this book explains, since I left Tajikistan, I have worked as a journalist and used my anthropology training to foresee and understand the 2008 financial crisis, the rise of Donald Trump, the 2020 pandemic, the surge in sustainable investing, and the digital economy. But this book also explains how anthropology is (and has been) valuable for business executives, investors, policy makers, economists, techies, financiers, doctors, lawyers, and accountants (yes, really). These ideas are as useful in making sense of an Amazon warehouse as in an Amazon jungle.

Why? Many of the tools we have been using to navigate the world are simply not working well. In recent years we have seen economic forecasts misfire, political polls turn out to be wrong, financial models fail, tech innovations turn dangerous, and consumer surveys mislead. These problems have not arisen because those tools are wrong or useless. They are not. The problem is such tools are *incomplete*; they are used without an awareness of culture and context, created with a sense of tunnel vision, and built assuming that the world can be neatly bounded or captured by a single set of parameters. This might work well when the world is so stable that the past is a good guide to the future. But it does not when we live in a world of flux, or what Western military experts describe as "VUCA," short for "volatility, uncertainty, complexity, and ambiguity." Nor when we face "black swans" (to cite Nassim Nicholas Taleb), "radical uncertainty" (as the economists Mervyn King and John Kay say), and an "uncharted" future (to quote Margaret Heffernan).[3]

Or to put it another way, trying to navigate the twenty-first-century world only using the tools developed in the twentieth-century, such as rigid economic models, is like walking through a dark wood with a compass at night and *only* looking down on the dial. Your compass may be technically brilliant and tell you where to aim. But if you *only* focus on the dial, you may walk into a tree. Tunnel vision is deadly. We need lateral vision. That is what anthropology can impart: anthro-vision.

This book offers extensive ideas about how to gain anthro-vision, using personal and third-party stories that explore questions such as: Why do we need offices? Why do investors misread risks? What matters to modern consumers? What should economists learn from Cambridge Analytica? What is driving green finance? How should governments Build Back Better? How does culture interact with computers? Before plunging into the details, however, there are three core principles of the anthropology mindset that are the most important to grasp, and which shape the structure of this book. The first idea is that in an era of global contagion, we urgently need to cultivate a mindset of empathy for strangers and value diversity. Anthropologists are experts in this since the discipline was founded around the goal of venturing to far-flung places to study seemingly "exotic" peoples. That creates a whiff of Indiana Jones. But that tag is misleading.[4] "Exotic" is in the eye of the beholder since *every* culture can seem strange to another and nobody can afford to ignore what seems strange in a globalized world (or dismiss other cultures as "shitholes," as former president Donald Trump did). Flows of finance, commerce, travel, and communication connect us, creating constant contagion, involving not just germs but money, ideas, and trends. However, our understanding of others has not expanded at the same pace as our interconnections. That creates risks *and* tragically missed opportunities. (Chapter Three explains that if only Western policy makers had bothered to learn some lessons from "strange" countries in West Africa or Asia, they would never have fallen prey to the COVID-19 pandemic.)

The second key principle of anthropology is that listening to someone else's view, however "strange," does not just teach empathy for others, which is badly needed today; *it also makes it easier to see yourself.* As the anthropologist Ralph Linton observed, a fish would be the last person to see water; it is easier to understand people in contrast to others. Or to cite an idea developed by another anthropologist, Horace Miner: "Anthropology alone amongst the sciences strives to make the strange familiar and the familiar strange."[5] The aim is to increase our understanding of *both.*

Third, embracing this strange-familiar concept enables us see blind spots in others and ourselves. Anthropologists are almost like psychiatrists, but instead of putting individuals on the couch, they place *groups* of people metaphorically under their lens, to see the biases, assumptions, and mental maps that people collectively inherit. Or, to use another metaphor, anthropologists use an X-ray machine to look at society, to see half-hidden patterns we are only dimly aware of. This often shows us that even if we think "x" is the reason why something has happened, it might actually be "y."

Consider an example from the insurance world. Back in the 1930s, executives at the Hartford Fire Insurance Company in Connecticut realized that warehouses which contained oil drums kept blowing up. Nobody knew why. The company asked a fire-prevention engineer named Benjamin Whorf to investigate. Although Whorf was a trained chemical engineer, he had also done research in anthropology and linguistics at Yale, with a focus on the Hopi Native American communities. So he approached the problem with an anthropologist's mindset: he observed warehouse workers, noting what they did and said, trying to absorb *everything* without prior judgment. He was particularly interested in the cultural assumptions embedded in language, since he knew these could vary. Consider seasons. In English, "season" is a noun, defined by the astronomical calendar ("summer starts on June 20," people say). In the Hopi language and worldview "summer" is an *adverb* defined by heat, not the calendar (it feels "summer(y)").* Neither is better or worse; but they are *different*. People cannot appreciate this distinction unless they compare. Or as Whorf observed: "We always assume that the linguistic analysis made by our group reflects reality better than it does."[6]

This perspective solved the oil drum mystery. Whorf noticed that

*Some academics, such as Ekkehart Malotki and Steven Pinker, have criticized Whorf's work, suggesting he said (wrongly) that the Hopi had no concept of time. That seems a misreading of Whorf's argument. Without wading into the controversy, the key point is this: people's vision of the calendar and time varies, and is not universal.

the workers were careful when handling oil drums marked as "full." However, workers happily smoked in rooms that stored drums marked "empty." The reason? The word "empty" in English is associated with "nothing"; it seems boring, dull, and easy to ignore. However, "empty" oil drums are actually full of flammable fumes. So, Whorf told the warehouse managers to explain the dangers of "empty" to workers and the explosions stopped.[7] Science alone could not solve the mystery. But cultural analysis—with science—could. The same principle (namely using anthro-vision to see what we ignore) is equally valuable when mysterious problems erupt in modern bank trading floors, corporate mergers, or pandemics, say.

That is because, "the least questioned assumptions are often the most questionable," as the nineteenth-century French physician and anthropologist Paul Broca reputedly said.[8] It is a dangerous mistake to ignore the ideas we take for granted, be that about language, space, people, objects, or supposedly universal concepts, such as "time."[9]

Or for another example, consider facial hair. In spring 2020, when the COVID-19 lockdown started, I noticed on video calls that many normally clean-shaven American and European men were sprouting beards. When I asked why, I heard answers such as "I don't have time to shave" or "I am not in the office, so there is no point." That did not make sense: in lockdown, many men had *more* free time and incentive to present a professional "face" (on a Zoom call your visage is in alarming close-up.) However, half a century ago an anthropologist named Victor Turner, who worked in Africa, developed a concept known as "liminality" that helped to explain the explosion of facial fuzz. Turner's theory posits that most cultures employ rituals and symbols to mark transition points, be they in the calendar (say, a new year), the start of a life cycle (entry to adulthood), or a big societal event (national independence).[10] These are called "liminal" moments, named after *limens*, meaning "doorway" in Latin. A common feature is that the usual symbolic order is inverted, presented in opposition to "normality," to mark a transition moment. When normally clean-shaven men suddenly sprouted beards during COVID-19, it seemed this was one such liminal symbol. Since beards were *not* "normal" for many professional men, sporting them signaled that they viewed the lockdown as abnormal—and, most crucially, transitional.

Did those fuzzy-faced financiers, accountants, lawyers, and so on explain their beards like that? Not usually. Symbols and rituals are powerful *precisely* because they reflect and reinforce cultural patterns of which we are (at best) only dimly aware. But if only corporate and political leaders had understood this liminal concept, they could have imparted more uplifting messages to their scared citizens and employees. Nobody likes limbo, or the thought of an indefinite lockdown. Framing it as a liminal time of transition, experimentation, and potential renewal would have sounded more inspiring. Not understanding the power of symbols created a missed opportunity. The same principle applies to face masks.

Or for a more serious example, consider a tale from a subsidiary of Google known as Jigsaw. In recent years, its officials have grappled with the spread of online conspiracy theories. Some seem harmless, such as a flat-earth theory. (Yes, these do exist.) Others are dangerous, such as "white genocide" tales (which suggest nonwhite groups plan to exterminate white communities) or the 2016 "Pizzagate" tale (alleging that presidential contender Hillary Clinton was running a satanic child-sex ring in a trendy Washington pizza parlor).[11]

Google executives have fought back using what they know best: technology. They have used Big Data analysis to track the dissemination of conspiracy theories; changed search engine algorithms to raise the prominence of fact-based information; flagged suspicious content and removed dangerous material. Yet tales keep spreading with deadly consequences (in late 2016 a gunman stormed the restaurant in Pizzagate).

So, in 2018, Jigsaw executives tried an experiment. Their researchers joined forces with ethnographers* from a consultancy called ReD Associates and fanned out to meet four dozen American and British theorists, in places ranging from Montana, US, to Manchester, UK.[12] Those encounters showed that some of the Google executives' assumptions were wrong. For one thing, the theorists were not monsters, as educated elites usually presumed; when heard with empathy, they were often friendly, even if you vehemently disagreed with their ideas. Second, techies did not understand what mattered to the theorists. In Silicon Valley it is assumed that information on slick professional websites is more trustworthy than that from amateur sites, *because that is how techies think*. But conspiracy theorists only trusted scruffy sites, since they presumed that the hated elites created the "smart" sites. This insight matters enormously if you want to debunk conspiracies. Similarly, the researchers had started with the assumption that their top priority was to rank the danger of different conspiracy theories (say, treat a flat-earth theory differently from white genocide). But face-to-face encounters showed that content was less important than the degree to which someone was down the rabbit hole and/or defined their identity and community with them. "It is more important to distinguish between types of theorists rather than types of conspiracy theories," they reported.[13]

They also realized another point: *none of those crucial insights could be gathered just with computers*. Big Data can explain *what* is happening. But it cannot usually explain *why*. Correlation is not causation. Similarly, psychology might explain why *one* individual turns to conspiracies. That

*The word "ethnography" is used to describe the method that anthropologists typically employ to study people, i.e., open-ended, intense, face-to-face observation. Not all ethnography is anthropology, since nonanthropologists sometimes use ethnographic techniques without drawing on academic anthropology theories. Almost all anthropologists, however, use ethnography. In business, "ethnography" is often used instead of anthropology, since it sounds less academic.

does not necessarily show how a conspiracy might define group identity. (In this respect the far-right QAnon tales, say, echo the role of folklore in earlier centuries.)[14] Sometimes there is no substitute for meeting people face-to-face, listening with an open mind, studying context, and, above all, noting what people do *not* say, as much as what they do talk about. Or as Tricia Wang, an anthropologist who worked for Nokia, has observed, Big Data needs "thick" data, or qualitative insights that emerge from the "thick description" of culture (to use a phrase posted by the anthropologist Clifford Geertz).[15]

Is this a magic wand to stop conspiracy theories? Sadly not. The battle continues (along with criticism of tech companies). But the insights gave the Google executives something crucial: *a way to see and correct some mistakes*. The tragedy is that such exercises remain rare. No wonder Jack Dorsey, cofounder of Twitter, says that if he could invent social media all over again, he would start by hiring social scientists alongside computer scientists. That might make our twenty-first-century digital landscape look quite different. And better.[16]

The book that follows is divided into three parts, which echo the three principles outlined above: the need to make the "strange familiar," to make the "familiar strange," and listen to social silence. The narrative arc is my own tale: what I learned about studying "strange" in Tajikistan (Chapter One); how I used those lessons to explore the "familiar" in the City of London and *Financial Times* (Chapter Four); and later uncovered social silences in Wall Street, Washington, and Silicon Valley (Chapters Seven, Eight, and Ten.) But the book also relates how anthropology has helped companies such as Intel, Nestlé, General Motors, Procter & Gamble, Mars, or Danica, among others, and how anthropology also sheds light on policy problems such as how to handle a pandemic, frame the economics of Silicon Valley, develop digital work, and embrace the sustainability movement. If you are just looking for practical "how-to" answers to modern problems, skip to later chapters; however, the early chapters outline where these intellectual tools arise from.

Three caveats. First, this book does not argue that anthro-vision should *replace* other intellectual tools, but complement them. Just as adding salt to food binds the ingredients and enhances flavor, adding anthropological ideas to disciplines such as economics, data science, law, or medicine creates a deeper, richer analysis. Blending computing and social science should be a particular priority today. Second, I would not pretend that these ideas are just found in the academic discipline of anthropology; some crop up in user-experience research (USX) studies, social psychology, linguistics, geography, philosophy, environmental biology, and behavioral science. That is good: academic boundaries are artificial, reflecting university tribalism.* We should redraw them for the twenty-first century. Whatever word you use to describe anthro-vision, we need it.

Third, this is not intended as a memoir. I only use my own tale as a narrative arc for a specific intellectual purpose: since anthropology is defined less by a single theory than its distinctive way of looking at the world, the easiest way to explain this mode of thought is to relate what anthropologists do. I hope my own story will illuminate this by addressing three questions: why should a study of Tajik wedding rituals prompt someone to look at modern financial markets, tech, and politics? Why does this matter for other professionals? And in a world being reshaped by artificial intelligence, why do we need another "AI," namely anthropology intelligence? The last issue lies at the heart of this book.

*Many anthropologists hate using words such as "tribe" and "tribalism," since they can sound pejorative, and do not reflect the more technical meaning these words have in relation to kinship structures. Fair point. But for ease of communication, I employ the words "tribe" and "tribalism" in the book, in the popular sense.

PART ONE

MAKING THE "STRANGE" FAMILIAR

The gist: When Donald Trump decried Haiti and African countries as "shitholes" in 2018, the comment sparked widespread criticism. Rightly so. But his offensive language revealed an uncomfortable truth that haunts us all: humans instinctively shy away from and scorn cultures that seem strange. One lesson that anthropology offers, however, is that it pays to embrace "strange" and culture shock. Anthropology has developed a suite of tools to do this, called participant observation (or "ethnography"). But these tools do not always need to be used in an immersive academic sense: the principles can be borrowed in business and policy contexts too, and should be embraced by any investor, financier, executive, and policy maker (or citizen) who hopes to thrive and survive in a globalized world.

ONE

CULTURE SHOCK

(OR WHAT IS ANTHROPOLOGY ANYWAY?)

"Anthropology demands the open-mindedness with which one must look and listen, record in astonishment and wonder that which one would not have been able to guess."

—Margaret Mead[1]

I stood on the threshold of a mud-brick house on a sunny autumn day. I could see a stunning vista behind the building: a steep rocky gorge, studded with golden foliage and green meadows, ascending to snowy peaks and a blue sky. It resembled the wild Afghan mountain scenes that I had occasionally seen on television screens in the late 1970s in Britain, when a Soviet invasion put Afghanistan in the news. But I was actually standing a hundred miles farther north, in Soviet Tajikistan in 1990, in a village I refer to as "Obi-Safed" in the "Kalon" Valley.*

"*A-salaam! Chi khel shumo? Naghz-e? Tinj-e? Soz-e? Khub-e?*" a middle-aged woman standing with me shouted out in Tajik. She was named Aziza Karimova, and worked as an academic in the Tajik capital of Dushanbe; she had traveled with me in a packed minibus on a bumpy

*Obi-Safed village and Kalon valley (literally "white water" and "big") are pseudonyms I used in my PhD to avoid any possible repercussions for the village during or after the civil war. The name of my supervisor and the villagers are also pseudonyms.

road for three hours to Obi-Safed, to introduce me to the residents. She wore clothing typical of the area: tunic and trousers, designed with a distinctive bright pattern known as *atlas*, and a headscarf. I wore it too, but my headscarf kept slipping down, since I did not know how to tie it properly.

A crowd appeared from behind the mud walls: the women wore the same *atlas* tunics and headscarves as I did; the men were sporting skull caps, shirts, and trousers. A babble of conversation exploded that I did not understand. They waved me into the house. As I crossed the threshold, I noticed that the inside walls were painted half-blue and half-white. *Why?* I wondered. A towering pile of embroidered, brightly colored cushions stood against the wall. *What's that for?* A television played loud Tajik music. More shouting erupted. The crowd threw cushions on the floor to act as "seats" and placed a cloth on the ground as a "table," then covered this with orange-and-white teapots, bowls, piles of sweets, and flat golden discs of bread; they heaped the latter with peculiar care, I noted.

A young woman materialized, poured green tea into a white bowl, tipped it back into the orange pot, and poured it in and out again three times. *Why?* Children scampered around the room. A baby screeched from underneath a rug. *What is a baby doing under a rug?* Then a formidable old woman with long white plaits shouted at me. *Who is she?* I felt as if I was on a fairground ride: the sights and sounds swirled in such a disorientating way I could hardly process them.

"What's happening?" I asked Karimova. I spoke to her in Russian, which I knew well; my knowledge of Tajik was more basic.

"They are asking who you are and what you are doing," she replied.

I wondered what she might say. There was a short answer to this question: I had arrived in Tajikistan in 1990—in what would later turn out to be the closing year of the Soviet Union, but nobody guessed that then—to do a PhD in anthropology, under an inaugural exchange program between Cambridge University in England and Dushanbe. Karimova had taken me to the Kalon Valley so I could conduct a study of marriage practices, which I hoped would answer a key question: Was there a "clash" between Islam and Communism in Tajikistan? But there was a much longer potential explanation too to my presence there. What had driven me into anthropology was a passionate desire to explore the world, and question of what it meant to be human. My training had taught me that one way to do this was to immerse myself in the lives of others, to understand a different viewpoint, with "ethnography." It had sounded like a neat—and noble—concept when I sat in a distant Cambridge University library. Not so, hunched on cushions in that blue-and-white room. *Is this completely mad?*

I asked Karimova what she had told the villagers. "I said you are doing research with me and asked them to help you. They said they would."

I took a deep breath and smiled at the crowd. "*A-salaam!*" ("Hello!") I said. Then I pointed to myself and said in Russian, "*Ya studyentka*" ("I am a student"), then in Tajik: "*Taleban-am.*"*

I later realized I had used the wrong word in Russian, which caused confusion. But at the time, I was just relieved to see smiles. I caught the eye of the young dark-haired woman who had been pouring the tea; she had a thin, intelligent face, with two small children clinging to her *atlas* tunic. She pointed to herself. "I-D-I-G-U-L," she said, speaking slowly and loudly, enunciating each letter, as if addressing a deaf idiot. One of the little girls copied her: "M-I-T-C-H-I-G-O-N-A." She pointed to her sister—"G-A-M-J-I-N-A"—and then waved at the rug that was emitting

*To Western ears, *taleban* (or *taliban*)is best known as the name of an Islamic movement, but it also means "student" in Tajik, Persian, and Dari (it became the name of the movement because its adherents depict themselves as "students" of Islam).

a baby's screech: "Z-E-B-I." Then she pointed to objects in the room: "*Mesa!*" ("Table!"), "*Choi!*" ("Tea!"), "*Non!*" ("Bread!"), "*Dastarkhan!*" (the word for the floor cloth that acted as a table).* I gratefully mimicked her, like a game. *If I act like a kid maybe I can learn how to do this!* I thought.

It was an instinct, as much as anything else. But it also illustrates a key point of this book, and one lesson of anthro-vision: the value of sometimes gazing on the world like a child. We live in an age when so many of the intellectual tools we use encourage us to solve problems in a pre-directed, top-down, and bounded manner. The method of scientific, empirical inquiry that emerged in seventeenth-century Europe champions the principle of observation but typically *starts* by defining the issue to be studied or problem to be solved, and then develops ways to test any conclusion (ideally, in a repeatable manner). Anthropology, however, takes a different tack. It also starts with observation. But instead of embracing rigid prior judgments about what is important or normal, or how topics should be subdivided, it tries to listen and learn with almost childlike wonder. This does not mean that anthropologists *only* use open-ended observation; they also frame what they see with theory and hunt for patterns. They sometimes use empirical methods too. But they aim to begin with an open mind and broad lens. This approach can be irritating for scientists, who typically seek data that can be tested and/or replicated on a large scale.[2] Anthropology is about interpretation and sense-making; it typically looks at the micro-level and tries to draw big conclusions. But since humans are not like chemicals in a test tube, or even data in an AI program, this deep, open-ended observation and interpretation can

*Although Tajik is a variant of Persian and the spelling of many Tajik words will look familiar to Persian speakers, there is no readily agreed way to write the Kalon version of Tajik since it is guttural and tends to turn "a" into "o." I have rendered the words as I heard them.

be valuable; particularly if we keep an open mind about what we might find.*

It is often hard in practice to live up to those ideals. I know: I had arrived in Obi-Safed flouting them myself. My research plan had been drawn up in Cambridge with a set of ideas and prejudices about Islam and Communism that were popular among Western policy circles, and which turned out to be wrong. But the whole point of anthropology is to make yourself open to colliding with the unexpected, widening your lens, and learning to rethink what you know. Which begs a question: what first inspired this cult of compulsive curiosity?

The word "anthropology" hails from the Greek *anthropos*, meaning "the study of man." That is no accident. Arguably the first "anthropologist" in history who described culture in a systemic way was the Greek writer Herodotus, who wrote an account of the Greco-Persian Wars in the fifth century BC that details the ethnic backgrounds of different armies and their merits as fighters.[3] Subsequently the Roman historian Tacitus described the traits of Celtic and Germanic peoples on the margins of the Roman Empire; Pliny the Elder, another Roman writer, authored a *Natural History* describing races like a society of dog-headed people who reportedly practiced cannibalism; the Persian polymath Abu Rayhan al-Biruni detailed ethnic diversity in the tenth century; the sixteenth-century French writer Michel de Montaigne penned an essay, "Of Cannibals," which described three Tupinamba Indians from Brazil, who were

*Some readers might conclude from this description that anthropology is a "soft" science compared to "hard" sciences such as physics or medicine, because it sometimes uses subjective analysis, not empirical research. Geertz, one of the most influential figures in the discipline, for example, viewed anthropologists as people who "read" or "interpreted" cultures. However, not all anthropologists accept Geertz's approach, and some use more empirical methods too. Hence I have avoided the word "soft," not least because it sounds pejorative.

brought to Europe by early booty hunters. Early anthropologists were often obsessed with cannibals, since they provided a counterpoint to define "civilization" against.

However, it was not until the nineteenth century that the idea of studying "culture"—and "others"—emerged as a proper intellectual discipline, born from the collision of several historical developments. The eighteenth century had been a time of revolution in Europe, when there was "a sustained effort to find the intellectual grounds for democratic overthrow of an Old Regime on its last legs," by studying "what everyone had in common, their human nature," as Keith Hart, an anthropologist, observes.[4] Then in the nineteenth century Charles Darwin developed the idea of biological evolution, which prompted interest in how humans had developed over time in not just a physical sense, but the social dimension too. The other impetus was imperialism. The Victorian Empire contained a plethora of cultures that seemed alien to the British rulers, and those elites needed information on how to conquer, tax, control, trade with, or convert these "strange" groups. So did the French, Spanish, and Dutch elites, and the emerging American elite, who were confronting native populations.

In 1863 a motley collection of adventurers and financiers created a "learned society"—a type of debating club popular in Victorian England—to study human nature. They christened it the "Cannibal Club" and hung a skeleton in a window of their headquarters, a white-stucco building at 4 St. Martins Place London, near Trafalgar Square. Christian missionaries next door begged them to remove the bones, but they refused.[5] The group's leadership included men such as British explorer Sir Richard Francis Burton, a former employee of the East India Company. Others were linked to the London Stock Exchange. By the 1860s Victorian England was in the grip of the type of mania later profiled by Anthony Trollope in his novel *The Way We Live Now*.[6] Investors were thus scrambling to buy railways bonds and other infrastructure projects in the "colonies" and needed information to assess risk. "The same individuals who puffed explorations of Africa or the promotion of mines and railways in Central or Latin America also puffed anthropology," notes the historian Marc Flandreau.[7] However, Burton and his ilk also had a distinctive philosophy: they believed that science showed that Europeans and Americans were biologically, mentally, and socially superior to others. "The savage is morally and mentally an unfit instrument for the spread of civilization except when, like the higher mammalia, he is reduced to a state of slavery," wrote August Lane Fox Pitt-Rivers, a British army colony and Cannibal Club member.[8]

These self-styled anthropologists backed away from this racist stance—a touch—after the American Civil War, when the Cannibal Club merged with another group of self-styled "ethnologists" run by Quakers (who had been campaigning against slavery) to create the Royal Anthropological Society. But the Victorian academics remained wedded to an evolutionary frame. So too in America: in 1877 Lewis Henry Morgan, a businessman and part-time scholar from Rochester, New York, published *Ancient Society*, which argued that "all societies run through the same stages in their evolution . . . from simpler forms of organization—families, brotherhoods, tribes—to modern, complex nation states."[9] One of Morgan's acolytes, John Wesley Powell—a former American soldier who'd fought in the Civil War on the Union side—persuaded the government in Washington to create a "Bureau of Ethnology" to map native American peoples. "There are stages of human culture," Powell declared in a speech in 1886. "The age of savagery is the age of stone. The age of barbarism is the age of clay. The age of civilization is the age of iron." It was considered so evident that American Indians, African-Americans, and Inuit were "primitive" that their artifacts were displayed next to animals in New York's Museum of Natural History (where they remained, largely unquestioned, until the advent of the Black Lives Matter movement).*

In the twentieth century an intellectual revolution took place, however, that not only laid the foundations of modern anthropology, but also underpins crucial twenty-first-century debates around civic values in company boardrooms, parliaments, schools, media, and the courts (even though few participants in these arenas know anything about anthropology). It started in the unlikely location of Baffin Island in Newfoundland, home to the Inuit. In the early 1880s an intense young German academic named Franz Boas earned a degree in natural sciences from Kiel University in Germany and then sailed to the Arctic. He hoped to study how animals interacted with snow and ice. But when bad weather hit, he was stranded in a whaling community for months, surrounded by the local Inuit population. Trapped and bored, he passed the time by learning the local language and collecting Inuit stories. That revealed something he did not expect: the Inuit were *not* just a collection of physical molecules, but humans who had feelings, ideas, beliefs, and passions—just like him. "I often ask myself what advantages our 'good society' possesses over that of the 'savages,'" he wrote in a letter from Newfoundland to an Austrian-American woman named Marie, who would later become his wife. "The more I see of their customs, I find that we really have no right to look down upon them contemptuously . . . since we 'highly educated' people are relatively much worse."[10]

Boas subsequently went to America, where he published a book in 1911 called *The Mind of Primitive Man*. This argued that the only reason why Americans and Europeans felt superior to other cultures was that "we participate in this civilization" and "it has been controlling all our actions since the time of our birth."[11] Other cultures could be equally valuable and

*Since 2018 the Museum of Natural History has attached material to its exhibits of Native American culture that explains the historical (i.e., racist) context of these exhibits. It has also removed a statue of Theodore Roosevelt from the front of the building.

worthy, if only we opened our eyes, he declared. In the New York intellectual circles of the day—at the start of the twentieth century—this was akin to a Copernican revolution of the social sciences.[12] Boas's ideas were considered so heretical that he struggled to find a proper academic job. He eventually wriggled into Columbia University, where he attracted like-minded students, such as Margaret Mead, Ruth Benedict, Edward Sapir, Zora Neale Hurston, and Gregory Bateson. From the 1920s on these academics fanned out across the world, to places ranging from Samoa to the American pueblos, to study far-flung cultures, aping Boas's intellectual frame.

A similar intellectual revolution also started on the other side of the Atlantic. One pioneer was Alfred Reginald Radcliffe-Brown, an English intellectual who decided in the early twentieth century that he "wanted to do something to reform the world—to get rid of poverty and war," and traveled to the Andaman Islands and Australia to see how the customs and rituals there made their societies work. Another, even more influential figure, was a Polish immigrant named Bronisław Malinowski, who enrolled in the London School of Economics in 1920 for a doctorate in economics, and then traveled to Australia to study the economics of Aboriginal communities.

When World War One started in 1914, Malinowski was detained as an "alien enemy" and dispatched to the Trobriand Islands in Polynesia. Stuck in a tent on a beach, he decided to salvage his doctorate by studying the complex gift exchanges of shells, necklaces, and armbands (known as *kula*) happening in the Trobriand Islands instead. He could not carry out the type of top-down economic survey he had planned. So he used the only tool he had available: eyewitness observations. Like Boas, Malinowski found that the unplanned detour changed his life: when he returned to London, he declared that the only way to understand strange "others" was to observe them firsthand, in an immersive way. This approach did not mean the researcher should become an insider, or "go native," to use the phrase common in the empire. "Not even the most intelligent native has any clear idea of the *kula* as a big, organized social construction, still less of its sociological function and implications," Malinowski wrote. But it was vital "to grasp the native's point of view, his relation to life, to realize his vision of his world."[13] You had to be an outsider *and* an insider to see clearly. Insiders took the *kula* for granted; outsiders thought *kula* was just a piece of trivia. An insider-outsider, though, could see that these complex *kula* exchanges had a de facto *function*: they kept the different islands interconnected, fostering social ties and embedding status systems.

Malinowski called that idea "participant observation." It spread, spawning a new academic tribe at universities in London, Cambridge, Oxford, and Manchester who—like the disciples of Boas—traveled to far-flung corners of the world to study other societies. The roll call included figures such as Edward Evans-Pritchard, Meyer Fortes, Audrey Richards, and Edmund Leach. In Paris, a new tribe of French anthropologists emerged too: Claude Lévi-Strauss headed to Brazil and Pierre Bourdieu analyzed France's former colony of Algeria. As they fanned out across the world, their endeavors shared a core idea: although humans tend to assume that their own culture is inevitable, it is not. There is a vast spectrum of cultural variation, and it is foolish to assume that our practices are either normal or always superior.

Today that point might seem so obvious that it is almost trite. The idea of tolerance is baked into the legal framework in many parts of the world, with laws that ban racism, sexism, homophobia, and so on (even though these ideals are often flouted). But, as the historian Charles King notes in a brilliant account of this intellectual revolution, it is difficult to overstate how radical this concept of cultural relativism sounded a century ago. Or how inflammatory. When Josef Goebbels, the Nazi leader, organized Nazi book burnings in Germany in 1933, the works of Boas were among the first to be tossed into the flames. The conflagration was front-page news in the Columbia University newspaper.[14] To non-anthropologists, the

discipline might seem like a dusty or exotic indulgence. To the Nazis—and Boas—the ideas in the discipline, such as cultural relativism, invoked an existential battle about what it meant to be "human" and "civilized." That is why the one of the greatest gifts that anthropology can offer the modern world is to be "the antidote to nativism, the enemy of hate [and] vaccine of understanding, tolerance and compassion that can counter the rhetoric of demagogues," to cite the anthropologist Wade Davis. We need it.

In 1986, almost a century after Boas sailed to Baffin Island, I arrived in Cambridge University to do an undergraduate degree with the odd name "arch and anth." The tag was short for "archeology and anthropology," and reflected the discipline's tangled—tortured—past. Victorian "anthropologists" assumed they needed to study culture, biological evolution, and archeology together to understand humans. By the late twentieth century, however, anthropologists no longer believed that biology was destiny, and the study of culture and society had become a discipline that was (mostly) separate from the study of human biology and evolution; the former was called "social" or "cultural" anthropology;* the latter "physical" anthropology. The boundary was not (and is not) rigid; writers such as Joseph Henrich, Brian Dunbar, Yuval Harari, and Jared Diamond have cleverly explored how human physiology, geography, and environment influences culture (and vice versa), and in American universities the physical and social anthropology is sometimes combined. In Britain, however, the disciplines tended to be kept separate. The name "arch and anth" was thus a misnomer or, more accurately, a sign of how institutions are creatures of their history.

*In the twentieth century, American anthropologists used the term "cultural anthropology" to describe their discipline, but their British counterparts preferred "social anthropology." The reason was that British anthropologists put more emphasis on social systems, but Americans (like Geertz) stressed culture patterns. Today, however, the phrases mean roughly the same thing.

There were other oddities about the course too. By the 1980s, the twin ideas of "cultural relativism" and "participant observation" dominated anthropology. This was interlaced with a desire to understand how social systems hung together (reflecting an approach called "functionalism" developed by Radcliffe-Brown) and how cultures created mental maps through myths and rituals (drawing on so-called structuralism theories pioneered by Lévi-Strauss) and cultural "webs of meaning" (described by the American anthropologist Clifford Geertz). But while the early academic descendants of Boas and Malinowski had a clear sense of purpose, by the 1980s the discipline had become more fragmented. Anthropologists were haunted with a sense of embarrassment about the discipline's colonial legacy and keen to refute it (even more so today.)[15] They had realized that true "participant observation" was hard to achieve, since the mere presence of a researcher in a society tends to change what is being studied, and researchers arrive with their own biases. They had also become uncertain about where the boundaries of their discipline should lie. Early anthropologists studied non-Western societies. However, in the twentieth century they increasingly turned their lens to Western societies. That was partly because academics such as Boas argued that *all* cultures are strange. It was also because the collapse of the nineteenth-century empires made it harder for them to do research in their old haunts, since some were hostile to them. (In the 1960s the premier of Ghana had a painting in his room depicting his country shaking off the chains placed on it by missionaries, colonial administrators, and anthropologists).[16] But studying Western cultures left anthropologists entering territory dominated by economists, geographers, and sociologists. So should they compete with those disciplines? Collaborate? As anthropologists groped for answers, the discipline spawned numerous subfields: economic anthropology, feminist anthropology, medical anthropology, legal anthropology, digital anthropology. It was a rich but confusing blend.

The one big unifying trait, however, was obsessive curiosity: anthro-

pologists are devoted to peering into cracks, immersing themselves into odd places, creeping into the undergrowth of society around the world. And as I read the vast range of studies they had done, in places ranging from remote jungles or islands to modern companies, I was hooked. In truth, my motives for choosing the course were as tangled as the discipline's past. I had grown up in a staid corner of suburban London, but in a family imbued with folk memories of Britain's colonial past (a great-grandfather fought in the Boer War; another great uncle worked in India's imperial administration; my father lived in Singapore, until he and his mother fled an invading Japanese army in World War Two and his own father was dispatched to an internment camp). I was eager to escape gray 1970s suburbia for "adventure," and keen, in a vague and idealistic way, to "do good." So in 1989 I enrolled for a PhD at Cambridge in anthropology.

I initially hoped to do fieldwork in Tibet, where I had spent months traveling as an undergraduate. But when the protests in Tiananmen Square erupted, Beijing slammed the door shut. "What about Tajikistan?" suggested an anthropology professor called Caroline Humphrey, as I sat, despondent, in her office in the magnificent surroundings of Kings College, Cambridge. Humphrey had done research on a Soviet farm in Mongolia in the 1960s, studying "magical drawings" and religion among an ethnic group called the Buryat, and then had written the first detailed firsthand study of a Soviet collective farm by a Western observer.[17] She had subsequently stayed in touch with Soviet academics.

I did not know anything about the country; indeed, I could not even locate it on the map. Humphrey, though, knew a Soviet academic in Tajikistan called Aziza Karimova, and although places such as Tajikistan had been off-limits to Western researchers during the Cold War, by 1989 the perestroika reform program was opening some long-closed doors. She reckoned Karimova might help. I applied for a Soviet research visa. To my great surprise, I received it, or, more explicitly, was enrolled in the department of ethnography (*etnografiya*) at the university in Dushanbe, the capital of Soviet Tajikistan. I had no idea what that meant in practice. Nor did anyone else; no one outside the Soviet bloc had ever done postgraduate work at the Dushanbe *etnografiya* department. But I reckoned that was part of the adventure. Like Malinowski, Boas, and Mead, I wanted to embrace culture shock.

In the summer of 1990 I flew out to Dushanbe. As the plane landed in the shimmering heat of the Soviet city, I could see Stalinist concrete apartment blocks set against a ring of mountains. A century earlier, it had been places like Baffin Island or Polynesia that represented the exotic "other." For a child of 1970s Britain, steeped in Cold War rhetoric and fears, the exotic "other" was the far-flung corners of the Soviet empire. To prepare, I had studied Russian intensively. I had also tried to learn Tajik. But that was hard since the only "teach yourself Tajik" book that I could find was an instructional tome written in Russian by the Soviet Communist party, which explained Tajik grammar with sentences such as "We must fulfill the five-year plan!" or "All praise to internationalism, socialism, and friendship!" and "We all love picking cotton!"

It was almost as challenging to embrace Soviet-style *etnografiya*. The Russian word sounded like a neat translation of the English "ethnography." But that was deceptive: a better translation was "the study of folklore"—but through a strictly Marxist lens. Ironically, this had been inspired by the ideas of nineteenth-century American anthropologists such as Powell and Morgan: after they published their arguments about how all societies were "evolving" from feudalism or barbarism toward civilization, Karl Marx and Friedrich Engels borrowed this frame to argue that humankind was "evolving" toward Communism. *Etnografiya* departments were thus stuck in the nineteenth-century evolutionary frame that twentieth-century British and American anthropology circles had so violently rejected. But I skim-read as many *etnografiya* books as I could find. (Or, more accurately, I read the middle sections of them, since the first and last chapter were always formulaic letters of praise to the Communist Party.)

"So what type of *etnografiya* will you study?" Karimova asked me when I appeared at the university department in Dushanbe. She was a dogged, vibrant woman who hailed from the historic city of Bukhara in Uzbekistan and had won a coveted position as a university academic through willpower and family connections to the Communist Party.

"Marriage rituals" was my prepared answer. It was not entirely true. When I had first started reading about Tajikistan in the hushed safety of a library in Cambridge, the issue which fascinated me was Islam and political conflict. Before the 1920s, the region called Tajikistan had been a pawn in the so-called Great Game geopolitical chess game between the Russian and British empires to exert control of the historic Silk Road realms.[18] The valleys around Dushanbe were nominally part of the Russian realm, but effectively ran their own affairs and had a proud Sunni Muslim culture. But after the 1917 Russian Revolution, Soviet Communists seized control of the area and tried dismantle the Islamic cultural heritage. In subsequent decades, it seemed peaceful. But during the Cold War, policy experts at places such as the CIA often suggested—or hoped—that the Muslim Central Asians were the "soft underbelly" of the Soviet Union, in the sense of being the people most likely to revolt against Moscow.[19] The Afghan War intensified that idea.*

I knew there was no chance of getting a visa from the Soviet authorities if I admitted that I planned to study this explosive topic. So I applied for a visa with a proposal to study marriage practices instead. It was a topic that had been extensively studied by Western anthropologists since one mantra of the discipline is that "marriage—its

*At this point you may be wondering "Was she a spy?" The short answer is: "no, never." If that answer makes you think, "She would say that, wouldn't she, if she really was a spy," ponder this: writing this book is *not* what a spy would do to stay under the radar.

ideology and associated practices—is the key to many societies around the world," as Nancy Tapper, an anthropologist who had conducted research in nearby Afghanistan, observed.[20] By an odd twist of history the Russian Communists agreed: when Soviet activists tried to eradicate Islam in the 1920s, they launched a so-called *khudzhum* (Uzbek for "onslaught") campaign to "liberate" women and attack traditional marriage rituals, hoping that these cultural reforms would "shake the nail" of Islamic culture, and make it Communist.[21] As part of *khudzhum*, activists forced thousands of women in Bukhara and Samarkand to rip off their veils, banned traditional Islamic customs such as arranged marriages, raised the marriage age, and introduced new Soviet marriage rituals.* The campaign was short-lived. But the legacy of *khudzhum* made the topic of marriage a good way to explore the issue that really fascinated me: the presumed clash between Islam and Communism. Or so I hoped.

My choice of topic thrilled Karimova, since Soviet *etnografiya* contained extensive research on "traditional" marriages, or *tui*, and she loved attending wedding parties, since they were jolly affairs. "I will take you to lots of *tui*!" she pledged, as she sat in a darkened study in the research institute in Dushanbe. She explained there would be lots of dancing. So, a few weeks later, we boarded a rickety, cramped minibus, traveled for several hours, and then climbed out in the sparkling beauty of the Kalon Valley, where Karimova led me up an unpaved mountain track through a gorge to Obi-Safed. "There will be *tui* to study!" she declared, waving at the mud houses. My fieldwork had begun. I had no idea what would

*This footnote in Central Asian history is little known outside the region, but it is fascinating. Ironically, the Russian Communists used an intellectual framework that was intensely anthropological: they argued that women were the "nail" pinning together traditional culture and that marriage and kinship were the key factors keeping that nail in place, so that liberating women would change society. This reasoning lead the Soviet activists to make dramatic efforts to promote female equality in the region, presaging what Western aid agencies would later do.

unfold, nor that what I was about to learn would eventually be so useful in studying Wall Street and Washington too.

In the following weeks, I tried to follow in the footsteps of Malinowski and Boas—or Humphrey and Gellner, my professors at Cambridge. I was not allowed to live in Obi-Safed all the time since my Soviet visa stated I was based at the Tajik National University in Dushanbe. But every few days I took a bus to the Kalon Valley and stayed with the large extended family that Karimova had introduced me to: a collection of adult brothers with their wives and children, plus a powerful, widowed matriarch called Bibigul. The dark-haired woman called Idigul, whose children had taught me my first local words, took me under her wing.

Life settled into a routine. Each day a collection of children would congregate in the house, around the *dastarkhan*, and play the game of teaching me new words in Tajik, giggling when I got them wrong. If they did not have school, they would pull me around the village, as the day's entertainment. In the evening they ran up the steep mountain paths to collect goats from the high pastures. I often followed. Running alone in the high pastures was a rare moment of privacy. *I am like a Tajik version of Maria in* The Sound of Music, I sometimes laughed to myself. Then I graduated to help with other household chores: I sat with the women and chopped carrots to make the local *osh-plov* recipe (a dish of greasy fried rice, carrots, and mutton that I loathed), fetched pails of water from a stream (although the village had electricity, it did not having running water), swept the floor, minded babies (and quickly discovered that what I had thought was an embroidered rug on my first day was actually a cradle).

I also did my "homework," to use the word deployed by Karimova when she described why I was in Obi-Safed. I walked between houses, with my notebook and camera, to ask questions about marriages and, most important, to use that as a gateway to talking about anything—and *everything*—else that I could. It was a classic technique of anthropology:

by focusing on one micro-level topic, ritual, or set of practices, an anthropologist hopes to gradually widen their lens to capture the entire landscape. In 1990 many of the marriages in the Kalon Valley were still partly arranged by families, in line with traditional Islamic norms. The villagers obsessed over marriage strategies and wedding parties with the same passion that middle-class American or European families might discuss the property market, job moves, holiday plans, or their children's education: Who was marrying whom? Who might marry whom? What bride price could they pay? Who had the best wedding? Day after day, the villagers pulled out faded photographs of previous brides and grooms, drew charts of their family trees, counted the stacks of brightly colored cushions and rugs that brides took to a new home as a dowry. The villagers also explained to me the long, confusing cycle of marriage rituals, which featured ceremonies around the *dastarkhan* with flour, bread, water, white clothing, and sweets. Sometimes a local villager described as a "mullah" officiated. However, old women often lead the rituals and prayers too. The couple also visited the local Soviet government office, to register the marriage with the state, and the wedding party often traveled in cars to a statue of Lenin farther down the valley, as if on pilgrimage, for photographs. I took notes about what people said—and what they did not.

The highlight of the ritual cycle, however, was the *tui kalon*—wedding feast. At dusk the villagers set out the tables in an open square, laden with bread, sweets, and *osh-plov*, and loud Tajik music would ring out, echoing off the rocky valley walls. Then everyone would congregate in the ring and dance for hours, swaying with movements similar to Indian or Persian dancing. "Dance with us!" the villagers shouted, as the music started. Initially I refused. But the children were persistent: in Obi-Safed, toddlers learned to dance by watching others, and by watching the Soviet television channels that constantly broadcast Tajik dancing, between Communist propaganda. "You won't find a husband unless you can dance!" Bibigul, the grandmother in the household, often shouted at me. So when the snow started to fall, leaving me trapped in the house, I started to copy the children's movements. By the early spring of 1991, the rhythm felt familiar enough for me to join the wedding dance. Then, by late spring, I noticed that my arms would twitch, involuntarily, if I simply heard the beat of a Tajik song. *My hands have gone Tajik*, I joked to myself. The habits of the village were slowly becoming "embodied" in me, to use a phrase developed by the anthropologist Simon Roberts.[22] Or as Miner might have said, actions that had once seemed completely "strange" were stealthily becoming "familiar" in a way I had never quite expected.

One day, in the middle of March 1991—many months after I had arrived in the village—I walked up the Kalon Valley to a squat gray concrete building. Dirty gray snow still lay on the valley floor; it was the end of a long winter. But there was a vibrant splash of red too: a picture of Lenin. This was the local *sovkhoz*, state farm. Inside sat a middle-aged man named Hassan, wearing a cheap gray suit adorned with Soviet medals. He ran the *sovkhoz.*

"I am doing *etnografiya*," I said, in Tajik. After six months of brutal immersion, my language skills had improved. "I want to talk about the *sovhkoz* and *tui*."

Hassan nodded. He had heard all about me from the rest of the village. He poured me some tea, put a circular disc of bread on the table, offered it to me.

"No Ramadan?" I asked. None of the women in the women were eating in the daytime, unless they were pregnant or working, because they were observing the Muslim fast.

Hassan laughed. "I am Communist!" he said, switching from Tajik to Russian.

"Are you Muslim too?" I asked Hassan, switching to Russian as well. The men in the village spoke both languages, and I tended to use the one they chose.

"Yes!" Hassan told me, back in Tajik, and then added by way of explanation. "My wife keeps the fast at home."

Aha! I thought. I had arrived in Obi-Safed hoping to use my study of marriage rituals to explore the "conflict" between Islam and Communism. Half a world away in Cambridge, I had taken it for granted that a conflict must exist, since the two belief systems were so opposed. But the time I had spent in Obi-Safed had presented me with a problem: the village did not seem to be seething with an ideological clash, in relation to marriage or anything else. The earlier *khudzhum* campaigns had aimed to crush traditional practices and replace them with Communist ones. In some senses the initiative had worked: my research showed that the marriage age had risen sharply[23] during the Soviet period. Polygamous marriages and forced marriages had largely vanished. Families, however, still paid a bride price and dowry, and they still arranged marriages. And while the official mantra of the Soviet Union was that ethnic identity did not matter since everyone was Communist, the Obi-Safed villagers hated the idea of marrying anybody outside the Kalon Valley.[24] Similarly, although the wedding cycle included a pilgrimage to the statue of Lenin, Islamic rituals had not vanished. "The picture that emerged is a complex bricolage of ceremonies," I later wrote. "Although Soviet rituals had been adopted, these did not exist as *alternatives* to 'traditional' rituals, but as *extensions*."[25]

Did this mean the villagers were hiding their Islamic identity? Was this a form of underground resistance against the Communist state? I initially assumed so. The area had faced so much repression in the past that I did not expect—as a foreigner—that I would be told the whole "truth."

But Hassan's comments in the *sovkhoz* office suggested there was another explanation for what was going on. The British culture I had grown up in, shaped by protestant Christianity, presumed that people should only have *one* religion or belief system. Western culture tends to prize "impartial principles over contextual particularism," as the anthropologist Joseph Henrich has observed, and assumes that "moral truths exist in the way mathematical laws exist."[26] Intellectual consistency is considered to be a virtue; a lack of it, hypocrisy. Yet this idea is not universal: in many other societies there is a presumption that morals are *context-based*, and it is not immoral to have different values in different situations. Hassan's behavior seemed to encapsulate that. A common theme in Central Asian cultures (and many other Islamic cultures) was that "public" space should be treated differently from "private" space. A gender divide was usually transposed on this: public space was male-dominated; private space was the realm of women. Hassan seemed to have extended the distinction between Islam and Communism onto this. The public sphere was dominated by the symbols and practices of the Soviet Communist state; the private sphere was a bastion of traditional Muslim values. Since women were associated with the domestic sphere, they had become the guardians of traditional Muslim culture.[27] Or to put it another way, when Hassan told me that he was "good Communist" who did not observe Ramadan—but still a "good Muslim" because his wife did—he was not necessarily *lying*, but invoking a compartmentalized mental, cultural, and spatial framework that appeared to be widespread.

Was this compartmentalization a *deliberate* strategy? I did not know for sure. But I suspected the best way to interpret the pattern was with the concept of *habitus* developed by Bourdieu, the French anthropologist.[28] This theory argues that the way humans organize space reflects the mental and cultural "maps" we inherit from our surroundings—but as we move about that space, with familiar habits, these actions reinforce these shared mental maps, and make them seeming so natural and inevitable that we don't notice them at all. We are creatures of our environment in a social, mental, *and* physical sense, and these aspects intensify one another (hence the reason "habit" and "habitat" have the same linguistic root in English). Whenever Hassan switched between Russian and Tajik—or ate bread at work while his wife observed Ramadan—he was reflecting *and* reproducing a sense of compartmentalization that alleviated the "clash" between Islam and Communism. Or to put it another way, "Communism" had been redefined in the village in a way that enabled there to be accommodation between the two systems, not conflict. The initial assumption that had driven my PhD—drawn from Western foreign policy circles and groups such as the CIA—had been wrong.

In the summer of 1991, I left the mountains of Obi-Safed and returned to the flat, familiar world of Cambridge University. I was excited about writing up my research since I felt that I had stumbled on an important idea—namely that the Cold War "soft underbelly" theory was misguided—and hoped this would enable me to build an academic career in anthropology or Soviet studies. But life then took a peculiar turn. Soon after my return, a coup erupted in Moscow, toppling Mikhail Gorbachev, the Soviet premier. The Soviet Union started to break up. That was a blow for my research since the topic at the core of my PhD was suddenly history, not current anthropology. But then a new opportunity materialized. I had always flirted with the idea of becoming a journalist, since that profession—like anthropology—seemed to be driven by curiosity. As the Soviet Union tumbled into chaos, an opening arose to be a temporary intern-cum-reporter for the *Financial Times* in the Soviet Union. I grabbed it.

Seven months later, in the late spring of 1992, I heard that political protest was bubbling in Tajikistan. So I took a plane down to Dushanbe, once again, but this time as a reporter. The streets initially looked eerily unchanged: rows of Stalinist apartment blocks and a jumble of flat mud-walled houses. But then events turned violent: protestors massed on the streets, clashes erupted, government troops fought back, and gun battles escalated that later produced a civil war that ultimately killed many tens of thousands.* Horrified and scared, I sheltered in a hotel in Dushanbe with a collection of other journalists, including Marcus, the reporter from the *Daily Telegraph* who appears in the Preface.

They peppered me with questions about what was going on. Initially, I was unsure how to reply. When I had lived in Obi-Safed a year before, this corner of the Soviet Union had seemed so peaceful that I had never imagined a world where society could crumble. It is always hard to imagine a systemic collapse and in spite of all the debate about the "soft underbelly" issue in Western policy circles, nobody in that world seriously predicted that the Soviet Union could really implode so fast. *Was my research all a complete waste of time?* I kept wondering.

But then, as I watched nervously in the Dushanbe hotel, I realized that what I had seen in Obi-Safed was more useful than I had realized. The "soft underbelly" theory had implied that the Islamic regions such as Tajikistan would be the *first* to rebel against the Communist system. However, it turned out that they were the last. Instead, the first republics to break away were the Baltic republics (and my first job as a freelance reporter for the FT was to file dispatches from the Lithuanian parliament, where protestors were standing behind concrete blocks, doing battle with the Communist Party). The Tajik government did not request independence until almost every other republic had already done so. Far from being the "soft underbelly" of the USSR, Tajikistan turned out to be a toughened hide, as I had suspected. *If only I had published my thesis a year earlier, I might have really looked prescient*, I sourly reflected.

My study of marriage patterns was also surprisingly relevant. I had arrived in Obi-Safed with a set of assumptions about national affiliations

*The civil war in Tajikistan was one of the least covered conflicts that erupted in the former Soviet Union, and as a result there is little hard data on the death toll. Pro-democracy groups guesstimate a death toll of between 30,000 and 150,000. Either way, it was tragically high.

that I had absorbed from my European heritage. These posited that the nation state was the preeminent political unit—because the concept of "nations" had shaped European history since the nineteenth century. Thus since the "Tajiks" lived in "Tajikistan" and spoke "Tajik," I started studying them through a national lens. But looking at marriage partner selection showed that this assumption was wrong: the villagers in the Kalon Valley only wanted to marry people like themselves, whom they defined as being *only* residents of the same region, if not valley—*not* as "Tajiks." They had not really embraced the idea of the Tajik state which had been imposed on the region by the Soviet Communists (much like European imperialists had created artificial boundaries and countries in Africa).

When I had been roaming about in Obi-Safed in 1991, this choice of marriage partners had simply seemed like a useful detail for my academic research. But as I sheltered in the hotel in 1992, the observation had assumed political—and tragic—significance. When opposition parties massed in Dushanbe demanding the removal of the Tajik government, some had described themselves as members of an "Islamic Party." Western journalists interpreted that label as a sign that the battles were about "Islamic extremism" versus "Communism," borrowing the tags often used to describe events in Afghanistan (and later in many other parts of the Middle East). Not so: when I talked to the "Tajik" factions on the streets of Dushanbe, I realized that what was really driving the clash was not "ideology," since members of both factions said they were Muslims and appeared to operate with the same public/private split I saw in Obi-Safed. Instead the key point of conflict was that the opposition party came from one group of valleys and the government from another. They were battling about who would have access to resources in a post-Soviet world. It was a regional, not religious, fight.

Did this matter? The answer was (and is) an emphatic yes if you want to understand the current trajectory of this volatile region, where

Russian-American-Chinese rivalry is creating a new type of "Great Game." So too if you are a historian who wants to disentangle why the CIA and others misread the areas of vulnerability in the former Soviet Union during the Cold War. However, there was (and is) a far wider lesson here that extends well beyond geopolitics. In our twenty-first-century world, there is a reverence for sweeping, top-down analysis with large collections of statistics and Big Data (and the bigger the data set, the better). This number-crunching can often be insightful. But my experience in Obi-Safed showed me that sometimes there is value in taking a worm's-eye, not bird's-eye, view and trying to combine these perspectives. It pays to do intensive local and lateral studies that explore a situation in three dimensions, ask open-ended questions, and ponder what people are *not* talking about. There is value in becoming "embodied" in somebody else's world—to gain empathy. That worm's-eye approach does not usually produce neat power points or flashy spreadsheets. But it can be sometimes be more revealing than any bird's-eye or Big Data view. "Ethnography is empathy," observes the anthropologist Grant McCracken. "You listen until you go, 'Oh, like that,' and you suddenly see the world as they do."[29]

It is not easy to embrace that worm's-eye approach. Culture shock is painful. It takes time and patience to immerse yourself in a strange world. Ethnography cannot be easily slotted into a window on the diary of a busy Western professional. Yet even if most people cannot venture to a place such as Obi-Safed, we can all embrace some of the principles of ethnography: to look around, watch, listen, ask open-ended questions, be curious like a child, and try to walk "in someone else's shoes," to cite the proverb. It is valuable, even if you are a politician, leader, corporate executive, lawyer, techie, or any other variant of the twenty-first-century professional world—or, more accurately, *especially* if you are a member of the tribe of the harried Western elite.

TWO

CARGO CULTS

(OR WHY DID GLOBALIZATION SURPRISE INTEL AND NESTLÉ?)

"Anthropology may not provide the answer to the question of the meaning of life, but at least it can tell us that there are many ways in which to make a life meaningful."

—Thomas Hylland Eriksen

The mood in the airy conference hall in the Computer History Museum in Mountain View, California, was earnest, if not geeky. It was September 2012. Just outside the hall, there were displays of artifacts from the cult of tech innovation that drives Silicon Valley, such as early prototypes of the Apple computer.[1] There was also a pile of salmon-colored *Financial Times* newspapers: the FT was hosting a corporate debate with representatives from tech companies and Stanford d.school. I was running the FT editorial operations in America.

It seemed a world away from the Tajik mountains. Or maybe not. On the platform next to me was Genevieve Bell, a vivacious Australian women with a mop of curly auburn hair who worked for Intel, the computing giant. She had spent her early years steeped in twentieth-century anthropology. She was born in Sydney, and when she was young her mother moved to the Australian outback to do fieldwork for a doctorate in anthropology. During the next eight years Bell lived in an Aboriginal community of about six hundred people near Alice Springs.* "I dropped out of school, stopped wearing shoes, and went hunting with people every chance I got," she said. She learned to extract water from desert frogs and snacked on "witchetty grubs," a type of Australian caterpillar that lives among tree roots. "I was very fortunate. I had the most blessed childhood."[2]

She did a PhD in anthropology, focused on Native American culture, and became a professor at Stanford University. "The joke in my family is that anthropology is less a vocation and more a mindset. It's a way of looking at the world that I don't know how to escape from. I had an ex-boyfriend once tell me I was a terrible person to go on a vacation with. He said, 'You treat vacation like fieldwork,' and I was like, 'I treat life like fieldwork.'"[3] But in 1998, her life took a curious turn.

One night she went to a bar near Stanford with a girlfriend, got talking to an entrepreneur called Rob, who suggested that Bell's background made her a good person to work in tech. Shortly after, an official at Intel, the world's largest maker of computer chips, asked her to visit their research laboratory in Portland, Oregon. "But I don't know anything about technology!" she protested. That was the point, the executives retorted: they already had plenty of engineers on staff who knew all about computers. What they did *not* know was how to make sense of humans in global locations who were buying tech devices that contained those computer chips. Intel offered her a job.

Bell knew that this was a strange career move. During the twentieth century, some anthropologists had migrated into business. But many anthropologists were wary about the idea of working for big companies or governments, since they feared this would reproduce the patterns of

*There is controversy in Australia about the best words to use to describe the indigenous Australian people. The commonly used word "aborigine" is not deemed respectful by the communities, so I have used the option suggested by Australian universities: https://teaching.unsw.edu.au/indigenous-terminology.

exploitation seen during the discipline's nineteenth-century imperial past. There was a cultural problem too: the type of students who migrated into anthropology tended to be nonconformist and antiestablishment; they wanted to analyze rules, not obey them—at a company or anywhere else.

Ever since Bell had feasted on witchetty grubs as a child, she had loved breaking the mold. And she could see that while Intel engineers might seem less exotic than Australian Aboriginal communities (at least, to Westerners), they represented a new frontier for anthropology. What would happen, she wondered, if you applied anthropological ideas to the twenty-first-century business and tech sector? Could anthropology have practical value?

"Can it?" I asked her, as we sat in the Computer History Museum.

"Yes!" Bell declared. She explained how she and a team of social scientists had been fighting to inject the lessons that she (and I) had learned into the corporate world. It was not easy. Engineers did not always like listening to strange—exotic—outsiders like anthropologists. She had gone head-to-head with Paul Otellini, the Intel chief executive officer, in meetings.[4] But what anthropologists told Intel had saved them costly mistakes and shown them opportunities. The reason was simple: one Achilles' heel of the Western corporate and tech world was that its highly trained engineers and executives tended to assume that everyone did (or should) think like them. They dismissed, ignored, or derided human behavior that looked strange. That mindset could be disastrous in a globalized world.

But how do you persuade twenty-first-century engineers and executives to change how they think? I wondered. The challenge seemed enormous.

To understand why a company such as Intel could—and should—use anthropological insights, it is worth pausing to ponder the profound paradox that hangs over twenty-first-century "globalization." In some senses, we live in a world of growing homogenization, or seeming "Coca-colonization," to use the phrase posited by the anthropologist Ulf Hannerz.[5] Flows of commerce, finance, information, and people have bound different corners of the globe increasingly tightly together in recent years. Thus, an item such as a bottle of Coca-Cola—or a computer chip—travels almost everywhere, creating an impression of "global homogenization," if not "cultural colonization" as David Howes, another anthropologist, says.[6] But there is a rub: even when symbols, ideas, images, and artifacts move around the world, they do not always mean the same thing to people who use them, let alone what the creator intended. A Coca-Cola bottle might look physically identical, but "in Russia [Coca-Cola] is believed to smooth wrinkles, in Haiti to revive someone from the dead, and in Barbados that it can turn copper into silver," Howes observes. In the movie *The Gods Must Be Crazy*, a !Kung tribe in the Kalahari desert turns a Coke bottle that has been tossed out of an airplane window into a ritual fetish. Although this story was fictional, the film was inspired by anthropologists' reports about so-called cargo cults seen in Melanesia and elsewhere that arose when Western military forces did airdrops of consumer goods, which locals embraced and then worshipped.[7] This might seem like merely an exotic piece of trivia. But it illustrates a key point: people create different webs of meaning around objects in different cultural contexts.

"Humans are symbolizing, conceptualizing, meaning-seeking animals," as the anthropologist Clifford Geertz—who was a towering force in the twentieth-century discipline—once observed. "The drive to make sense out of our experience, to give it form and order, is evidently as real and as pressing as the more familiar biological needs."[8] Moreover, one irony of globalization is that even as commerce and digital technology spread common cultural memes, digital technology also makes it easier for communities to express their cultural and ethnic distinctiveness. Mediums such as television, radio, and (more recently) the internet help minorities in nation states promote their own languages. Digital platforms enable a diaspora to rally together and communities to coalesce around symbols of ethnic difference or reject symbols of globalization. (For a delightfully humorous glimpse of this watch the 1985 film *The Coca-Cola Kid* about a tiny Australian town that resists the global drink brand.) Globalization fosters uniformity in some spheres and separation in others, making the concept of "Coca-colonization" a contradictory one.[9]

This creates traps. Coca-Cola executives found this out the hard way. At the start of the twenty-first century, they decided to sell bottled tea in China, but Chinese consumers shunned the product. They were baffled and asked some anthropologists to investigate. A group from the consultancy ReD Associates duly did so and pointed out that the meaning of green tea to Chinese consumers was different from its meaning to Americans. "To the corporate culture of Coke, based in Atlanta in the southern United States, the word 'tea' means a refreshing sweet drink that goes well with BBQ. For this [American] culture, tea is all about addition: adding sugar and caffeine for a late-afternoon kick," notes Christian Madsbjerg, cofounder of ReD. "[But] tea is about *subtraction* in the Chinese culture. Tea—like meditation—is a tool for revealing the true self . . . and should take away irritants and distractions like noise, pollution and stress."[10]

Similarly, in the late 1990s Merrill Lynch tried to expand its brokerage operations in Japan by using an advertising campaign that depicted its bull logo, a symbol that in America invokes market optimism.[11] The Merrill Lynch executives were delighted when surveys showed high consumer recognition in Japan. But then they realized that the bull was "recognized" because it was associated with Korean barbecue—not money. The so-called semiotic codes around consumer goods, to use a concept developed by Ferdinand de Saussure, are context-dependent. Or, to cite Geertz again, "webs of meaning" around objects and practice can vary—widely.

Gerber, the American baby food company now owned by the Swiss giant Nestlé, reportedly made an even worse mistake with cross-cultural messages, according to a tale often taught on Western marketing courses. In the mid-twentieth century, Gerber tried to expand its international operations by selling baby food in West Africa using jars decorated with a picture of a smiling baby, a common advertising image in America and Europe. But in some African cultures the picture on a tin is expected to represent the *ingredients* of the food.* "Accustomed to seeing the contents of packaged food depicted on product labels, [some] villagers assumed that the jars contained not food made *for* babies, but food made *of* babies," Howes writes. "Are Americans cannibals, they wondered?"[12]

But while cultural difference in a globally connected world creates traps, it can also create opportunities, or it can if people are willing to realize that not only do webs of meaning vary, but they are also *fluid*. This matters, not just for a company such as Intel but almost anybody operating in a globalized world. Cultural variation and fluidity can produce some surprising consequences—as shown by an entirely different story from Nestlé, in relation to the humble Kit Kat chocolate bar in Japan.

During most of the twentieth century Kit Kat was an object that seemed utterly "British." It emerged from the confectionary company founded by (and named after) Joseph Rowntree, a Victorian-era Quaker, and in the twentieth century the bar was advertised to British factory workers with the slogans "Have a break, have a Kit Kat" and "The biggest little meal in Britain."[13] Then, in the 1970s, Rowntree's (which later merged with the British group Mackintosh) exported the biscuit to other countries, with British branding, such as Japan. Sales there were mediocre,

*Nestlé cannot confirm the historical accuracy of this. The story might thus be apocryphal. However, the tale probably stems from a real incident of some sort, and the fact it has been widely repeated illustrates the key point: it is dangerous to assume others thinks like us.

since many Japanese mothers considered the biscuit too sweet for their children.

But in 2001, the Japanese marketing executives working with the Kit Kat brand in Japan—which had subsequently been acquired by Nestlé—noticed an odd development: although sales of Kit Kat were normally stable, they were surging in December, January, and February on the southern island of Kyushu.[14] There was no obvious reason. But when the local Nestlé executives investigated, they discovered that teenagers and university students in Kyushu had noticed that the name "Kit Kat" sounded similar to the phrase *kitto katsu* in the Kyushu dialect of Japanese, meaning "you must overcome." That had prompted them to buy Kit Kat bars as a lucky token when they took their exams for university and high school, an ordeal known as *juken*, which takes place between December and February.

Initially, the team at Nestlé's Japanese regional branch in Kobe did not think this cultural wrinkle—or mutation—had practical value. The corporate headquarters in Vevey, Switzerland, had strict rules about global branding, so the biscuit could not be renamed the "*kitto katsu*" bar in Japan. However, the news came at a crucial juncture: as Philip Sugai, a local business school professor points out, sales of Kit Kat in Japan were ailing and the Nestlé executives were under intense pressure to find a new strategy. The marketing tag "Have a break" did not work in Japan, but consumer surveys did not explain why. So the marketing team tried an experiment: instead of asking shoppers *directly* what was wrong with the tag, over several weeks they asked teenagers to take photos that illustrated how they imagined the concept of "having a break," paste them on a board, and then explain what they meant in an undirected way, *on their terms*. This approach had first emerged in the American marketing world in the late twentieth century, borrowing ideas from ethnography (of which more later). Western companies operating in Japan were keen to employ it, since the cross-cultural clash often seemed so confusing.

The teenagers' photos showed them listening to music, painting their toenails, sleeping, and so on. But none were eating chocolate. That revealed a crucial point: Japanese *juken* students did not think "having a break" with chocolate was remotely relaxing. The only good break they craved was a really long rest. So Kohzoh Takaoka, the head of marketing for Nestlé in Japan, along with colleagues such as Masafumi Ishibashi and Ryoji Maki, decided to downplay the "Have a break" tag and use the phrase "*Kit(to) Sakura Saku!*"—meaning "Wishes Come True!"—in local advertising instead, with pictures of cherry blossoms, or *sakura*.

If any executives from the Nestlé head office in Vevey had seen the images, they might have presumed it was just a pretty picture. But *sakura* are also a Japanese symbol of exam success—and were as close as the Nestlé Japan team could get to rebranding Kit Kat without disobeying the rules set by their Swiss bosses. Then they persuaded hotels near exam centers to distribute free Kit Kats to their guests with a postcard saying "the *sakura* are sure to bloom." "We didn't exactly tell the headquarters of Nestlé in Vevey what we were doing, because we knew that it would sound so strange," Ishibashi later told me. "We wanted to start quietly and see if it would work."

It did. Sales of Kit Kat soared, as students began to treat the chocolate bar as a new variant of an ancient Japanese phenomenon called *omamori*, a good luck charm that the Shinto religious shrines sell to devotees in Japan after it is blessed by a priest. To outsiders, chocolate might not seem sufficiently sacred to qualify for this label. But the Japanese are often pragmatic—and, as in all cultures, their semiotic codes are more fluid than they (or others) might realize. In 2003, a consumer survey carried out a by the internet portal Goo showed that no less than 34 percent of students had started using Kit Kat as *omamori*—second only to the 45 percent who were using proper Shinto tokens blessed by an actual priest. By 2008, 50 percent of all Japanese students taking exams reported that they were using a Kit Kat as *omamori*. Social media became filled with pictures of teenagers cradling the red-wrapped bar in their hand as they sat at exam desks, their head bowed as in prayer (or, more accurately, a state of terrified stress).[15]

The Japanese team in Kobe eventually told the senior Nestlé managers in Vevey what was going on. The Swiss executives were startled but—wisely—did not stop the experiment and cultural mutation. The Japanese team launched a Kit Kat box with space for the families of students to write good luck messages. Then they persuaded the Japanese postal system to turn these red boxes into quasi envelopes with prepaid stamps. When the Fukushima earthquake struck in 2011, Nestlé executives persuaded the local train company to accept Kit Kat boxes as train tickets. The team also experimented with taste. In Britain, the chocolate bar was a biscuit with three wafer layers separated by vanilla and covered in brown chocolate coating. But in 2003 the Japanese team added strawberry powder to create a pink Kit Kat. The next year they added green tea (*matcha*) to the mix. Soon there was an entire rainbow spectrum of bars: a purple bar flavored like sweet potato; another green bar flavored with wasabi; others flavored like soy, corn, plum, melon, cheese, and butter. The company even launched a special "throat lozenge" flavor as a tribute to the fans supporting the Japanese soccer World Cup team. "Called Kit Kat *Nodo Ame Aji*, which translates to Kit Kat Cough Drop Flavour, this new chocolate actually delivers a dose of 2.1 percent throat lozenge powder in every serving . . . to provide a fresh and invigorating flavor," a local Japanese website explained. This "lozenge" flavor was supposed to help the fans cheer more loudly.[16]

By 2014 the bar had become the best-selling single type of confection in Japan, and the Kit Kat bars had become so closely associated with Japanese culture that they were being sold as "local"—*Japanese*—souvenirs for international tourists at airports. Then came another twist: in 2019 Nestlé started selling the green *matcha* Kit Kat in European markets, including Britain. Strictly speaking, this did not represent a

Japanese import as such: the *matcha* bars were actually manufactured in a factory in Germany. But it was far from anything that Rowntree, the Victorian English Quaker, might have imagined would happen to the British chocolate he launched in York. The senior executives in Vevey, Switzerland, were so impressed that they took a once-unimaginable step: they promoted Ryoji Maki, the young(ish) executive who had executed much of the *kitto katsu* campaign (with Ishibashi and Takaoka), to run global marketing strategy for Kit Kat at the Swiss headquarters. This was the first time that a Japanese person had held this role. "What this story shows is that you have to think outside the mainstream," Maki told his Swiss colleagues, as he showed them pictures of Japanese teenagers praying in exams to the red-wrapped Kit Kat bar. Or as Ishibashi echoed: "The point is that you have to listen to consumers, where they are. You cannot assume anything." Neither for chocolate—or, it would turn out, computer chips.

When the Australian anthropologist Genevieve Bell arrived at Intel's research division in Portland, Oregon, in 1998, the company was at a strategic crossroads. In the previous years, the West Coast group had become the world's largest producer of semiconductors, putting it at the center of the personal computing ecosystem. Now the landscape was changing. Although Intel dominated Western markets, it was the emerging market regions, like Asia, that now offered the most growth. And while Intel had previously sold chips to companies that made computers for office use, consumers were now a fast-swelling source of demand. Intel executives needed to understand these new non-Western users, including women. Those were a particular mystery since most Intel engineers were men. "I packed up and moved to Oregon and started at a company I knew little about in an industry I knew nothing about in a field nobody knew anything about," Bell later explained. "My boss told me they needed my help understanding women—all women!

"I said, there are 3.2 billion women on the planet. And she said, 'yes, if you could tell us what they want, that would be great.'"[17]

Bell joined a group called "People and Practices Research" staffed by several dozen designers, scientists, and cognitive psychologists—plus a few other anthropologists, such as Ken Anderson and John Sherry. Anderson, like Bell, came from a classic anthropology background: he had done his fieldwork studying music culture in the Azores. The research group had already developed some novel ways to study consumers inside America; at one point they stuck a modified calculator on a fridge door, as a self-styled "fridge pad," to see how consumers might react to the (then) utterly shocking idea of letting a computer enter a kitchen. "The fridge pad really got the engineers' attention," Sherry chuckled. But Bell's mission was to look outside America at places such as India, Australia, Malaysia, Singapore, Indonesia, China, and Korea. Her assistant referred to them with the acronym I AM SICK.[18]

Bell started by recruiting local ethnographers from universities and consultancies, who stayed in households in those countries for several days, watching how families worked, lived, prayed, and socialized, and how technology fitted into that. This was not full-scale participant observation of the sort venerated by the descendants of Malinowksi and Boas. But it borrowed some ideas: instead of relying on statistics and surveys, the researchers used observation and open-ended conversations. The aim was to look at the "webs of meanings" that people gave to objects in their lives and provide a "thick description" of these cultural patterns, to cite Geertz. So instead of starting the research by asking consumers "What do you think about computers?" the anthropologists *first* looked at the context of people's lives and tried to see—and imagine—where computers might fit in. This begged a question: If the anthropologists were looking at the entire picture and providing "thick description," how could they know what to focus on? The answer lay in hunting for patterns and semiotic codes. Just as a Kit Kat bar could have different "webs of meanings" in Japan and Britain, the treatment of computers could vary with context. In Malaysia, Bell saw there were Muslim communities using the GPS capabilities of their phones to locate Mecca for their prayers. In other parts of Asia there were families who burned paper models of cell phones as a prayer offering for their ancestors to use in the next world. In China, people were taking their mobile phones to a temple to be blessed.[19] Indeed Bell encountered a phone shop manager in China who refused to sell her a phone—even with plenty in stock—because he did not have access to a lucky "number." "It was like a scene from a Monty Python show," she later recalled. "I could see all the phones stacked up but he kept saying he had none for sale."[20]

Spatial patterns mattered too. "I had a lovely moment with some guys in the States and some guys in Malaysia," she noted. "I was explaining to them that one of the differences between Asia and the U.S. has to do with the physical size and configuration of people's homes. Intel is very interested in the digital home, and we have to be careful about the assumptions we're making about what that home looks like." When an American designer said that each of his kids had a PC in their room, she explained, "the guys in Malaysia said, 'Wow! Your kids have their own rooms? Aren't they lonely?' "[21] The Americans were surprised by the Malaysian reaction. The Malaysians were startled that the Americans were even surprised.

It was not easy for Bell and the rest of the team to communicate the insights back to the engineers working at Intel in America. Engineers were trained to solve problems with hard numbers, but the anthropologists preferred to tell stories to interpret cultures. "You have these 'softer' scientists sitting next to hard scientists designing chips and things very familiar to Intel, and it's much harder to justify and measure the qualitative research," Pat Gelsinger, then Intel's chief technology officer (and later Intel CEO), admitted to a reporter a few years after Bell's arrival.[22] Or as Sherry said: "What you are facing is a problem of cultural translation on many levels"—between scientists and anthropologists.

But the Intel anthropologists tried to bridge this divide. Bell plastered the walls of the Intel offices in Portland with gigantic photos of people in "ROW"—Rest Of the World—using computing products. She used storytelling to communicate the ideas to engineers. Sometimes they rejected the messages. Early in their research, the anthropologists reported back to the Intel executives that consumers were embracing cell phones around the world with startling alacrity and suggested the company should focus on that. The suggestion was initially brushed off (which analysts later concluded was a strategic mistake on the part of Intel). There was also a big battle around the question of paper. Many of the Intel engineers were convinced that the future of the office would be "paperless," since they were used to working online themselves—and assumed everyone else wanted to do that too. But when the anthropologists spoke to people who were *not* Silicon Valley engineers, they realized that consumers liked paper for emotional reasons. "It's what anthropologists call a persistent and stubborn artifact," Bell observed.

In other areas the anthropologists did have "a real impact" on strategy, Gelsinger said. Until the early twenty-first century the Intel managers tended to assume that it would be hard to sell PCs into a market such as Malaysia because per capita wealth was low. However, the anthropologists could see that extended families were pooling resources for investment for numerous other products, and placed a high value on education. So they pitched an idea: Why not try to position the PC as a product that an *extended* family could use for the next generation to engage in education? It worked: sales of PCs rose. Then Bell noticed that among Chinese families there was widespread concern that a PC might distract children from their homework, and the anthropologists suggested to the engineers that Intel designers create a special "lock" that could be placed on computers to prevent children from playing computer games. The Intel engineers subsequently worked with a Chinese PC maker to create this "China Home-Learning PC" and released it in 2005.[23] It sold well. "At first the engineers didn't want to hear us at all, or not until they had seen an example of success," Sherry observed. "But once they had seen what could happen, they didn't want to do anything without us."

As the years passed, the anthropologists slowly won respect in the company. Bell was promoted to become "director of user research" and put in charge of a business unit called "Digital Home"; two other social scientists—Eric Dishman and Tony Salvador—were respectively asked to oversee "Digital Health" and "Emerging Markets" teams. Then the experiments intensified: as engineers inserted computers, and chips, into every corner of people's homes, offices, and cars, the anthropologists followed along, watching everything they could.[24]

In 2014, for example, Bell and another anthropologist named Alexandra Zafiroglu went to an underground parking lot in Singapore to meet a man called "Frank" who drove a white SUV. They started by asking him to take out every single object that was sitting inside the car and then put it on a plastic sheet, so that they could climb onto a stepladder and photograph it. A vast pile of items appeared. Some were expected: a car manual, manuals for the electronic devices, Bluetooth headset, and a detachable GPS system. Much of the haul, however, was not. There were iPods, calculators, a collection of CDs and DVDs, remote controls for the car's DVD players, wireless headphones, and "umbrellas, golf clubs, credit cards, toys, candy, hand sanitizer, a small Buddha given to Frank by his mother, and an anti-slip pad on which the Buddha rested," a reporter later noted.[25] To engineers this seemed like "rubbish"—and irrelevant for the beautifully crafted computing technology that the engineers were designing for cars. Frank himself seemed embarrassed by the "junk." So did all the other car owners that Bell and Zafiroglu met; they never voluntarily talked about these items. The clutter was not exactly hidden, but it was not seen either; or not until Bell and Zafiroglu spread it out on a plastic sheet.

But, as anthropologists, Bell and Zafiroglu believed that nothing is just "mess"—or irrelevant. What we consider embarrassing is revealing. The display on the plastic sheet showed two things. First, people "were using their cars to keep them socially safe, not just physically safe," by retaining symbols and rituals that delineated their territory. "In Malaysia and Singapore, for example, we were surprised to find people kept *ang pow* packets (lucky envelopes of money given at Chinese New Year) in their cars all year round."[26] Secondly, car drivers were *not* using the tech as expected or planned. Engineers had installed "embedded voice-command systems" in cars to reduce distracted driving and blithely assumed this innovation was being used. That was because when drivers were asked direct questions about the technology, they told researchers they used it. But when the anthropologists observed what drivers actually did—not what they said they did—they saw that whenever drivers got bored in traffic, they reached for their personal handheld devices and used those, not the voice-command systems that engineers had so lovingly designed. Rhetoric diverged from reality.

Bell urged the engineers to embrace this pattern—instead of merely ignoring or deriding it. Rather than assuming that drivers would simply use the devices already inside the car, Bell suggested that the engineers should design products that would enable consumers to *sync* their own personal devices with their cars. There was a bigger lesson here: the engineers had previously tended to start with an innovative idea and impose it on others; the anthropologists were urging them to *begin* by looking at the world through users' eyes, in all their variety, and respond to that. Or as Bell told me in the Computer History Museum, the lesson she kept trying to impart was this: "*That may be your worldview, but it is not everybody's!*" It was simple to say, but painfully hard to remember.

By 2015, the focus of the social science team was shifting. When Bell first joined, the research group spent most of its time studying how consumers reacted to the artifacts of technology—like computers—and how those might fit into people's lives. This echoed the way that the intellectual descendants of Malinowski, Mead, and Boas had studied the interaction between people, artifacts, rituals, space, and symbols. However, as the twenty-first century wore on, and cyberspace became increasingly dominant, the focus shifted more toward networks. Machines were no longer merely passive objects. They were interactive devices that almost had agency. That created new questions for the anthropologists: What do humans do when machines start to have their own forms of "intelligence"? Can culture be programmed into AI? Should anthropologists study intelligent machines like a new "other"? How can they explore networks, not just "things" and people? "What anthropology offers now is not just about user experience. It is about taking a holistic view of tech, thinking, for example, about what kind of guardrails we need to develop products in an ethical way," Sherry argued. Or as Anderson observed: "Anthropology started as a study of 'man' [sic] the animal, in an evolutionary and comparative framework. Today, new instantiations of A.I. challenge us to consider what it means to be human, or nonhuman. It pushes . . . anthropology beyond the human."[27] This created a host of new questions for engineers too. "We are moving away from a mentality with engineers of just asking what is technologically possible to design, to a world where we say what *should* we design?" Lama Nachman, chief scientist at Intel observed. "That is quite different. For that we need to look at social context."

So the anthropologists started to study the "webs of meaning" around AI. This revealed some subtle but striking distinctions. In Germany, for example, it seemed that consumers were happy to accept the use of AI in devices for elderly home care, but only if the data from those AI devices was not shared outside the house. The researchers reckoned that was because of folk memories about past government surveillance. In America, by contrast, there was less focus on whether or not data collected by AI devices would be shared inside or outside the home, and more unease about whether consumers would have "agency" over a machine.

One of the most striking—and sensitive—pieces of research revolved around the use of facial recognition technologies in China and America. Anderson led this, as part of a four-strong team. It was long way from the research he had done as an academic anthropologist among traditional musicians in the Azores. However, the approach was similar: patient observation and listening, without prior assumptions. The project was based around half a dozen sites. Four were in China, mostly located in Hangzhou, including retail and office complexes, and a couple of schools that were described with the pseudonyms "High School X" and "High School Z." Two sites were in America, and described with the pseudonyms "St. Nicholas of Myra, a private Catholic Pre-K to 8th grade school in a gentrifying urban neighborhood," and "the Sheriff's Department of Rock County."[28] Over a couple of years, the anthropologists visited the sites, and observed how facial recognition technology and AI systems were being used.

Some of the observations were not particularly surprising. In the American locations, the team observed a sense of "moral panic" around AI that echoed the tone in the Western media, which had been warning that these technologies threatened core American values, such as privacy and liberty. However, when the anthropologists watched what people were actually *doing*—not saying—they saw as many inconsistencies as they had seen with the "mess" in people's cars. "The principal at St. Nicholas of Myra has recently deployed a facial recognition system . . . to monitor who comes in and out of the school," the research team noted. However, the school only monitored adults, not kids, to make it "safe" and "ethical"—even though it was the children they were actually trying to keep safe. When the researchers asked why a school even needed an AI system, the teachers declared that "the system allows the principal and receptionist to identify and greet everyone by name, which they feel fosters a feeling of community . . . [and] makes sure the kids are safe, happy, healthy and holy." No one could explain, though, how AI helped kids be "holy." Similarly, in the Sheriff's Department of Rock County, Anderson found that while the police were permitted to use "facial recognition software in a distributed crime solving team . . . the guidelines for the sheriff's department are very clear in that the video does not come from any city or county public cameras, it only comes from private residential or commercial cameras." Why footage from residential cameras was deemed acceptable, while government camera footage was not, was a mystery—to the researchers and police.

In China the situation was different. The team found that facial recognition devices were ubiquitous in buildings, shops, banks, and schools, and "so ordinary and uneventful that [their use] often goes unnoticed, both to users and to researchers who are supposed to be in the field keenly observing." On one occasion, for example, the team asked a woman they were working with to walk through the facial recognition system at her residence. She duly did so—but in such a casual manner that the Intel anthropologists had to ask her to repeat the action over and over again, because interacting with facial recognition cameras was so "normal" that it was hard to see these interactions at all. On another occasion the Intel team asked to accompany a Chinese man to take money out of the facial recognition ATM, and they encountered the same problem. "You could almost see him thinking, 'Oh yeah, foreigners think facial recognition is interesting? Is this a scam to take my money?' We also had to ask him to log in three times to catch the process."

To American observers, this situation was apt to spark horror, not least because reports had emerged from 2017 on that the Chinese government was using surveillance tools—including facial recognition—to engage in repression and human rights abuses against the Uighur population in the Xinjiang province. Many Americans assumed that Chinese consumers must secretly hate the idea of this surveillance, since the Americans did.

The Intel team argued, however, that it was a mistake to presume that the Chinese must view things as Americans did. They did not pretend to fully understand what was happening in the minds and lives of the Chinese people they were studying: their studies were "shallow" by academic standards (of a relatively short duration), the team relied on translators (since Anderson did not speak Chinese), and they knew they were operating in a country with government controls. "The snapshots don't tell a complete story—there isn't one to tell," their report explained.

Yet even allowing for these caveats, they could see a big difference in how the Chinese were reacting to facial recognition systems, compared to the Americans. "The overwhelming presumption in China is that the government exists to keep people safe," the team explained. "In a society that has had overt and everyday surveillance in human and institutional form for over 70 years, the emergence and deployment of recognition through cameras has been less controversial than in the USA." There were some rebellions. The Intel team tracked a "Chinese High School Z," which used facial recognition to determine what the students could—or could not—eat in the school canteen, giving students who were deemed to be overweight steamed fish, say, instead of barbecued pork. But when the parents and students "complained fiercely," the system was scrapped. The Intel team also noted unease among some Chinese students about the intrusive surveillance. "I've had cameras in my schools all of my life," June, one student, told Anderson's team in "High School X," which deployed more than forty cameras to track the students. "They are watching us to protect us, but it is a little creepy. I mean, they know so much about us that they could know when you go to the bathroom or if you were dating and who." (It turned out that her suspicions were justified: a teacher later told the Intel team that "we've known . . . [June] has been dating for over a month" but had not banned it since "she and her boyfriend are both getting very good grades.")

However, these signs of resistance—or concern—did not mean that

Americans could project their own assumptions onto China. In China real-world facial recognition was so ubiquitous that it had become boring. "We watched as customers at a KFC quickly ordered on a screen then smiled briefly to pay," Anderson noted. These are just normal, everyday, "nothing to see here" parts of urban life. Most Chinese regarded tech innovation as inherently positive, since they thought this would spark more growth and make the country stronger on the world stage. There was also a subtle, but important, difference in how Chinese and Americans viewed the merits of machines relative to humans. Americans were scared of the idea of machines making decisions, partly because of the impact on popular culture of movies such as *2001: A Space Odyssey* (which shows an AI system called Hal taking over a spaceship, with terrible consequences). But in China, there was so little trust in human bureaucrats, because of events such as the Cultural Revolution, that dealing with computers instead of people sometimes felt like an improvement. Robots were likely to be less capricious and cruel, and an AI-enabled facial recognition platform did not demand bribes. There was another subtle difference around the idea of "individuality." Americans feared that AI and facial recognition systems would rob them of privacy and individual rights. But in China there had been so little preexisting respect for individual rights that it seemed almost flattering that a facial recognition camera could make judgments based on how a unique individual looked—instead of "just" an anonymous number. Or as Anderson said: "In a curious way, [in China] AI facial recognition technologies highlight the individual, a hallmark of Western culture and traditions."

This did not mean that the Intel team *endorsed* how China was using these technologies, Anderson stressed. But the research showed that it was a mistake for Americans to assume that they alone knew how technology was being incorporated into people's lives—or how it could and should be. That meant that studying differences was valuable because it could throw each culture's ideas into sharper relief. It could also offer clues about the future, given that it was not just technology that was jumping across borders, but ideas and attitudes too. When Anderson started the study in 2017, many Americans were horrified by the idea of having any type of facial recognition technology in their lives. By 2020, however, they—like the Chinese—were becoming almost nonchalant about some manifestations of the once strange innovation since it had become embedded in some devices such as the new Apple smartphones. And that raised another urgent question: if ideas and technologies kept jumping across borders and mutating, faster than almost anyone expected, how could anyone define the limits? "The focus now is on meeting the needs of users in sectors like AI in an ethical way," explained Nachman. "For that you need social scientists and engineers to work together."

Americans presumed that it was only Westerners who asked such questions or expressed these scruples. However, that assumption was also wrong. When Intel had first entered the Chinese market in 2008, the idea of "anthropology" was barely known in most Chinese universities.* However, in the early years of the twenty-first century Intel hired some Chinese academics who had been trained in other branches of social science in places such as Fudan University to do research. So did other consumer companies. The concept spread, and a group of Fudan academics subsequently created a consultancy called Rhizome that billed itself as "the first consulting company in China to feature applied anthropology," blending ethnography and data science.[29] Then, in the summer of 2020, a self-styled business anthropologist named Zhang Jieying, who worked at the Chinese Academy of Social Science in Beijing, posted a heartfelt memo on the internet.[30]

"The value of anthropology is to provide transnational cultural

*China did actually have a fledgling social science tradition in the early years of the twentieth century: the sociologist Fei Xiaotong wrote a masterful study of Chinese society in 1947. However, social sciences were subsequently crushed in the Cultural Revolution.

translation for the era of globalization," she declared, pointing out that American companies such as Microsoft, Intel, and Apple had created teams of social scientists to do precisely this. Jieying urged Chinese companies to copy the idea, since they needed to understand the peculiar cultural contradictions—and "webs of meaning"—created by globalization too. "Today's Chinese technology companies and digital products want to go out of China . . . [and] need cultural translation of anthropology."

Jeiying stressed that there was another reason why Chinese companies needed to import the idea of anthropology: ethics. "The potential value of anthropology for the development of science and technology is also that it is a buzzer with [a] warning effect," she declared. It sounded uncannily similar to what the Intel team was saying. Ideas can sometimes move around and mutate in ways that are even more surprising than the evolution of a chocolate bar.*

In late 2020, or some eight years after I first met Bell in Mountain View's Computer History Museum, I caught up with her again by phone. By then the world of business anthropology—and Bell—had moved on. Three decades earlier, very few anthropologists worked at companies. By 2020, however, social scientists equipped with ethnography skills had moved into numerous tech groups. Shortly before Intel built its team, for example, anthropologists such as Lucy Suchman, Julian Orr, Jeanette Blomberg, and Brigitte Jordan at Xerox developed pioneering research ideas (of which more later). Blomberg then worked at IBM with Melissa Cefkin (who subsequently joined Nissan). Nelle Steel, Donna Flynn,

*The word "globalization" is often tossed around as if it is a single thing. It is not. As displayed in an excellent set of metrics from DHL and NYU Stern Business School, globalization has (at least) four components: the movement of goods, money, people, and ideas. In this century, the latter category of globalization has exploded much faster than the others, due to the internet. https://www.stern.nyu.edu/experience-stern/about/departments-centers-initiatives/centers-of-research/center-future-management/dhl-initiative-globalization.

and Tracey Lovejoy built a research team at Microsoft which eventually became one of the biggest employers of anthropologists in the world. Abigail Posner developed social science at Google, using anthropologist consultants such as Tom Maschio and Phil Surles. Apple built a team with Joy Mountford, Jim Miller, Bonnie Nardi, and others. Consumer goods companies were using anthropologists too. Indeed, the trend became so marked that in 2005 Intel's Anderson joined forces with Microsoft's Lovejoy to create a dedicated forum to develop business ethnography, called "Ethnographic Praxis in Industry Conference," better known as EPIC. The ugly name baffled most outsiders. But that had a benefit: the mysterious title sounded more impressive to techies than "anthropology" since the latter phrase had an exotic, prehistoric image.

Not all anthropologists regarded this as a victory for the discipline. Far from it. Even as EPIC gained legs, some academic anthropologists hated the idea that anthropologists were working for companies at all. An encounter that Kathi Kitner, another anthropologist at Intel, had with an academic she described with the pseudonym "Trip" during a research trip to India was typical.[31] One night Trip and Kitner got talking over a cigarette and "as [we] smoked, Trip took a deep drag, and asked: 'How do you continue as an anthropologist and work at a place like Intel?' " Kitner later recalled. "I knew what she really meant. Don't they suck your soul out from within you? Don't you hate having to sell out people's lives for a corporate profit? What is it like to be working from the belly of a capitalistic beast? How can you work under such *unethical* conditions? Haven't you *sold out*?"

Kitner replied "No." She believed that her work at Intel was valuable because she was helping engineers gain empathy for people different from them. Or as Bell explained: "What we are trying to do is show people that tech is not just designed for and by a group of white men in their twenties in California." However, unease continued to bubble among some academics. Even enthusiasts for business anthropology fretted that their methods might become so diluted that they would be subsumed into activities like "user experience" (known as USX or UX) research, human computer interaction (HCI), human-centered design, human factors engineering, and so on.[32]

There was another problem: working for a company left anthropologists at the mercy of changing corporate fashions. Intel was no exception. During the first decade of the twenty-first century, the company scrambled to hire anthropologists because it wanted to use that research to win clients. But in the middle of the second decade, there was a wave of corporate restructuring, the social scientists were scattered into different business units, and their numbers reduced. That was partly because Intel's own clients were hiring ethnographers of their own, and the company no longer sat at the center of a single ecosystem based around the PC. The other reason was that Intel was facing mounting strategic challenges, since Asian rivals were grabbing market share in the chip sector. Indeed, by late 2020 the challenges were so serious that Intel was being targeted by activists. In theory that meant there was *more*, not less, need for the company to hire innovative thinkers who could look around corners, imagine the future, and analyze the cultural patterns inside and outside the company. In practice, Intel (like almost every other company in this situation) responded by cutting back on activities that harried managers viewed as "non-core."[33]

So Bell reinvented herself—again. In 2017 she returned to Australia, and while she remained a senior fellow at Intel, she became director of an innovation institute called 3Ai at Australia National University. There she assembled an unlikely mix of anthropologists, nuclear scientists, sociologists, and computer experts with a mission to create a new branch of engineering that could build an AI-enabled "future safely, sustainably and responsibly."[34] She recruited Alexandra Zafiroglu from Intel to join her. The idea was that just as the invention of programmable computers had led to the emergence of software engineers in the twentieth century, in the twenty-first century cyber-physical systems will lead to a new type of engineer—albeit one that does not yet have a name. She also joined a Australian government advisory committee on AI, science, and tech.

"It's a long way from where you started," I laughed as we spoke over the phone. An image popped into my mind of her eating witchetty grubs, as a child, in the Australian outback. *It's a long way from where we both started,* I might have added, thinking about my days in Obi-Safed. But Bell argued not. When anthropologists had first studied Australian Aboriginal peoples, they had been exploring new frontiers, or cultures which seemed "strange." At Intel, Bell had embraced a similar goal in unlikely places such as an underground Singaporean parking lot. Now she was exploring a new frontier of "strange"—AI. The thread that linked all these endeavors was the same goal she had told me in the Computer History Museum: the need to tell powerful Western elites, "That may be your world view, but it's not everybody's!"

Business executives needed to hear it, she argued. So did techies. However, there was another group that needed to listen to this message too: policy makers. Ignoring alternative viewpoints was (and is) detrimental for business in a global age. So, too, for governments tackling contagion risks—like pandemics.

THREE

CONTAGION

(OR WHY CAN'T MEDICINE STOP PANDEMICS?)

"Human diversity makes tolerance more than a virtue; it makes it a requirement for survival."

—René Dubos[1]

Paul Richards, a white-bearded anthropology professor, sat in an ornate eighteenth-century conference room inside the Admiralty Building in Whitehall, headquarters of the British government. The walls were festooned with oil paintings of British dignitaries. Facing him, across a highly polished mahogany table was Chris Whitty, a balding doctor-turned-bureaucrat who was chief scientific advisor for the British government's overseas aid and a respected expert on issues such as infectious diseases. It was the late summer of 2014.[2]

Whitty had reason to be worried. Some months earlier a highly infectious disease called Ebola had started to sweep through Britain's former colony of Sierra Leone and neighboring Liberia and Guinea. Groups such as the World Health Organization and Médecins Sans Frontières had rushed to halt the contagion. So had the UK, French, and American governments: Barack Obama's American administration had even sent four thousand troops to Liberia. The world's best medical experts at places such as Harvard were hunting for a vaccine, and computer scientists were using Big Data tools to track it.

But nothing had worked. Ebola kept moving through the vast forests of West Africa. The governments in Europe and the United States were braced for it to arrive imminently on their shores. The Centers for Disease Control in Washington was warning that the world was "losing the fight" against the disease and more than 1 million people would die unless something—anything—could turn the tide.[3] So Whitty had summoned Richards and other anthropologists with a question: Why had computing and medical science apparently failed in West Africa? Had Western scientific experts missed something?

Richards hardly knew whether to laugh—or cry. A couple of decades earlier a British cabinet minister named Norman Tebbit had announced, while working in a similar white stucco building, that it was a waste of public money to fund anthropologists since they just did irrelevant research, such as "studies of the prenuptial habits of natives of the Upper Volta valley."[4] Richards epitomized Tebbit's target. He hailed from the British Pennines and had started his career as a geographer, but then spent four decades doing patient participant observation among the Mende people in the forest regions of Sierra Leone, living among them, speaking their language—and marrying a local woman, Esther Mokuwa. She was a seasoned researcher in her own right, and also sat at the mahogany table facing Whitty. Richards was an expert on agricultural practices but also fascinated by Mende ritual since he espoused a "Durkheimian" philosophy, named after the French intellectual Émile Durkheim, that argued that cosmology shapes behavior (and vice versa). Richards passionately believed that rituals matter, be they marriage ceremonies, death rites, or anything else.[5]

Tebbit had scorned this. But in 2014, history had taken a peculiar twist. As Ebola spread, reports had emerged about behavior and beliefs that seemed horrifyingly strange to Western ears: patients were running away from hospitals, hiding from aid workers, attacking (and killing) healthcare professionals, holding funerals where they touched the infected—and highly infectious—corpses of Ebola victims. "I heard people kiss dead bodies," Whitty said. Western journalists had reported this detail with baffled horror; it evoked the type of exotic—racist—images from Joseph Conrad's novella *Heart of Darkness*.

"They don't just kiss bodies for no reason!" Mokuwa retorted. She had arrived at the Whitehall building stricken with grief for her dying compatriots. But she was also furiously angry. The main reason why the anti-pandemic policy was going so wrong, she told Whitty, was that Western medical "experts" were only looking at events through their own assumptions, not locals' eyes. Without some empathy—or an attempt to make strange seem familiar—medical and data science would be useless.

The meeting drew to a close. As they trooped out, Richards spotted a historical plaque at the side of the ornate room—and burst out laughing. The meeting room had once hosted the corpse of Lord Admiral Nelson, the revered British naval hero, who had died in the Battle of Trafalgar in 1805. After death, his body was apparently pickled in a cask of brandy, brought back to Britain in a ship called the HMS *Pickle* (yes, really).* It was then displayed in Greenwich and Admiralty House, Whitehall. Some fifteen thousand mourners came to pay respect—by touching and kissing his brandy-soaked corpse.[6]

"If Nelson had Ebola, everyone in London would have caught it!" Richards pointed out. Whitty laughed. However, Richards was trying to highlight a serious point: no culture has a right to dismiss other cultures as "strange" without realizing that their own behavior can also look odd. Particularly in a pandemic.

*No, I am not making this up: it really happened. If you are chuckling or wincing, ask yourself this: Why? What does it reveal about your view of "normal?" Then watch the Netflix series *The Crown* to see how the body of King George VI was embalmed and displayed as recently as 1952. Ideas of "normal" change.

The word "Ebola" comes from the name of a river deep in the African Congo. In 1976, doctors reported a strange—terrifying—new "hemorrhagic fever" around that Ebola River. It started with a fever, sore throat, muscular pain, headaches, vomiting, diarrhea, and rashes, but often led to liver and kidney failure and internal bleeding. The Johns Hopkins Medical Center observed that "25 percent to 90 percent of those infected" died, with "average case fatality rate . . . around 50 percent."[7] That was comparable to Europe's thirteenth-century Black Death plague.*

In the subsequent three decades, the disease sporadically flared up in different African regions, but then ebbed away because its victims expired so fast. That changed in December 2013 when a two-year-old child became infected in a village in Guinea, near the town called Guéckédou, located near the wiggly—artificial—borders that nineteenth-century colonial rulers had used to divide the vast West African forests into countries called "Guinea," "Sierra Leone," and "Liberia." The local population were tightly entwined with one another, constantly moving across the borders, and the disease spread quickly.

A dark-haired American called Susan Erikson was one of the first Westerners to hear about Ebola. Early in her life she had spent a couple of years in Sierra Leone, as an idealistic volunteer with America's Peace Corps. She then returned to college in the 1990s to do a doctorate in anthropology but with a twist: she combined cultural analysis with medical studies. This branch of the discipline, called "medical anthropology," champions a core idea: the human body cannot be explained by "hard" science alone, since sickness and health need to be put in a cultural *and* social context. Doctors typically view the human body in terms of biology. However, in

*The reason for the wide range in mortality rates is that the impact of Ebola varied enormously between communities, depending on poverty levels, healthcare, and infrastructure, as Paul Farmer, the medical anthropologist, has stressed.

most cultures the body is also treated "as an image of society" that reflects our beliefs about issues such as pollution and purity, as Mary Douglas, the anthropologist, points out.[8] This affects how health, sickness, and medical risk are viewed. Or, as Douglas observed in a book she coauthored on nuclear, environmental, and medical risks, since "the perception of risk is a social process," each culture "is biased towards highlighting certain risks and downplaying others."[9] During a pandemic, for example, people typically cling to "their own" group, however they choose to define it. That means people typically overemphasize risks that arrive from outside the group and underestimate the ones that are inside the group. Throughout history pandemics have been associated with xenophobia, even if people are complacent about domestic infection risks.

Erikson initially hoped to use medical anthropology to study reproductive health in Sierra Leone. But in the 1990s a brutal civil war erupted in the region. So she switched her focus to Germany before eventually returning to Sierra Leone, from her academic base at Simon Fraser University in Canada, to explore how digital health technology was impacting public health. On February 27, 2014, she woke up in a rented room in Freetown, Sierra Leone's capital, reached for her phone, and read about a "strange hemorrhagic fever presenting like Ebola" in an online newsfeed. "I just went, 'OK,' better note that. But I wasn't too concerned. I see a lot of 'dread disease' feeds like that,"[10] she recalls. Then, when the health ministry called a meeting to plan its response, with government officials and representatives from groups such as Médecins Sans Frontières (MSF), UNICEF, and the World Health Organization, Erikson's research team attended to do some participant observation.

"An administrator begins the meeting with an overview of Ebola and the threat of its spread," the research team's field notes say. "Then [the administrator] moves to the task: 'We have a template [to fight Ebola], but we need to bring it home, to make it Sierra Leonean.' He explains that the template is a WHO document from [an earlier Ebola episode in]

Uganda that needs to be wordsmith[ed] for Sierra Leone. 'We are here to make surveillance and laboratory plans.' "[11]

"People in the audience respond as though they've done this before," the notes continue. "The group begins discussing surveillance tools—reviewing the standards for evaluating suspected and confirmed Ebola cases. . . . People begin debating about the number of people that need to be trained for RRTs (Rapid Response Teams). People calculate that with 1200 Public Health Units (PHUs) (health posts) throughout the country plus private sector clinics, 2 RRTs per PHU means that 2500 people need to be trained."

To participants, the conversation seemed unremarkable. The Sierra Leonean officials were following a script to fight contagion created by international organizations such as WHO and legitimized by global health science. But as Erikson listened, she felt worried. Officials were tossing around acronyms like talismans to ward off danger, signal power, and unlock funding from Western donors. She had seen this many times before. However the Sierra Leoneans lacked the sovereignty to make their own decisions about Ebola and nobody was asking the Sierra Leoneans what was best—or what would-be Ebola victims might want. *Is this really the best way to fight a pandemic?* Erikson wondered. She feared not.

Two weeks later, on March 11, a Boston-based tech platform called HealthMap issued a global alert about Ebola. It seemed a victory for American innovation. Until that point, it had always been WHO that warned the world about a new disease outbreak. But HealthMap, which won funding from Google, had beaten it to the punch. "Meet the Bots That Knew Ebola Was Coming!" trumpeted a headline from *Time* magazine, next to some terrifying photographs of healthcare workers wearing white hazmat suits and goggles, in an African jungle.[12] "How This Algorithm Detected the Ebola Outbreak Before Humans Could!" declared Fast Company.[13] The news sparked excitement among Western medical groups and techies. It seemed that these computing tools could not only track the disease, but also predict where it might move next in a way that would enable Ebola to be crushed swiftly. At Harvard Medical School, a British researcher called Caroline Buckee had analyzed the records of 15 million Kenyan cell phones to track the spread of malaria. She hoped to do same with Ebola and asked the telecoms company Orange for permission to use cell phone data in Liberia for this purpose. "The ubiquity of cell phones is really changing how we think of diseases," she observed.[14]

Half a world away in Freetown, however, Erikson was getting worried. With a bird's-eye view, the data science seemed impressive. Not so with a worm's-eye perspective. One reason was that sites such as HealthMap tended to track news in English, not local African languages or even the French used in Guinea. There was no guarantee that models developed for malaria could be transposed onto Ebola.[15] There were few reliable cell phone towers to dispatch the all-important "pings." Most important, there was the problem that Intel had grappled with: it was a mistake for anybody (especially Western techies) to assume that everyone shared their attitude to life. In America or Europe, people typically have a one-on-one relationship with their phone, and these devices are regarded as "private" property, an extension of self. Losing a phone feels to Westerners almost like losing part of themselves. Not so in Sierra Leone. "Cell phones are loaned, traded, and passed around among family and friends, like clothes, books, and bicycles. A single phone can be shared by an extended family or, in rural areas, a neighborhood or a village," Erikson observed.[16] Thus while the phone records suggested that phone ownership in Sierra Leone equated to 94 percent of the population, this did *not* mean that everyone had a phone, as Western tech experts tended to assume; some people had a phone for each network, but others had none. "Pings" were not people. That made it impossible to build accurate predictive models with "pings" alone. Computer science needs social science, if you want to make sense of data.

By the early summer of 2014, Ebola was spreading fast. On the advice of global health groups, the governments of Sierra Leone, Guinea, and Liberia rolled out the standard protocols that Erikson had heard discussed in March: they imposed quarantines and lockdowns, ordered sick people to go to isolation centers, known as Ebola Treatment Units, and banned victims from seeing (let alone touching) families and friends. They also insisted that the corpses of anyone who died be buried in a "safe" manner, without human contact, since they were extremely infectious. Messages about all this were placed on posters, in radio bulletins, and on pamphlets.

It made perfect policy sense to Western eyes. But something was going tragically wrong. Another anthropologist, named Catherine Bolten, had a grisly—ghastly—view of the problem. She had done her fieldwork in a bush town called Makeni, the northern regional capital, a few years before Ebola hit. After she returned to America, she stayed in close touch with friends there, such as a local lawyer who worked at the University of Makeni, named Adam Goguen. When Ebola arrived in his district in the early summer of 2014, Goguen sent Belton daily emails on real-time events.

Goguen's own village was one of the few that obeyed the government's orders, since his local village chief spoke English, regularly tuned in to the BBC, had good relations with a local NGO, and thus understood the WHO pandemic-fighting rules. He sealed off the village to the outside world and imposed a quarantine. Everybody lived. The chief who ran the neighboring village, however, took another tack. He decreed that the source of Ebola was a witchcraft curse and refused to send anybody infected with Ebola to "exclusion" hospitals or to impose a lockdown. "Every resident targeted for quarantine had another household to shelter them, and this was exactly how they reacted to the prospect of the authorities isolating them from the only people they believed would care for them properly," Goguen and Bolten subsequently explained in a joint article. "Even residents who suspected that Ebola was a contagious disease, and not [a witchcraft curse], nursed family in secret."[17] The villagers also rejected the "no touching" rule for the living—and the dead. When Ebola victims died, the so-called secret societies that ran village rituals organized traditional burial ceremonies—with infectious corpses.

A local nurse tried to stop people touching the living and dead bodies of Ebola victims, explaining the medical risks. "The nurse had conducted contact tracing from the first funerals and accurately predicted who would fall ill [after touching the corpse]," Goguen told Bolten. However, the villagers attacked the nurse, accusing her "of slaughtering them with witchcraft." When soldiers stepped in and buried infected corpses, locals later dug up the bodies and reburied them—touching them. With great bravery, the local nurse kept trying to spread the WHO message. However, when she visited a family whose members had just died from Ebola, she was "prevented from quarantining the house by the village youth, who were armed with machetes, and the residents of the homes targeted for quarantine . . . dispersed among related households, whose members concealed them." That lead to forty-three more infections.

Similar scenes were unfolding across Guinea, Sierra Leone, and Liberia. The WHO officials, MSF, and local governments tried to fight back by intensifying the lectures about medical risks and using soldiers to impose its orders. "It was assumed that if communities had correct information on Ebola risks then appropriate actions would follow," Richards explained.[18] But that backfired. Villagers continued to blame the virus on witchcraft or a government plot. An angry mob attacked a MSF isolation unit in Guinea.[19] In southern Guinea, villagers killed eight members of a so-called national Ebola awareness team and dumped their bodies in a latrine. By the autumn, an average of ten attacks per month were taking place in the region against medical burial and infection control teams.[20]

In September 2014, the Centers for Disease Control in Washington warned that the contagion was so bad the disease would soon spread to the West and could kill up to 1.2 million people. There was no prospect of a cure or vaccine in sight. "Medical education seemed helpless against 'pavement radio,'" Bolten recalls.[21] "In the United States there was near panic about the prospect of it coming here."

In October 2014, some of the American anthropologists who had worked in Sierra Leone, Guinea, and Liberia held an emergency meeting at George Washington University. Emotions were running high. "We were sitting there in this room feeling just overwhelmed with grief for the . . . people we knew [in West Africa]," Bolten recalls. She had just learned that two of her friends had died and could hardly concentrate "since I kept checking my phone for news" to see if a truckload of rice she had dispensed as aid had arrived. She also felt frustrated and guilty. The anthropologists in the room had spent years patiently trying to understand the cultures of West Africa, hoping to spread a little empathy in a globalized world. Now prejudice and racism was exploding.

"I had an American journalist call me up and ask why the Africans kept behaving in this barbaric and stupid way," Mary Moran, one of the anthropologists in that Washington room, observed. She argued that these labels were unfair. Until the early decades of the twentieth century, Americans had routinely kept the bodies of deceased family or friends in their houses after death, for a few days, posing them in "lifelike" tableaus with living people for photos. What happened to Admiral Nelson's body—or that of King George VI—was not an outlier. Yet Western journalists, doctors, and aid workers were now decrying the West Africans' "primitive" rituals and claiming (wrongly) that Ebola was caused by strange "natives" eating "bushmeat."

The anthropologists considered this not just unfair but also cruel. The West Africans were facing terrible trauma in a place with little—or no—infrastructure. They wanted to grieve their losses in a way they considered proper. Their local belief system asserted that when somebody died, their living friends and family needed to pay respects by participating in a funeral, with the body present; without that, the deceased would be consigned to permanent hell and everyone else around them would suffer. That rite had often been interrupted during the civil war, creating the risk of a curse. Nobody wanted that cycle to continue. "An Ebola death is not nearly as bad as an Ebola burial," Goguen explained to Bolten. "Only the body dies from Ebola, but an Ebola burial kills the spirit."[22]

There was another crucial point that scornful Western critics failed to understand: there were also real-world, practical impediments to following the WHO advice, since there was so little preexisting health infrastructure. While the academic anthropologists were meeting in Washington, another medical anthropologist, named Paul Farmer, was arriving in West Africa. Twenty-five years earlier he had cofounded a nonprofit called Partners in Health to offer medicine to emerging market regions such as Latin America, Haiti, and (latterly) Central and West Africa. Although Farmer was a trained physician who believed in the power of medical science—and the need for tangible "stuff, staff, space and systems" to fight disease—he believed that healthcare needed to be offered with respect for local cultures and an awareness of social context. He was appalled by what he saw in Sierra Leone, Guinea, and Liberia.[23] Ebola victims were collapsing in pools of vomit, sweat, and diarrhea on the road, in taxis, at hospitals, and at home. Large numbers of doctors were dying. The already weak medical infrastructure was falling apart. And while medical groups such as MSF and WHO were trying to *contain* the disease, they were not really trying to offer therapeutic care. The Ebola Treatment Units had "too little 'T' in the ETU," he fumed. Given that, it was not surprising that Ebola victims kept running away or ignoring orders, and it was wrong for outsiders to scorn people for doing that. After a long civil war and with a history of colonial oppression, there was little reason for ordinary people to trust their government or hectoring Western "experts." A lack of empathy was quite literally killing people and fueling the spread of the disease.

Could anthropologists do anything to counter this? Opinions in the room in Washington were divided. Some academic anthropologists were leery of working for a government of any hue. Others felt that only West Africans should speak for the region, not Europeans or Americans. Many academics had little practice at engaging with policy makers; they preferred to observe, not agitate.[24] "Economists don't have any problems with standing up and saying clearly: 'This is what is going to happen next!' They have the networks to reach people in power and the confidence to forecast the future—and if this turns out to be wrong it doesn't matter, they just carry on!" says Erikson. "Anthropologists are not like that." But the anthropologists knew they had a moral obligation to do something. Or as Bolten observed: "We sat there [in the room] and asked: Is there any point to what we have been doing all these years if we don't speak out?"

In subsequent weeks Farmer and his colleagues at PIH angrily campaigned for a policy change, to focus on patient *care*, with empathy, not just disease containment. The academic anthropologists also did something they had almost never done before: tentatively organize themselves to offer advice on culture. In America, the AAA society produced memos for the Washington administration about local culture. French anthropologists did the same in Paris. A United Nations Ebola-fighting team hired a medical anthropologist named Juliet Bedford. "It was a watershed moment," she recalls. "There was a real sense in the UN that they had to change the standard operating procedures [for medical help] but didn't know how."[25] In London, a group of anthropologists, including Richards, Melissa Leach, and James Fairhead, created a dedicated website called the Ebola Response Anthropology Platform.

"The objective [of Ebola-fighting measures] is to combat a virus, not local customs," one memo sternly declared.[26] Whitty, the British doctor-turned-bureaucrat in Whitehall, convened meetings with them in the ornate Whitehall buildings to hear their advice. Then Mokuwa volunteered to go to the forested region in eastern Sierra Leone where the epidemic was raging. For weeks she walked the arduous off-road tracks to visit communities she knew well from earlier fieldwork and sent reports to Whitty and others, hoping to offer a local, worm's-eye perspective to balance the top-down view of scientists. "I walked and walked and tried to listen," she recalls.*

The dispatches were a revelation to the British bureaucrats. Until that point, Western medical experts—and Whitty—had assumed the best strategy to contain Ebola was to put sick people in large, specialized isolation centers. But Mokuwa explained that approach did not work, since the ETUs were far from the villagers and victims could not travel more than a few miles. It was also a terrible mistake to build exclusion centers with opaque walls; if nobody knew what was happening inside the buildings, sick people were more likely to run away. Sending young outsiders into villages to dispense medical advice was equally disastrous since the villagers usually only accepted advice from village elders. So the other anthropologists offered some policy ideas: Why not change the style of the exclusion centers to make them transparent? Put lots of small treatment centers in local communities? Use village elders to transmit messages about Ebola safety? Devise funeral rituals that would be safe in medical *and* social terms? Recognize that many people would insist on

*Mokuwa, like other anthropologists, stresses that she would have preferred to have had more local voices speaking to Western governments; or have the message coming from a group of West African anthropologists. But one failing of twenty-first-century Western anthropology is that there are relatively few non-Western adherents. Mokuwa and Richards have been trying for many years to build the discipline in local West African universities, but it is uphill work, since these departments are very underfunded (like so much of the wider infrastructure in the region).

caring for their sick relatives at home and advise them on how to make their homegrown solutions safer? It echoed, in a sense, what Bell had told the Intel engineers when she saw that drivers kept using their own devices in cars, in defiance of the engineers' ideas. Why not work *with* the local culture, not against it?

The messages slowly had an impact. Inside MSF, some doctors started to call for more emphasis on therapeutic care, not just containment.* The international agencies changed the design of exclusion centers to make the walls transparent.[27] In Whitehall, Whitty switched policy on the ETUs and declared that the British government would fund the construction of dozens of smaller triage and treatment points close to communities. Medical teams began to talk with local communities about how to modify their funeral rituals to make them safe while also respecting the dead. One template for how to do this was set down when an ugly incident erupted in a village in the forest of Guinea. When a pregnant mother died, the local WHO officials initially tried to bury the body rapidly away from the village. But local villagers were determined to do funeral rites and remove the fetus to avoid a curse. A dangerous battle exploded. However, Julienne Anoko, a local anthropologist, stepped in and worked with the community to adapt existing rituals to remove potential curses—and persuaded the WHO to pay for that ritual. It worked: the body was buried safely, mourning rites were held "in the presence of administrative officials, the WHO team" that left villagers so reassured that "the community thanked everyone involved with traditional songs of peace," she later observed.[28]

Local communities also started to devise their own solutions to care for patients outside the hated ETUs, at home—and Western doctors

*The internal fight about MSF and WHO policy in West Africa was (and is) a matter of great controversy that I cannot give justice to here. However, for details see the account in Farmer's magnificent book *Fevers, Feuds, and Diamonds: Ebola and the Ravages of History* (New York: Farrar, Straus and Giroux, 2020).

reluctantly began to accept these. In Liberia, villagers donned raincoats, worn back to front, over garbage bags as a rudimentary form of personal protective equipment. Villagers created homegrown protocols to use survivors to perform contact tracing and treat sick patients. Then the old men and women who ran the *Poro* and *Sande* secret societies, which controlled funerals for members, got involved too. "We held a seminar at Njala University [in 2015] where a paramount chief came with some elders who asked us for some white hazmat suits," Richards later recalled. "When we asked why, they said they wanted to create a dancing 'devil' that would teach the girls of the chiefdom about the Ebola hazard." It was radically different from the messaging tactics used by WHO and the governments. But it was far more effective.

By the spring of 2015, Ebola patients were no longer running away from exclusion centers, nor were communities digging up bodies to rebury them or attacking the medical staff. The contagion slowed. By the summer WHO had declared that the Ebola epidemic was over. The final death toll was estimated to have been between eleven and twenty-four thousand.* Tragically high, it was also a mere 2 percent of the worst scenario projected by the CDC in the summer of 2014. "It was a good news story—in the end," Rajiv Shah, the man whom President Barack Obama put in charge of the White House Ebola response, later told me. "What we learned was that you can make policy much more effective when you work with the communities and bring them into solutions."

To which the anthropologists might have replied: "Of course."

Five years later, Richards and Mokuwa—along with other veterans of the Ebola fight—found themselves beset with unexpected déjà vu. This time

*There is obvious uncertainty about the numbers given the weak health care infrastructure. The WHO put the final toll in the summer of 2016 at 11,000; observers such as Farmer consider this a gross underestimate: https://www.ids.ac.uk/opinions/a-real-time-and-anthropological-response-to-the-ebola-crisis/.

the disease was COVID-19, not Ebola. However once again the problem had started in a place that seemed so exotic to Westerners that it was easy to demonize: Wuhan, China. "Blaming the neighbors [in a pandemic] is an eternally popular sport and so is mocking their food," Farmer tartly wrote in April 2020, as COVID-19 spread across Europe and America. "The Ebola-era obsession with bushmeat is neatly enough reflected in commentary about Wuhan's wet markets, where (one imagines) caged civets pace, eels and strange fish squirm and flop and pangolins shed scales like golden tears."[29] However, COVID-19 did not stay in exotic lands. "Ebola happened in the dark heart [deep corners] of Africa. Much of the general population in the global north thought it was 'out there,' a long way from them," Bedford observed. "But then they discovered that COVID was happening in parts of the world where they [the general population] never expected to be facing this threat."

Could Western governments learn from the past to devise a better response? The anthropologists initially hoped so. By 2020 the British bureaucrat Whitty had been promoted from the development agency in the UK into an even more influential role as chief medical officer for the entire British government. He was thus advising on the COVID-19 campaign. He seemed perfectly placed to draw the right lessons from the Ebola saga about the need to blend medical and social science since he had written joint pieces with social scientists in 2014 championing precisely that.[30] Groups such as WHO had also used the Ebola experience to improve their tactics to fight other infectious diseases, such as a 2016 outbreak of Zika. Computer scientists were becoming wiser too, blending social and data science. At HealthMap, the disease tracking platform that John Brownstein had created in Boston, the doctors and scientists had increasingly realized the need to put data into social context. "Big data is not the holy grail. We know it is only useful if you understand the social context," Brownstein told me. "For COVID-19, we need a hybrid: machine learning and human curation."[31] Or as Melinda Gates, cochair of the Bill & Melinda Gates Foundation, which focuses on global healthcare, also told me: "We have been forced to rethink some of the way we use data. At the beginning there was a lot of excitement about Big Data, and we still firmly believe that getting better statistics is very important and technology can do amazing things. But we cannot be naive—understanding the social context matters."[32]

So, with a sense of optimism, the anthropologists presented ideas about how to harness cultural awareness to fight COVID-19.[33] They suggested that policy makers recognize that kinship patterns affect transmission rates (intergenerational households in Northern Italy, say, posed risks). They warned that cultural attitudes toward "pollution" can distort people's perception of risks, leaving them fearful of outsiders but ignoring insider threats. The US president, Donald Trump, demonstrated that: he referred to COVID-19 as a "Chinese invasion," and shut the US border, but downplayed risks from "insiders" to such a degree that an outbreak of COVID-19 erupted in the White House.[34]

The anthropologists also warned that the messaging around COVID-19 needed to be clear, sympathetic, and in tune with the needs of communities. Top-down orders alone did not suffice. "The name for Ebola in Mende, one of the main languages of Sierra Leone . . . was *bonda wore*, literally 'family turn round.' In other words, it was clearly recognized that this was a disease requiring families to change behavior in major ways, especially in how they cared for the sick," Richards wrote in a memo posted on the Oxfam website in the spring of 2020.[35] "Covid-19 will require similar changes at the family level, especially in terms of how the elderly are protected. The buzz words for epidemic responders include self-isolation and social distancing, but the details of how to implement these vague concepts have been left to local social imagination. Should grandpa be packed off to a shed?"

The anthropologists also stressed that the need to blend social and medical science was demonstrated not just in evidence from West Africa but from Asia too. The tale of face masks was particularly striking. After the SARS epidemic swept through Asia in the early years of the twenty-first century, several anthropologists and sociologists—such as Peter Baehr, Gideon Lasco, and Christos Lynteris—studied the emergence of a "mask culture" in the region. They concluded that masks had helped combat contagion, but *not* just because of hard science (whether masks stopped the inhalation or exhalation of virus particles), but also because the ritual of putting on a mask is a powerful psychological prompt that reminds people of the need to modify their behavior. Masks are also a symbol that demonstrates adherence to civic norms and community support.[36] The ritual of "masking up" changes other behavior.

Some government officials listened. In New York, for example, local officials swiftly unleashed a campaign to persuade residents to embrace masks. It initially seemed unlikely to work since masks were associated with stigma in New York and wearing one appeared to offend New Yorkers' individualistic culture. But billboards around Manhattan were festooned with messages that tried to change the "webs of meaning" around masks, as Geertz might say, redefining them as a sign of strength, not stigma. "No mask? Fuggedaboutit!" read one. "We are New York tough," declared another, and (at Thanksgiving), one read, "Don't be a Turkey, Wear A Mask!" It was the Big Apple's equivalent of the *Sande* secret society dances that Richards and Mokuwa had noted in Sierra Leone. It worked: New Yorkers quickly adopted masks with near religious zeal. If nothing else, it demonstrated the point that Richards often stressed: while cultural belief systems mattered deeply, they were not fixed in stone.

In Boston, Charlie Baker, the Republican governor of Massachusetts, was also creative. He hired Farmer and his PIH team to import the lessons they had learned from West Africa and elsewhere for the COVID-19 fight. "This is reverse innovation," Farmer explained. He told Baker that the best way to curb COVID-19 was to offer care and empathy, working with communities rather than just relying on top-down orders or digital apps. "No [contact tracing] app can provide [a COVID victim] with emotional support or address their complex and unique needs," explained Elizabeth Wroe, a Harvard-trained doctor at PIH.[37] "You have to walk with the person and address whatever they need."

Yet in many other places, officials ignored the lessons from Ebola—and social science. In Washington, Daniel Goroff, a scientist at the National Science Foundation, created a dedicated network to help "decision makers at all levels of government" build effective pandemic policy with social and medical science.[38] But Trump's White House displayed no desire to embrace behavioral science or reverse innovation. In Britain, the Scientific Advisory Group for Emergencies (SAGE) invited a behavioral scientist into their group, David Halpern, who circulated memos suggesting (sensibly) that the British government should import lessons about masks from countries such as Germany and South Korea.[39] But SAGE was dominated by politicians and scientists from fields such as medicine and unveiled policies that were often the precise opposite of what anthropologists (or behavioral scientists) suggested. First, Prime Minister Boris Johnson declared that people should *not* wear face masks. Then, he backed masks but shunned them himself. Policies were imposed in a top-down manner (even though Britain had excellent local community health centers), and the government poured money into expensive digital contact tracing technologies (which barely worked). "The government's incorporation of expertise from behavioral and other human sciences has been woeful," lamented Gus O'Donnell, the former head of Britain's civil service, in November. "When the government says it 'follows the science,' this really means that it follows the medical sciences, which has given it a one-sided perspective and led to some questionable policy decisions."[40]

Why? Politics was often one explanation.* In America, Trump had

*I realize I am ignoring other Western countries, such as those in continental Europe, which had varied responses, but for reasons of space I am focusing on the Anglo-Saxon world.

risen to power with an anti-immigration, America-first message that derided poor countries in places such as West Africa as "shitholes." In London, Johnson relied heavily on advice from Dominic Cummings, who often seemed dazzled by empirical science.[41] There was also hubris; the British and American government presumed their medical systems were so world-beating that there was no need to embrace reverse innovation.[42] However, the anthropologist Richards suspected there was another problem too: that deceptive label "exotic." When Whitty had summoned anthropologists for meetings in Whitehall in 2014, he had done so because British government officials thought they were dealing with strange *others*. In 2020, they thought they were in a "familiar" landscape. They thus felt little need to learn from others or hold a mirror to themselves, even though a mere two years earlier a Halpern-led behavioral insights team created by the British government had stressed the importance of thinking about "how elected and unelected government officials are themselves influenced by the same heuristics and biases that they try to address in others."[43]

This produced tragic mistakes. If only Western governments had looked at themselves in the mirror at the start of the COVID-19 crisis, they might have seen the weaknesses of their own pandemic-fighting systems. If they had looked at the experience of West Africa or Asia, they would have also (re)learned another essential lesson: when doctors work with communities, with empathy, it is far easier to beat a pandemic. Or as Richards said: "The government knows you need anthropologists to help if it is culturally difficult like in Afghanistan. They don't think they need anthropologists in inner Manchester or South Yorkshire.

"They do."

PART TWO

MAKING THE "FAMILIAR" STRANGE

The gist: It is human nature to assume that the way we live is "normal" and everything else is weird. But that's wrong. Anthropologists know that there are multiple ways to live, and everyone seems weird to someone else. We can use this in a practical sense: when we look at the world through someone else's eyes, we can look back and see ourselves more objectively too, seeing risks and opportunities. I have done this as a journalist. A host of consumer goods companies have used variants of this tool to understand Western markets. But it can also be used to understand what is happening inside institutions and companies, particularly when you borrow ideas and tools from anthropology, such as the power of symbols, the use of space (habitus), foot-dragging, and the definition of social boundaries.

FOUR

FINANCIAL CRISIS

(OR WHY DO BANKERS MISREAD RISKS?)

"What we are familiar with we cease to see."

—Anaïs Nin[1]

I sat in the back row of a darkened conference room in a modernist municipal hall in Nice, on the French Riviera, feeling stupid. Next to me sat ranks of chino- and pastel-shirt-clad men. They had big plastic lanyards around their necks holding nametags that read "European Securitization Forum 2005." This was a gathering of bankers who traded complex financial instruments such as derivatives linked to mortgages and corporate loans. I was there to report on it as a journalist for the *Financial Times*.

At the front of the hall, at a podium, financiers were discussing innovations in their field, wielding power points with equations, charts, Greek letters, and acronyms such as "CDO," "CDS," ABS," and "CLO" on them. *It's like being in Obi-Safed again!* I thought. Once again, I felt culture shock. It was far more subtle than in Tajikistan since the cultural patterns felt more familiar. But the language was gobbledygook: I did not know what a CDO was or what was happening at the forum.

An investment banking conference is just like a Tajik wedding, I thought. A group of people were using rituals and symbols to create and reinforce their social ties and worldview. In Tajikistan this occurred with a complex cycle of wedding ceremonies, dancing, and gifts of embroidered cushions.

On the French Riviera, bankers were exchanging business cards, rounds of drinks, and jokes, while engaging in communal golf tours and watching PowerPoints in darkened conference rooms. But in both cases the rituals and symbols were reflecting *and* reproducing a shared cognitive map, biases and assumptions.

So, as I sat in the darkened French conference hall, I tried to "read" the symbolic map that underpinned the conference, just I had once tried to "read" the symbolism—and webs of meaning, to use Geertz's frame—in a Tajik wedding, paying attention to what people did not talk about, as well as the topics they wanted to discuss. Patterns emerged. The financiers thought they wielded control over a language and knowledge to which few other people had access—which made them feel elite. "Almost nobody else in my bank really knows what I do either!" one financier joked when I asked him to explain what a "CDO" or "CDS" was (they stood for "collateralized debt obligation" and "credit default swap," I learned). The fact that the financiers shared this common language created a shared identity; they were tied together with bonds of knowledge and social links forged through work, even though they toiled in scattered locations, in New York, London, Paris, Zurich, and Hong Kong. They communicated on a dedicated message system attached to a Bloomberg trading terminal. *It's like a Bloomberg village*, I joked to myself. The financiers also had a distinctive "creation myth"—to use another common anthropological term—to justify their activities. Outsiders sometimes claimed that financiers only practiced their craft to make money. However, the bankers did not present their activities to themselves that way. Instead they invoked concepts such as "efficiency," "liquidity," and "innovation." The creation story behind the craft of securitization—which was what the conference was about—was that this process made markets more "liquid," in the sense that debts and risks could be traded and flow as easily as water, making it cheaper to borrow money. They insisted this would be good for financiers and non-financiers alike.

Another telling detail was that the financiers' PowerPoints lacked one feature: faces or other images of real humans. In some senses this seemed odd, given that the creation myth asserted that "innovation" benefited ordinary mortals. But when the financiers talked about their craft, they rarely mentioned living, breathing *people*. Greek letters, acronyms, algorithms, and diagrams filled their PowerPoint slides instead. *Who is borrowing this money? Where are the humans? How does this connect to real life?*

Initially, these questions left me curious—not alarmed. A defining trait of the anthropology mindset—like journalism's—is compulsive curiosity, and I felt as if I had just stumbled into a whole new frontier crying out to be explored. It could be valuable for the readers of the *Financial Times* if I set out to offer a travel guide to this new land, I told myself, imaging that I might cover it like my journalist colleagues were writing about Silicon Valley. Both sectors, after all, had a creation myth that was evangelical about innovation and its purported benefits for mankind.

Later it became clear that this creation myth also contained a terrible "flaw," to cite the word later used by Alan Greenspan, former chair of the Federal Reserve;[2] the cultural patterns I observed on the Riviera were creating risks that would later spark the 2008 financial crisis. Precisely because the financiers were such a close-knit intellectual tribe, with little external scrutiny, they could not see whether their creations were spinning out of control. And because they had such a strong creation myth about the benefits around innovation, they were averting their eyes from risks. An anthropologist named Daniel Beunza later dubbed this the problem of "model-based moral disengagement";[3] another, Karen Ho, blamed it on a "liquidity cult";[4] a third, Vincent Lépinay, highlighted the "mastery" of complex maths.[5] Whatever metaphor was used though, the problem was that financiers could see neither the *external* context of what they were doing (what cheap loans did to borrowers) nor the *internal* context of their world (how their clubbiness and peculiar incentive schemes fueled risks).

This is why anthro-vision matters. One benefit of anthropology is that it can impart empathy for the strange "other." Another is that it can offer a mirror for the familiar—ourselves. It is never easy to draw clear lines between what is "familiar" and "strange." Cultural difference exists in a shifting spectrum, not rigid static boxes. But the key point is this: wherever you sit, in whatever blend of familiar and strange, it always pays to stop and ask yourself a simple question that the bankers on the Riviera were not asking: If I was to arrive in this culture, as a total stranger, or as a Martian or child, what might I see?

My journey into the Great Financial Crisis started, indirectly, in 1993, or six months after I had sheltered in a hotel room in Tajikistan listening to gunfire amid the civil war. Soon after I had completed my fieldwork, I did an internship for the FT, was hired as a freelance foreign reporter—and then (while completing my PhD), was offered a position as a graduate trainee. I grabbed it gratefully, since I was fascinated by journalism.

When I arrived at the FT's head office in London, my supervisors placed me for training in the "economics room" (or team). It was meant to be an honor. But I was dismayed. When I had decided to enter the world of journalism, I had done so because I was fascinated by culture and politics. Economics and finance were a mystery, and the jargon seemed so impenetrable that I was apt to dismiss it as boring. *This is not why I became a journalist!* I thought, as I sat in the economics room and skim-read "teach yourself finance" books. But then I realized that fear and prejudice drove much of my reaction. At university, anthropology students had often clustered in a different social "tribe" from students who wanted to become financiers, and the language of the financial students baffled me. Jumping that cultural gap required skills similar to anthropology. Or as I later observed to Laura Barton, a fellow British journalist who interviewed me after the financial crisis had exploded in 2008: "I thought, you know what, this is just like being in Tajikistan. All I have to do is learn a new language. This is a bunch of people who have dressed up this activity with a whole bunch of rituals and cultural patterns, and if I can learn Tajik, I can jolly well learn how the FX market works!"[6]

The mental shift delivered dividends. The more I looked at how money moved around the world, the more fascinated I became. "People who come from a background of arts and humanities and social studies tend to think that money and the City is boring and somehow dirty," I explained to Barton. "If you don't look at how money goes round the world, you don't actually understand the world at all." Of course, one problem was that many people who worked in the world of money assumed that money was the *only* thing that made the world "go round." That was also wrong. "Bankers like to imagine that money and the profit motive is as universal as gravity," I told Barton. "They think it's basically a given and they think it's completely apersonal. And it's not. What they do in finance is all about culture and interaction." However, I thought—or hoped—that if I could find a way to link the two perspectives, studying money and culture in tandem, it might add insight. So, in subsequent years, as I built a career at the FT—first on the FT's economics team in Europe and then for five years as a reporter and bureau chief in Japan—I kept asking myself the same question, over and over again: How does money make the world go round? How is this process viewed by different people in the world? What, in other words, are the "webs of meaning" around finance?

In late 2004 I sat at another "desk," at the FT's head office in London, and it went by the odd name of the "Lex team."* This division of

*The Lex column started in 1945, but the origin of the name is unclear. It is sometimes attributed in FT lore to the Latin phrase *lex mercatoria* meaning merchant law; it may also have started as a pun around the phrase "*de minimus non curat lex*" or "the law bothers not with trifles," since a rival 1940s paper had a column named after a character who snapped up "trifles." See https://www.politico.com/media/story/2014/08/the-60-second-interview-rob-armstrong-head-of-the-lex-column-financial-times-002617/.

the paper required journalists to provide pithy pieces of commentary about corporate finance. I had ended up there more by accident than design (after working in Japan, I had hoped to go to Iran as a foreign reporter but switched plans when I became pregnant). But my official title was "acting head" of Lex, which meant I had strategic oversight for how the FT commented on corporate finance. *It's like being acting editor for the church newsletter of the Vatican*, I sometimes laughed to myself.

One day, in the autumn of 2004, I received a request from the editor: Could I write a memo outlining the topics that Lex was covering—and how this coverage could or should change? I started by responding to the memo in the normal way, following the protocols that media groups use: I examined our past columns, read what rivals had written, looked at our news coverage, and then tried to guess whether our balance seemed sensible or not. That analysis suggested to me that we were not paying enough attention to Asia and the tech sector in our Lex columns. I dispatched a memo outlining that.

Then I had a second thought: *What would this memo look like if I wrote it as an anthropologist?* If I were to crash-land into the City of London or the *Financial Times* news desk as an insider-outsider, what would I see? I could not answer that by replicating what somebody such as Malinowski had done when he pitched his tent in the Trobriand Islands to do his anthropology. Nor with the method I had done in Obi-Safed: walking around a village to peer into other people's lives. In Tajikistan I had enjoyed remarkable freedom to ask questions and watch people. As I had gone around the valley doing my "homework" with a gaggle of kids, camera in hand, the villagers were so excited about the idea that I could take photographs, and then distribute these, that they let me see different corners of their life (even those which an unmarried girl might not usually see). In the City of London, however, banks did not let journalists wander around their offices unaccompanied; reporters were not usually permitted to enter the buildings without a public relations official monitoring them (or acting as a "minder," as journalists joked). Nor did institutions such as the Stock Exchange or public institutions such as the Bank of England, or their American counterparts. It was thus hard to see financiers in their natural habitat at all. There was, in other words, a problem around hierarchy that the early anthropologists had not faced. When people such as Malinowski went to the Trobriand Islands, they were coming from a society that was more powerful than the one they were studying. In the City of London, financiers were far more powerful than journalists or anthropologists; the challenge was how to "study up."*[7] "The very notion of 'pitching tent' at the Rockerfellers' yard, in the lobby of J. P. Morgan, or on the floor of the New York Stock Exchange is not only implausible but also might be limiting and ill-suited to a study of 'the power elite,'" observed Karen Ho, an anthropologist who studied Wall Street in the late twentieth century and early twenty-first century by getting a job in the back office of Bankers Trust.[8]

So, I improvised. Whenever I interviewed financiers to write Lex columns, I tacked on some unstructured, open-ended questions; I tried to listen to what people said—and what they did *not* talk about. On a couple of occasions, I borrowed a strategy I had once used in the Tajik village: I gave somebody a blank sheet of paper and pencil and asked them to sketch out how the different pieces of their world fitted together. In Obi-Safed I had used this technique to understand kinship links and how these family patterns affected the physical location of houses in the valley. In City restaurants I asked financiers to draw pictures in my

*This problem of how to "study up" was first detailed by the anthropologist Laura Nader in the 1970s and has sparked endless soul-searching. Some anthropologists have responded by getting jobs in the institution they are trying to study. Lépinay and Ho both worked at banks. But this raises ethical issues about whether researchers should identity themselves. Another option is one followed by Dinah Rajak, which is to work in a "corporate social responsibility" team that is partly on the outside, that monitors the company.

notebook, showing how the different pieces of the financial markets fit together and their relative sizes.

It was surprisingly hard for insiders to draw this "map" of all the financial flows that shaped the City. They could see *pieces* of this picture. There was excellent data about equity listings, say. But none of the people working in private sector banks or government institutions could offer an easy-to-follow idiot's guide to show how all these flows interacted. This seemed odd given that financiers seemed obsessively keen to measure things. Or maybe not: as Malinowski had first noted in *The Argonauts of the Western Pacific*, it is always hard for insiders to see an overarching "map" of their world.

I also noticed that insofar as any picture could be painted showing the relative size of the financial flows and activities, this did not necessarily reflect the volume of conversation about them. More specifically, outlets such as the *Financial Times* wrote extensively about the equity markets. But there was less coverage of corporate bonds, and almost nothing about derivatives—even though the bankers kept telling me that the world of corporate credit and derivatives was large, profitable, and expanding. Rhetorical heat and real action diverged. Once again, that pattern was not so surprising from the perspective of an anthropologist: in every society, there is a divergence between what people say they do and what they actually do. In Tajikistan the villagers spent a lot of time talking about weddings but did not talk about other parts of their life that absorbed equal amounts of time, such as their work in the state farm. While the mismatch was not surprising, it had a practical implication for me as a journalist. "The financial system is like an iceberg!" I told colleagues. A small part—equity markets—was visible, in the sense that it was subject to obsessive media coverage. The bigger piece—derivatives and credit—was largely submerged. That created an opportunity for scoops, or so I hoped.

After sending the FT editor my official memo about the future of the

Lex column, I wrote a second memo titled "The Financial Iceberg." That argued that the FT should devote more coverage to the "submerged" bits of the financial-world-cum-iceberg, such as credit and derivatives. Since coverage of the equity markets was so widespread that it was almost commoditized, I reckoned it made more sense to write about a topic nobody else was covering. Initially nothing happened. Then, a staff reshuffle occurred, I was moved from Lex—and offered a job running the capital markets team. "You can do that iceberg stuff there!" the editor told me. I was not thrilled. The Lex team commanded high status within the ecosystem of the FT. So did the economics team: it sat in a plush office near the editor with wonderful views of the River Thames and St. Paul's Cathedral. The capital markets team seemed sleepy and low status by comparison. The stories it generated tended to be buried in the back of the paper, and it was located at the other end of the building from the editor, overlooking the trash cans.

Am I now on the mommy track? I wondered. I was pregnant, for the second time, and feared my career was stalling. A female friend on the Lex team tried to cheer me up. "Capital markets is a great place to work with a baby because nothing really happens!" she declared. "You can go home at five o'clock each day!" It made me feel worse.

In March 2005 I started my new job with the title "head of the capital markets team." I was eager to explore this strange new frontier of finance. But I faced a practical problem: the only place I could ever see bankers "in their natural habitat"—as I joked to friends—was financial conferences. This was the one venue where they roamed in the same space as journalists, without PR minders. So I attended every conference I could find, starting with the European Securitization Forum in Nice, and supplemented this with more formal—controlled—visits to meet bankers in their offices, trying to craft a travel guide to the world of financial innovation.

It was hard. The sector was swathed in so much jargon that it was difficult for an outsider to make sense of what was going on. The idea of "securitizing" debt, to use the financial jargon for what financiers were doing, was not new: bankers had been chopping up pieces of debt and issuing new securities (like bonds) with this for two decades, partly because they were responding to a tough set of bank regulations called "Basel One" (named after the Swiss town). But by 2005 multiple new variants of this practice were emerging, because the bankers were trying to take advantage of (or in banker speak "arbitrage") an updated version of these rules, called Basel Two, using not just corporate loans but risky "subprime" mortgage debt too. There was no readily available data about the size of these new submarkets, or manuals or an idiot's guide to what the jargon meant. When I asked a banker to explain what an instrument such as "CDO"—or "collateralized debt obligation"—was, he (or rarely she) would explain that it referred to a bundle of different pieces of debt that could be sold to investors, with different levels of risk attached. If I asked what a "CDS"—or credit default swap—meant, I would be told it was an instrument that let investors make bets about the risk that a piece of debt would go into default.

But how can I communicate these ideas to FT readers? I kept wondering. Eventually I decided that the easiest tactic was to use metaphors: a CDO could be likened to a sausage since it entailed chunks of financial "meat" (debt) being sliced up and reassembled into new casings (CDOs) and seasoned according to different tastes (with corporate or mortgage loans and different levels, or "tranches," of risk) that could be sold around the world. Sometimes investors would slice and dice those CDOs and then reassemble those new fragments into a new instrument, called a "CDO squared"; that, I joked, was like sausage stew. Similarly, a CDS could be described with the metaphor of horse racing: what people were trading was *not* horses, but bets that had been placed to see if the horse would win; or, more accurately, insurance bets taken against the risk that the horse might collapse and die. To reinforce the point, I asked the graphics team at the FT to produce diagrams and pictures of horses—and sausages—to put next to our stories. I also scrambled to put pictures of faces on the pages too, to make the topic seem less abstract. But it was hard to find these: few of the human financiers involved in debt, derivatives, or securitization world wanted to be quoted or photographed, and it was almost impossible to see the human borrowers at the end of the complex financial chains.

As 2005 wore on, the contours of this strange landscape started to fall into shape—and my access to financiers improved, as they became increasingly curious to talk to me. *Why are they willing to speak?* I wondered. I eventually realized I had stumbled into a pattern similar to Obi-Safed. Back in Tajikistan, the villagers had often seemed happy to see me because they knew who I was—the strange student who was studying marriage rituals. They also knew I was talking to numerous households and were eager to know what *other* people were saying, since I had more social freedom to ask questions than they did. The City of London felt oddly similar. The financiers who worked in the markets were supposed to be seamlessly connected with digital technology. Their banks were supposed to have unified internal operations too. But in reality, information flows between different desks inside the same bank were often poor, because the bankers were paid according to how their team performed, and thus had overwhelming loyalty to that team. Different desks at different banks could not see how the entire CDO or CDS market was evolving, since their view tended to be restricted to whatever sat beneath their nose too; the world was oddly opaque to insiders—and even more opaque to outsiders. "I am like a bee in a field of flowers," I joked to my colleagues. I was picking up pieces of information "pollen" and spreading it around, between banks—just as I had once done as I walked between houses in Obi-Safed.

What was even more striking was the institutions that were supposed to be monitoring this activity—namely central banks and regulators—faced fog too. The FT sat near the Bank of England, which had a departmental structure similar to the one at which I worked: one high-status (and highly visible) department monitored macroeconomic statistics; another less visible (and somewhat lower-status) group monitored capital markets and the systemic risks in the financial system. The man who ran that second group, Paul Tucker, was also trying to create a "travel guide" for the shadowy parts of the financial iceberg for British regulators and politicians. We often swapped notes. But Tucker also lacked hard data and faced similar communication challenges: his colleagues and politicians tended to consider the technical issues of derivatives far less exciting than, say, monetary policy. The jargon further tarnished it. Tucker tried to invent new words that might make complex finance sound more exciting. "Russian doll finance" was one of these, "vehicular finance" another.[9] But they did not catch on.

Initially, this pattern just irritated me. But as the weeks passed, I started to get alarmed. The story seemed so complex to outsiders that there were precious few people besides insiders who understood what was going on. The financiers insisted that there was no need to worry. These instruments, after all, were supposed to reduce overall risk in the financial system, not increase it; that was the theory behind the liquidity creation story, namely that innovation would enable risks to flow so smoothly, like water, across markets that they would be priced accurately and distributed.[10] Back in the 1970s and 1980s, banks had run into trouble because they had concentrated risks on their books (because, say, they had lent to lots of mortgage borrowers in the same town). But securitization distributed credit risks so widely that if losses occurred lots of investors would each take a tiny blow—but no single investor would take a painful enough hit to suffer serious damage. Or so the theory went. The driving principle was the same as the old saying "A problem shared is a problem solved."

But what if that logic is wrong? I wondered. I could not tell if it was, precisely because it was so opaque. But there were some oddities—or contradictions—that I could not explain that were starting to ring alarm bells. One was that in 2005 the cost of borrowing in the markets kept falling even though central banks kept raising rates. Another was the fact that while innovation was supposed to make markets so "liquid" that assets could be traded easily, the CDOs were barely being traded at all, because they were so complex. Indeed, it was so hard to get market prices for these instruments, because of the lack of genuine trades, that accountants were using prices extrapolated from rating models to record the value of CDOs in accounts, even though the system was supposed to be based on mark-to-market principles, or using market prices. This was a profound intellectual contradiction. Another oddity was that securitization implied that banks should sell their debts to other investors, and thus *shrink* their balance sheets—but these balance sheets kept expanding according to Bank of England data. Something did not smell right.

I wrote a few articles asking whether risks were building inside this strange, shadowy world.[11] Financiers protested. Then, in the autumn of 2005, I went on maternity leave. The timing dismayed me. "I am going to miss all the fun!" I complained to colleagues; I had a hunch that the pattern in the markets was becoming so odd that a market correction would occur while I was out of the office. I was wrong: when I returned to the FT in the spring of 2006, I discovered that not only had the market failed to "correct"—or decline—but the cost of borrowing had fallen even lower, the volume of credit being extended had risen, and the innovation turned even wilder. *Was I totally wrong?* I wondered; ever since I had been forced to rethink the thesis behind my PhD in Tajikistan, I had keenly been aware of just how misguided my prejudices could sometimes be.

But then my unease became more intense—and I penned increasingly critical articles.[12] It felt like a lonely path: even as the activity became more frenzied, few outsiders were peering into the strange world, far less trying to ring alarm bells. The bankers had concocted such a potent "creation myth" for their craft, based around theories like the "liquification of markets" and the value of "risk dispersion," that few outsiders felt able to challenge them. The bankers had little incentive to question themselves either. That was not because they were necessarily telling *deliberate* conscious lies to themselves (or others); the more important—and far more pernicious—issue was the issue of the "habitus," or the concept developed by Bourdieu that I had once used to explain the split between public and private space in Obi-Safed.[13] The financiers lived in a world where it seemed entirely natural that trading desks competed with one another, and that nobody outside the bank (or even on other trading desks) knew what was happening on those trading desks. It also felt natural that the messy business of executing trades was outsourced to a back office—in another part of the bank, with lower social status. It also seemed unremarkable to the financiers that they were the only ones who understood the jargon of their craft and that this baffling language scared others away. And since financiers conducted their trades on electronic screens, using abstract math, it did not seem odd that their minds—and lives—were utterly detached from the real-world implications of securitization.

Exceptions to this pattern did exist. As the film *The Big Short* (based on a book by Michael Lewis[14]) shows, in 2005 and 2006 a few hedge fund investors decided to bet against (or "short") subprime mortgage instruments at the center of this CDO and CDS boom. What sparked this maneuver was that a financier went to Florida and bumped into a pole dancer who had taken out multiple mortgages she could not possibly repay. The experience of seeing a living, breathing human at one end of the financial chain showed the contradictions in the craft. But what was startling—in retrospect—was how rare such faces were. Few financiers bothered to talk with borrowers, pole dancers or not, or look at what was happening on the ground in a holistic sense. The bird's eye mindset of the financiers was the polar opposite of the worm's-eye view of an anthropologist. Which was precisely what made the situation dangerous.

Sometimes I tried to point this out to financiers. They did not usually seem keen to listen. "We had enormous kickback from the bankers in the City saying, 'Why are you being so critical of the industry? Why are you being so negative?' All that kind of stuff," I later explained to the *Guardian* journalist Barton. During a trip to the World Economic Forum in Davos in 2007, I was denounced from the stage. "One of the most powerful people in the US government at the time stood up on the podium and waved my article[s] . . . as an example of scaremongering," I told Barton. On another occasion, in the late spring of 2007, a senior financier in London summoned me to his office to complain that I kept using words like "murky" and "opaque" to describe credit derivatives. He felt this vocabulary was needlessly alarmist. "It's not opaque! Anybody can find anything they need on a Bloomberg machine!" he scolded me.

"But what about the 99 percent of the population that is not on Bloomberg?" I asked.[15] The financier looked baffled; it did not seem to have occurred to him that they might have a right—or desire—to peer into finance. *It's that Bloomberg village again*, I thought. What financiers were *not* thinking or talking about mattered. So did the fact that this oversight was so habitual that it felt natural. As Bourdieu had once observed "the most successful ideological effects are those which have no need of words."[16] Or as the American novelist Upton Sinclair posited, more punchily: "It is difficult to get a man to understand something, when his salary depends upon his not understanding it!"[17]

The problem did not simply lie with the financiers, however. Cultural patterns in the media mattered too. It was more difficult for me as a journalist—insider—to see those patterns, since I was (and am) a creature of my own environment and biases. However, anthropologists have always been fascinated by the question of how narratives are created in different societies, whether through myth (studied by academics such as James Frazier in the nineteenth century and Lévi-Strauss in the twentieth century)[18] or movies (studied by the anthropologist Hortense Powdermaker, who turned her lens onto Hollywood in the twentieth century).[19] The media is also part of the modern narrative flow—and thus shaped by cultural biases too, although it is often hard for journalists to see that given that they are reared at work on the (admirable) principle of offering dispassionate, neutral reporting. Outsiders often focus on the contentious question of journalists' political bias. A more subtle and little-discussed issue, however, revolves around the much broader question of the way journalists are taught to define, construct, and transmit a "story" in relation to politics, finance, economics, or anything else. Western journalists are trained to put information into that "story" category if it contains several key components: a "person" (or people); tangible numbers and facts; on-the-record quotes; and a narrative, ideally with drama. As I looked around the financial world in 2005 and 2006, I could see that those elements defining a "story" existed aplenty in the sphere of equities: companies did tangible things; share prices moved in visible ways; analysts gave colorful quotes; corporate executives could be photographed; there were narratives that had a beginning and an end.

The big problem with the tale of debt and derivatives, however, was it lacked almost all of these features that created "stories." There were very few faces. It was hard to get on-the-record quotes that were interesting. Hard numbers about the sector were rare. Events emerged as slow-moving, elliptical trends, not dramatic step changes. Worse still, the sector was drowning in ugly acronyms that were gobbledygook to outsiders. That made it seem complex, geeky, and utterly dull, and thus as easy to ignore as the "empty" oil drums that Whorf had watched in warehouses in Connecticut, or the "mess" in people's cars that Bell had photographed in a Singapore parking lot. "Western journalists still typically assume that a 'good story' is one with plenty of human element," along with drama, I subsequently explained to the Banque de France, the French central bank, in a memo.[20] Or as the journalistic gag goes: "If it bleeds it leads." Securitization lacked that, since it was a slow-moving, opaque tale where change occurred in elliptical arcs. Precious few people outside the derivatives world wanted to wade through the messy alphabet soup to find out what was happening in this seemingly dull world and, "since this topic did not fit the usual definition of a 'good story,' most newspapers had little incentive to invest in this tale—particularly at a time when the media resources were dwindling," I told the French central bank. That, rather than any deliberate cover-up or dastardly plan to conceal activity, was the main reason why finance spun out of control, with the problems hidden in plain sight. Or as I sometimes laughed to colleagues: "If you want to hide something in the twenty-first-century world, you don't need to create a James Bond–style plot. Just cover it in acronyms."[21]

In 2011 I bumped into Alan Greenspan, the legendary figure who had run the Federal Reserve from 1987 to 2006. We were at the Aspen Ideas Festival, a conference which took place each year in the town of that name in Colorado. He asked me where he could find a good book on anthropology. "Anthropology?" I asked, stunned.[22] Until that point the mighty former central banker—dubbed the "maestro" because of his influence over financial markets—seemed the very last person likely to express any interest in cultural studies. He epitomized the group of policy makers and economists who believed in free-market theories—and who thought that humans were driven by profit-seeking, rational self-interest that was so consistent that it could be tracked with models taken from Newtonian physics. That stance had prompted Greenspan to champion financial innovation and adopt a hands-off policy on finance; even when he feared bubbles were developing, with credit derivatives or anything else, he assumed these would self-correct because markets were liquid and efficient.[23] Although he occasionally warned of the risks inherent in derivatives, he agreed with financiers that products like the CDO and CDS would make markets more "liquid" and efficient—and thus approved of them.

I asked why he wanted to know about anthropology. With a wry smile, Greenspan pointed out that the world had changed—and he wanted to understand it. That seemed an understatement. In the summer of 2007 a financial crisis had erupted after some of the creditors in the chains of debt—such as American mortgage borrowers—started to default. The initial losses from these defaults were not that large. However, they created the financial equivalent of a food poisoning scare which—once again—was easiest explained with the metaphor of a sausage: if a small piece of rotten meat gets into a butcher's mixing bowl, consumers will shun *all* minced meat and sausages since they cannot tell where the poison might lie. When defaults cropped up on mortgage loans, investors refused to touch CDOs since they could not track the risk, because these instruments had been sliced and diced so many times. Tools that were supposed to disperse risk among investors and thus make it easier to absorb blows had introduced a new risk into the system—a loss of confidence. Nobody could tell where the risks had gone.

For almost a year, the financial authorities scrambled to contain this "financial food poisoning" problem by propping up markets, bailing out banks, and then isolating (and removing) the financial vehicles—or instruments—that contained the bad mortgages, or poison. It did not work: in October 2008 a full-blown financial crisis erupted. It was a painful intellectual blow for men such as Greenspan. An entire generation of policy makers had believed that free-market economic incentives could create such an efficient financial system that if any excesses emerged—like a credit bubble—these would self-correct without causing real damage. That now seemed wrong. Or as Greenspan told Congress in late 2008: "There was a flaw [in my thinking]."[24] That was why he wanted to read some books about anthropology: he wanted to know how "culture" had messed up the models.

I was impressed. When Greenspan had first made his comment about the "flaw" to Congress, this admission had sparked widespread scorn, particularly from people who had lost money in the crash. But I considered that reaction to be wrong. It was rare for any leader, let alone someone dubbed a "maestro," to admit to an intellectual mistake in public. Even fewer tried to rethink their ideas by exploring a new mode of thought, such as anthropology. I thought Greenspan deserved credit for embracing a spirit of inquiry. But as we discussed anthropology, I also realized that the reason why Greenspan wanted to understand "culture" was not quite the same as what drove most anthropologists. To him, studying "culture" was mostly about an attempt to understand why *other* people behaved strangely. Thus he was turning to anthropology for the same reason that Whitty had asked anthropologists for help in Britain during Ebola: to make sense of "strange" others. What Greenspan was particularly curious about when I met him in Aspen was how cultural patterns might be influencing the 2011 Eurozone debt crisis, for example, since he found the behavior of the Greeks particularly baffling. To him, in other words, the Greeks were a strange "other," particularly in contrast to the Germans, and he wanted to know if the Greeks' cultural patterns could blow apart the Eurozone.

That was a valid concern to have. And anthropologists often explored "others." But it was only half of what anthropology could offer, and in the aftermath of 2008 it was not just Greece that offered interesting material for cultural analysis; what had just happened with debt on Wall Street or over in the City of London was equally interesting. So I suggested he also read some of the studies that anthropologists had done of Western finance. There were plenty to choose from. An anthropologist, Caitlin Zaloom, for example, had lived among traders in the Chicago trading pits and London markets in 2000 and tracked how the shift to electronic markets had shaped financiers' cultures.[25] Karen Ho had deconstructed the liquidity ideology on Wall Street, and noted that one key reason why finance kept spinning out of control was that financiers transposed this frame into the real economy—without realizing how odd (if not inappropriate) it seemed to others.[26] "Instead of recognizing constant dealmaking and rampant employee liquidity as their own local culture, my Wall Street informants conflated their organizational practices with their culture roles as interpreters of the market," she observed. "They confused 'natural' market laws and financial cycles." Similarly, a Scottish financial sociologist, Donald MacKenzie, had analyzed how traders' tribalism prompted them to create different valuation models for financial products, even with the same (supposedly neutral) math.[27] An American legal anthropologist—or someone who applied anthropology to law—named Annelise Riles did a startling piece of analysis of the cultural implications of derivatives contracts in Japan and America.[28] Another, Melissa Fisher, analyzed the peculiar issues around gender imbalances on Wall Street.[29] Daniel Souleles studied private equity players' networks.[30] Alexandre Laumonier did fascinating work looking at how the locations of cell phone towers shaped hedge funds' trading strategies around Chicago and London.[31] Vincent Lépinay, another Francophone anthropologist, worked as an equity derivatives trader in a French bank and wrote a masterful study that illuminated how hard it was for even financiers to understand "disruptive financial engineering" and "the risks generated by the innovative financial products."[32] There was a host of work that tried to put macroeconomic models in a wider cultural context, and embed the economy in social life, as Keith Hart, the anthropologist, put it.[33] There was even a brilliantly provocative piece of research about Greenspan's own "tribe." Douglas Holmes, an American anthropologist, had studied the rituals of institutions such as the Bank of England, Riksbank (Sweden), and the Reserve Bank of New Zealand. That led him to conclude that central bankers exerted (and exert) influence on the economy not so much by mechanically changing the price of money (as usually presumed in economists' models) but by casting verbal spells. Narrative and culture mattered, even for central bankers; or *especially* in central banks.[34]

But Greenspan did not seem particularly eager to read about studies of culture in his own backyard; like the vast majority of non-anthropologists, he thought that anthropology was about studying the exotic (in his case, Greece). No wonder: it is never easy for anyone to peer back at themselves or their own world objectively, least of all if they are elite. Using an anthropological lens on ourselves can reveal uncomfortable truths about our world, and the elite rarely have much incentive to do that, whether they are in finance, government, business, or the media. "The problem for businesses that hire anthropologists is that they might give you messages you don't want to hear," observes Lucy Suchman, an anthropologist who once worked for Xerox (of which more later).

However, it is *precisely* because it is hard for elites to "flip the lens," that it is important to do so. That became clear during the tale of COVID-19. It was (and is) true in the world of money. If only financiers had operated with an anthropologist's lens before 2008, the financial bubble might never have become so large—and then burst with such terrible consequences. Similarly, if only more central bankers, regulators, politicians—and, yes, journalists too—had thought like anthropologists, they would not have been so blind to the mounting risks and so trusting of bankers.

But this is *not* just a tale about finance or medicine. Far from it. Almost all business leaders and policy makers could benefit by asking the basic question that dogs anthropology: If a Martian were to land here suddenly and look around, what would they see? What am I ignoring since it seems so familiar, not "strange"? If I was to employ concepts such as the "webs of meaning" or habitus in my life, what might I see?

FIVE

CORPORATE CONFLICT

(OR WHY DID GENERAL MOTORS' MEETINGS MISFIRE?)

"To see what is in front of one's nose needs a constant struggle."

—George Orwell[1]

Bernhard, a German engineer, sounded furious. In front of him, in a drab conference room in Warren, Michigan, on the campus of the mighty American auto giant General Motors, were a group of fellow engineers. Some hailed from a GM subsidiary called Saturn, which was producing cars 500 miles away in a plant in Springfield, Tennessee. Others were based in Warren, working in a group known as the "the Small Car Group" that made brands such as Chevy Cavalier and Pontiac Sunfire. But Bernhard worked in Rüsselheim, Germany, 4,000 miles away. He was head engineer for a company called Adam Opel that was supposed to be working with Saturn and the Small Car Group to build a brand-new vehicle as part of a high-profile partnership. It was December 9, 1997.

Much was riding on this partnership: the board of GM—and its investors—hoped it would show how to revitalize the ailing auto group. Several hundred engineers from each group had already spent a year holed up on the second floor of a GM building in Warren, working on the project, code-named Delta Two; it was their second attempt at collaboration. But something was going wrong. And in the corner of the room an anthropologist named Elizabeth Briody was trying to work out why—using essentially the same type of participant observation skills that I had once employed in Tajikistan.

"The last time I met I talked with you [in November] we had narrowed the park-brake-cable-routing to two routing [systems]—the Saturn routing and the Honda routing," announced Mary, a representative from the Small Car Group; the meeting had been called to discuss where to place the wiring for a parking system for the putative Delta Two car. "We decided we needed to have must-and-wants sets of criteria and rated them. The Saturn routing came out with a score of 2301.5 and the Honda came out with a score of 2107.5. This suggests we should use the Saturn routing." Mary waved a piece of cabling made by GM's rival, Ford, for emphasis. Then she dropped the bomb: "Opel isn't happy with this decision."

The chief engineer from Saturn stated, "You can't buy into the process and then say you don't like the numbers."

Rory, the chief engineer from the Small Car Group, who had previously worked at Saturn, jumped in. "When we make a decision, we have to have consensus. You have to be 70 percent comfortable with something. . . . If there was no support by the Opel folks, then we don't have a decision. Everyone will walk out of a decision with some discomfort."

"My guys didn't buy into it," Bernhard, the Opel chief engineer, abruptly declared. His colleague added: "We were overruled."

"It is not acceptable to have a team recommendation and then say 'No, my team didn't buy into it,' " Rory retorted. The group had already spent a total of 280 hours discussing this issue, without conclusion. Sullen fury permeated the room.

Elliott, another Small Car Group executive, pointed out—unhelpfully—that a similar fight was underway around the "EPS," or electronic power steering, for the new car. But Bernhard pressed on. "I have two concerns with the Saturn solution: the carpet and noise and vibration."

"We are one and a half weeks late," countered a member of Mary's team.

"I need to keep this issue open," Bernhard retorted.

"We need for you to accept this team's decision," Rory insisted.

"But the team didn't come out with a consensus decision," Bernhard said.

"What does it to take for consensus around the team's decision?" Rory asked, seemingly in despair. Nobody appeared to know.[2]

Briody jotted notes, trying to observe *everything*. The GM workers usually ignored her since she was technically one of them: she worked at a unit of the automaker called GM Research and lived in Michigan herself. But while she seemed like an insider, she knew her job was to think like an outsider too. And as she listened, she noticed two striking—important—points that the engineers themselves, as insiders, could not see. The fights that were underway were not just between the "Germans" and the "Americans." There were almost as many fights *between* different American groups. GM was beset by tribalism. Second, the reason why the meetings were so disastrous was *not* just because of a difference in engineering views (say, where to put the cable), but something insiders had failed to see: even before discussing engineering issues, the different "tribes" had different cultural assumptions about what a meeting was. They had never noticed these differences, let alone reflected on them, because they took "meetings" for granted. However, just as a Kit Kat can look physically similar around the world but carry different webs of meaning, the modern ritual that is called an office meeting might *seem* universal, but it is not. A failure to realize that can be disastrous in terms of how institutions work—or do not function at all.

"What I do is make explicit what has been implicit," Briody explained to a journalist, shortly after the Delta Two project. "Sometimes that makes people uncomfortable. But that's the anthropologist's job. We help people see patterns more clearly."[3] Moreover, these patterns not only explained why a once great company such as GM was going wrong in the late twentieth century—but why numerous risks were (and are) stalking other companies that were (are) trying to jump across borders, conduct mergers, or simply combine different professional skills, of the sort needed, say, if an auto company tries to create a self-driving car.

GM was not the first big company to use anthropologists to study itself. That honor arguably goes to a business called Western Electric, a forerunner of the AT&T telecom group, which used to have its main factory in Hawthorne, Illinois. In 1927 the company management invited some researchers at the fledgling so-called School of Human Relations at Harvard University into their operations, to study some of the twenty-five thousand workers who were making telephone equipment and components. The reason they did this was that the company leaders wanted to analyze a question that remains a staple of business school studies and management consultancy: Were the practices used at Western Electric productive, in terms of getting the workforce to do their jobs well? It was an issue that sparked great anxiety since in the 1920s—as today—rapid technological change and globalization were turning business upside down.

The Harvard University team pulled into the project was run by a psychiatrist named Elton Mayo, but included an anthropologist named William Lloyd Warner, who had previously studied Aboriginal communities in Australia and then moved into studying American corporate systems, foreshadowing the transition taken by Bell at Intel.[4] The researchers conducted two experiments. First they subjected different teams of workers to different levels of light, and observed them to see if this affected their performance. Then they did the same while changing the timing of their work schedules and rest breaks.

The results were startling—but not in the way anyone had expected. The observations showed little change in productivity among workers when the lighting and rest-break schedules were changed. But there was a dramatic improvement when the workers thought they were being watched, compared to when they thought the researchers were not present. This created a headache for the researchers, since it showed that the mere presence of the researchers changed what they were supposed to study (a phenomenon that came to be called the "Hawthorne effect"). It also carried a lesson for business executives that matters as much in the twenty-first century as it did in the early twentieth century: sometimes the simplest way to improve worker productivity is just to make the workers *think* they are being watched.

Mayo, the psychiatrist, then conducted surveys among the workers. But this experiment did not proceed as planned either. When they filled in the survey, workers invariably just gave the answers they thought the researchers wanted to hear. So Warner suggested that it might be wiser to employ the tools he had used for his research among Australian Aboriginal peoples: unstructured observation and open-ended interviews. It was not easy for elite academics to listen "without interruption" to what the workers wanted to say, notes Gabriel Santiago Jurado Gonzalez, another anthropologist.[5] High-status professors and executives were used to doing the talking, not watching with the type of "child-like wonder" Mead described. But over the course of three years, the company permitted the researchers to conduct twenty thousand unstructured interviews. These showed that the management of Western Electric had entirely the wrong assumptions about their employees. The managers assumed that workers responded best to economic incentives and that the official bureaucratic employee hierarchies in the factories described how power patterns worked. But the researchers discovered that there was "an informal structure within the company created from the existing social relationships among colleagues . . . separated from the formal structure established by the organizational chart and internal regulations of the company," as Gonzalez notes. Moreover, economic incentives were *not* the only motivation affecting performance; instead the researchers uncovered tales like that of an eighteen-year-old female worker who reported that she "was being pressured to request a pay raise at the factory" at home but feared that "receiving a raise meant separating herself from the group of workers among whom she felt happy."

Chastened, the company leaders asked the Harvard team (which, by then, was also collaborating with the University of Chicago) to study what incentives might increase productivity. Yet again, the research did not produce the answer they expected. "Workers had created a rumor according to which the most efficient people were 'servants' of the management who increased the average production of the group to obtain individual benefits. Consequently, no worker wanted to stand out," notes Gonzalez. The executives did not know what was really going on with staff—or even what they did not know.

When the Great Depression hit, the research project at Western Electric stopped. In the aftermath of World War Two, the concept of using social science—or the type of observational techniques that anthropologists had employed—fell out of favor. Postwar America was dazzled by engineering and the hard sciences; would-be executives were taught about systems of scientific management, corporate efficiency, and effective planning. Talking about tribalism seemed old-fashioned when industrial technology seemed so exciting. Nor did there seem to be any incentive for an ambitious American executive to think about cultural differences since the Western allies had triumphed in the War—and American companies were swelling in power.

However, as the twentieth century wore on, the mood started to shift. Away from the limelight, General Motors embarked on an experiment. In the early years of the century, the auto giant had been one of the most powerful and successful companies in America, if not the world. Indeed, in the 1950s the company was so dominant that almost half of all American cars bought by consumers emanated from GM factories in Michigan, and Charlie Wilson, the then GM president, declared,

"What's good for General Motors is good for America." However, by the 1980s GM's halo was slipping—fast. From the 1960s on, German and Japanese cars entered the market, first as imports and then via the construction of factories in America. The "foreigners" rapidly won market share. Then industrial discontent grew: in 1970 the United Auto Workers staged a strike at GM that lasted sixty-seven days and cost the company $1 billion in profit. Doubts arose about the Americans' management systems. GM and Ford had enjoyed dazzling success in the first half of the century by using a mass production system which presumed that the most efficient way to treat workers was like cogs in a machine, allocating each human to one—and *just* one—proscribed job in a clear-cut hierarchy. The new Japanese rivals, however, used a different system (sometimes called the "Toyota Production System," or TPS) which asked workers to collaborate in small teams and take responsibility for the entire production of a car in a more flexible manner, rather than treating each worker as a preordained cog. Initially the Americans scorned this arrangement. But by the 1980s, scorn was turning into introspection.

The GM executives—like the other automakers—responded by throwing money at research and development, hiring engineers and scientists to improve auto design. One of these was Robert A. Frosch, a physicist and former NASA administrator, who was put in charge of the R&D team. Frosch had cut his teeth in the world of hard science. But early in his career he had encountered an in-house anthropologist who was working with scientists and was intrigued by the idea of blending the perspectives. "He was a Renaissance guy," Briody observed. So Frosch decided to bring a social scientist into GM's R&D team.

Like most anthropologists who migrated into business, Briody had never expected to be pulled into this world—or thought that her path might cross that of a man such as Frosch. She did postgraduate studies in anthropology at the University of Texas in the early 1980s, an era when her counterparts usually headed to developing countries to do fieldwork.

Since Briody spoke some Spanish, Latin America or Central America seemed a natural destination. But she was desperately short of money. So she switched tack and studied the community of (mostly Spanish speaking) janitors who cleaned the buildings at her university. Nobody had done this work before since this "tribe" did not seem at all exotic or glamorous. But Briody was curious about what she might find, hidden in plain sight. "I spent hours sitting with the janitors in their lunch breaks just listening to the stories of their lives and work—everything," she later explained. "They were happy to talk to me, since they were not used to people being interested."

She subsequently studied migrant farmworkers from Mexico who picked oranges and grapefruits in Texas orchards. This was another part of half-hidden America. Then some GM researchers heard about her work and invited her to use the same research techniques to look at the workers on the company's assembly lines. So Briody visited the GM offices in Michigan in the mid-1980s, and she "became hooked." To her, studying a factory and its seemingly "troublesome" union members was as thrilling as going to the Amazon or the Trobriand Islands; it represented a new intellectual frontier that Frosch, the NASA physicist, was almost as keen to explore as she was.

Shortly afterward, Briody arrived on the assembly lines at a noisy factory in Michigan. By the mid-1980s the GM managers had already used all manner of supposedly scientific management tools to measure what was happening in its factories—and, above all, to try to explore what was going wrong. Briody, however, took a different tack. Her brief was to observe how manufacturing work got done; so in classic ethnographic style, she set about observing *everything* that caught her eye, whether or not it fitted the usual definition of a management "problem": material handlers whizzing by on their jitneys; storage areas strewn with arriving inventory; assemblers working in the "pit" attaching bolts to the vehicle underbodies;

repair zones chock-full of trucks. She tried to avoid having preset ideas about what mattered, but instead to observe like a child—or a Martian.

One day she was shadowing a material handler when he made a striking comment. "A lot of people hoard parts," he declared, gesturing at the lockers. Briody's ears pricked up. By then the auto industry was in the grip of a so-called quality movement, inspired by the remarkable results Japanese manufacturers had achieved. The plant had been conducting "quality training"—and messaging these ideas to everyone. This was supposed to create a slick logistics system. So why, Briody asked, did anybody ever "hoard" parts?[6]

"If your line is about to run out of a certain part, you are responsible [and] if the line shuts down for even five to ten minutes, it would reflect on your foreman, general foreman, superintendent, and plant manager and also cost GM a bunch of money," one material handler told Briody. "Consequently a lot of people stock up on certain parts and store them in their lockers [or] in the wrong stock area where only they will know where it is." Or as another material handler explained after Briody watched an assembly line shut down due to a lack of parts: "If the material handler had set some extra [parts] aside from before, he wouldn't be facing this problem. Over and over again I have found parts hidden in different places in the plant." The neat inventory systems were being ignored. Instead a game of hide-and-seek was underway. Or as one handler observed: "We [are] part of a board game or race to see who [can] locate the parts and get back to home first." The hide-and-seek "game" was so intense that Briody calculated it absorbed a quarter of the handlers' time. That was startling. What was even more surprising, through, was that the senior GM managers had no idea this "game" was even occurring.

That begged a question: *Why* would workers want to hide parts in their lockers, like naughty children? Briody concluded that the answer was that workers were in a near impossible position. The model of mass production, which had shaped American auto production, measured workers according to how they performed, as cogs, using quantitative metrics. If more vehicles rolled off the assembly line, bonuses were paid; if not, they were not. The new "quality movement," pioneered by Japanese and German car makers, judged workers by different metrics, such as whether products had flaws (or not). That shift in emphasis sounded impressive when presented to investors. But there was a rub: even amid the "quality" rhetoric, American workers were still being judged and paid by metrics of "quantity," and the factories still had hierarchical structures that treated workers like cogs.

The workers had responded to this with a distinctive coping strategy: a "blame culture." Whenever something went wrong, the *first* response among the workers was to blame somebody or something else—rather than seek their own solutions—because they did not feel they had enough agency to fix anything. "If you admit that a particular thing was your fault, you have to do something about it," a material handler explained to her. "It's so much easier to blame another department on another shift. . . . The first rule of thumb is 'Cover thy ass.'" Indeed, when Briody reviewed the transcripts from the factory conversations she heard, she discovered that "plant personnel were seven times more likely to blame than to praise each other."[7]

This meant, she concluded, that it was wrong to assume that the battles between the unions and managers were the *cause* of GM's problems, as investors, top managers, and some politicians claimed. Instead the fights were the *symptom* of bigger structural challenges and contradictions. Thus you could not hope to "fix" the productivity problem at GM just by taking a top-down view; you also needed to look at the world bottom-up, through the workers' eyes. And although journalists, investors, politicians, and managers were obsessed with the visible battles around the unions, what was arguably even more important, but largely ignored, was the continual stealthy subversion of rules in the factories through, say, the games around auto parts in assemblers' lockers.

There was—and is—a bigger lesson here for investors and managers alike. When business school students are taught about companies, they typically focus on official institutional hierarchies and "org charts," and ponder what happens when open conflict breaks out between different teams or layers of the hierarchy. However, anthropologists have always known that power is not exercised just through an official hierarchy, but through informal channels too, and conflict does not always take place in overt ways. A study by the anthropologist James Scott of Malaysian peasants illustrates this well: in this study, Scott shows that when agricultural peasants are faced with oppressive landlords, they do not usually fight back with open conflict, but instead with delaying tactics and subversion—or what he described as "foot-dragging."[8] Malaysian farmers might seem to have little immediate connection to Michigan unions. But what Briody was observing was simply another potent form of "foot-dragging," as an adaptation to an inventory system that was going haywire. The "foot-dragging" was having wide, corrosive effects—but in a way that most Western business executives were not able to see since it never occurred to them to go into the locker rooms.

Twenty years later, on the eve of the 2008 Great Financial Crisis, Briody returned to the factory floors where she had watched the "hide-and-seek" games around the assembly lines. In those intervening years, GM's Asian rivals had grabbed even more market share, and in response companies such as GM had moved some production out of their birthplace—Michigan—into other corners of America, such as Tennessee, where the unions were less powerful. They had also put factories into places such as Mexico. This "outsourcing" had been carried out to cut costs, since salaries in Mexico were much lower than those in Michigan. But it had an unexpected additional consequence: the Mexican plants not only produced cars cheaply, but often did so with higher quality too.

Why? Briody was sent back to investigate, with two GM colleagues—

Tracy Meerwarth and Robert Trotter—using similar modes of research. In some senses, what they found was cheering. When Briody had done her initial study in the 1980s, she had the impression that many of her recommendations ended up being ignored by the top managers—despite a GM board review. However, two decades later she discovered that a surprising amount of change had occurred. Top-down statistics showed this: productivity at the company rose 54 percent between 1986 and 2007; customer complaints fell 69 percent between 1989 and 2008 (although this was badly marred in the next decade by a scandal over faulty ignition switches)[9]; workdays lost to occupational injury and illness fell by 98 percent between 1993 and 2008.[10]

More striking still, ethnography suggested that the "blame culture" was fading. An episode that Meerwarth witnessed in one Michigan factory captured this change. One day she visited a newly occupied stamping plant, still not completely furnished with all the stamping presses and other equipment, and only running one shift. A plant manager, called Davis, had asked a team of workers—called the "skilled trades" group—to choose a site on the brand-new factory floor for their recreation room. The workers duly taped their chosen corner away from the noise of the presses.[11] But Davis wanted the room to be close to the managers' office. A standoff ensued. "We were upset," "Don," a leading member of the UAW (union of autoworkers), told Meerwarth. "It's a slap in the face for us to say you have a choice and then no choice!" Two decades earlier, the fight might have sparked a union-management fight. But now Davis backed down—and Don's team got their recreation room in the part of the factory that they had selected. "Sometimes I feel like I am banging my head against a wall. The old way at GM was a sort of perception that 'Hey, I'm the new boss. This is my way,'" Don said. "[But] I can honestly say that we have made more improvement than ten years [ago] and far more improvement than twenty years ago. We have a recipe for success here . . . in spite of our problems." A more empowered culture was emerging.

Briody's group never got a chance to present these findings to the top GM management. Just after they completed their study, the Great Financial Crisis exploded, sparking a deep recession. That lead to the bankruptcy of GM, which was placed in government control, and Briody and the other researchers lost their jobs, along with thousands of other GM staff. "It was very sad what happened," Briody later observed. "I don't think that GM gets nearly enough credit for what was going on in the early years of the twentieth century—it was finally starting to move in a better direction. But by then it was too late."

In subsequent years Briody found that the lessons she learned at GM could be applied in many companies. She advised some global groups on how to cope with internal culture clashes between different ethnic groups. She cowrote a best-selling manual to help Western expatriate business leaders who were sent outside their home country cope with seemingly "strange" cultures.[12] However, as she offered her advice about crosscultural miscommunication, she also stressed a crucial—but oft-ignored—point: the worst misunderstandings sometimes happen between different teams within the supposedly same ethnic group, particularly if they came from different locations or had different professional training (say, IT workers mingling with engineers). Miscommunications are sometimes more dangerous when people appear to speak the same language or have the same national identity, precisely because nobody even notices or questions the assumptions they use—or ask whether other people have the same assumptions.

That point has been stressed by anthropologists studying other aspects of Western professional culture. Back in the 1980s, Frank Dubinskas worked with a team of researchers to look at how the concept of "time" was imagined in several different communities: particle physicists, biologists doing genetic research, semiconductor engineers, medical professionals, as well as lawyers and financiers. "Time—or better, times—means different things to each of the communities of scientists, engineers, doctors and executives that we investigate," he observed. "We are accustomed to speaking of them all as parts of 'Western culture,' as if there was some uniform context or hegemonic framework that patterns time. However, differences in the social construction of times are crucial factors in doing scientific and technical work and in shaping the communities of professionals who do it."[13]

When Briody later looked back at notes around the ill-fated Delta Two project at GM, she could see that her research had started—as so often—around a set of wrong assumptions. Most people at GM assumed that the problems that dogged the project arose because "Germans" (i.e., the engineers from Opel in Rüsselheim, Germany) were fighting with the "Americans" (from Saturn in Spring Hill, Tennessee, and the Small Car Group in the Detroit area). It seemed temptingly easy to use these ethnic labels since the different teams had different languages and were defending different car technologies. But when Briody observed the teams in action, she saw that ethnic labels only explained part of the problem. One striking point was that Americans working in Rüsselheim behaved like the rest of the Adam Opel team, i.e., like "Germans," and Germans in the Detroit area acted like their majority American team. It was not ethnicity that mattered but the cultures that emerged inside different institutions and locales. The other striking point was that the "Americans" were far from uniform, but had cultural divides too. One of the teams was based in Michigan, near the traditional headquarters of GM. However the second team hailed from Spring Hill, Tennessee, where GM had built a factory in the 1980s, when the American giant was frantically trying to stave off competition from Japanese rivals. Back then, the GM executives had deliberately placed this new venture away from Michigan to break the power of the unions—and remodel factory work and create more "collaborative" manager-worker practices. As a result the Spring Hill factory had a different culture from its counterpart in Michigan—and that split was as important as the "German-American" divide.

The workers themselves could not easily describe the defining features of their own culture since they each assumed the way that they worked was "natural." But Briody kept trying to compare them to see the differences and, like any anthropologist, she found that looking at rituals and symbols helped to clarify the patterns and comparisons. In Tajikistan I had done this with wedding rituals; Briody focused on corporate meetings.[14] Normally, office workers never spend much time pondering the meaning of this word.[15] But when Briody pored over the transcripts of the disastrous meetings she watched during the Delta Two negotiations, she realized that the three groups each had different assumptions about what a "meeting" should be. The Opel team from Rüsselheim assumed these rituals should be short, with a clearly preset agenda. Since most day-to-day work was performed *outside* meetings, it was presumed that the only function of these gatherings was to make a concrete decision, and the phrase "I am holding a meeting" was *not* equated with "I am doing work." Moreover, the Rüsselheim group assumed that insofar as decisions were made at a meeting, this should be done by a leader; a hierarchical power structure existed—at least in their mind.

However, the engineers from the so-called Small Car Group, based out of the Detroit area, thought that "having a meeting" *was* equivalent to "doing work." They expected to spend much of their work time sitting inside meetings. That was because the Detroit team operated with another assumption that differed from that of the Rüsselheim team: meetings were the proper place for ideas to be shared. Thus the Detroit group assumed that the agenda for a meeting should *not* be predefined; they instead wanted it to evolve as information was exchanged. And while Rüsselheim had a hierarchical, leadership-driven system, the Detroit group thought that the decisions should be "majority preferred"—meaning that most people had to back them.

The Tennessee group had yet another mental and cultural pattern. Like the team from Rüsselheim, the engineers in Tennessee expected meetings to be brief, since they also thought that most of the work should be done elsewhere; but *unlike* Rüsselheim, the Tennessee group thought that the point of a meeting was to develop consensus, rather than make decisions, and did *not* like preset agendas. Moreover, they hated the idea that a decision might be taken in a hierarchical manner by a leader. Instead the Spring Hill plant had a formal rule in place that a decision could only be made when everyone agreed that an idea was at least 70 percent correct. The "Americans," in other words, were not a single group.

Briody later studied the meeting rituals of three other branches of GM—GM do Brasil (the automaker's Brazilian operation), GM Truck Group (a unit based in Pontiac, Michigan), and Isuzu (an entity in Fujisawa, Japan, that had struck a joint venture deal with GM). There she saw even more variants on these themes. The GM Truck Group in Pontiac used a pattern of "individual empowerment" to get work done. GM do Brasil used "collaboration," and Isuzu used a single "voice of authority." The key cultural ideal at Isuzu was "harmony," while at GM do Brasil it was "interdependence," and at GM Truck Group it was "individualism."[16] None of these cultural patterns was necessarily "right" or "wrong." But they were different and those differences tended to go unnoticed because the concept of a meeting was so familiar. Or, to put it another way, most of the GM engineers and executives had never learned that sometimes the simplest way to improve operations is to step back and ask: *What would happen if I was to look at this organization from the eyes of the lowest member of staff—instead of the lofty heights of the C-suite? How is space being used to reinforce social and mental divisions? What, in other words, might an anthropologist see? If he or she was permitted to enter—and leaders listened.*

In 1999, Briody presented the results of her study to the Delta Two team. By then it was clear that the project was in trouble. Indeed, soon after that the GM senior product development leaders concluded it would be impossible to ever get the three different teams to produce together a small car with a common system below the seats, and stopped the project. Some engineers blamed the issue on science. But Briody tried to outline the different assumptions about meetings. Initially her messages came as a shock to everyone. Then it was almost a relief.

"The senior engineer sank back into his chair and put his hands in his head and said: 'At last I get it!'" Briody later recalled. "He kept saying: 'I just didn't understand this before, but now I do.' It was a real moment." Culture mattered.

SIX

WEIRD WESTERNERS

(OR WHY DO WE REALLY BUY DOG FOOD AND DAYCARE?)

"It is weird not to be weird."

—John Lennon

In the spring of 2015 Meg Kinney, an executive who ran a consultancy called Bad Babysitters, received an urgent message from a digital strategist in Los Angeles: "A client needs your help."

The entity in need was Primrose Schools, based in Georgia. On paper, the business seemed a raging success. It had been founded in 1983 to offer care for children aged six weeks to five years old and built its operations so effectively across America that it was close to becoming a billion-dollar operation, with 400 different nurseries and 11,500 staff. The executives had achieved this by embracing data and educational expertise to an impressive degree. They offered a proprietary "Balanced Learning" program based on developmental research combined with the best thinking of renowned early learning philosophers. They also relied on economic models to predict future supply and demand, and used Big Data to model trends and prospective audience profiles in a manner normally associated with Silicon Valley. "If Mom is upstairs researching preschool ratings and reviews on her iPad and Dad is downstairs checking football scores on his phone with the TV on, Primrose knows this and will push them both unique versions of some awareness-building content," Kinney observed in a report.[1] This was not your parents'—or grandparents'—nursery.

But the Primrose executives had a problem: the KPIs (key performance indicators) were odd. The key issue was that conversion rates were low. Parents were browsing the website, interacting with content, and visiting social media. But at that moment of truth—visiting the school—parents were not enrolling at the predicted rates. It seemed baffling. The level of brand recognition seemed adequate. Consumer inquiries were rising. The offering had not changed, nor had the predictive models. But something had gone wrong. And although Big Data information collected from parents' digital journey described *how* the parents were behaving, it did not explain *why*.

Kinney set to work. The name of her strategy consultancy—Bad Babysitter Productions—did not reflect any specialization in early education; she mostly worked with consumer goods companies and retailers and selected the tag as a piece of irreverent branding, to be memorable. But what really set the consultancy apart was its approach: it used ethnography. Kinney had spent most of her career as an account planner in advertising, running accounts for companies such as Procter & Gamble. But later in her life she stumbled on the ideas embedded in ethnography and anthropology and embraced them. She was not the only one. The discipline of anthropology had first emerged in the nineteenth century to study the rituals, symbols, myths, and artifacts of other "strange" cultures, along with their institutions and social systems. In the twentieth century, some anthropologists—like Briody at GM—used these tools to look inside Western institutions too. However, these tools could shed light on Western consumer culture too, particularly if you looked at what American consumers consider "normal" with outside eyes.

In the 1950s the anthropologist Horace Miner did this in a memorable way in a landmark satirical essay looking at "body ritual" among the

"Naricema" tribe, or "America" in the mirror."[2] In his essay Miner writes as if an anthropologist had stumbled on a "North American group living in the territory between the Canadian Cree, the Yaqui and Tarahumane of Mexico and the Carib and the Arawak of the Antilles" who display a peculiar obsession with the human body and engage in such customs as a twice-daily ceremony in a shrine with a font, using ritualistic movements taught to children at a young age by a "holy man"—better known as the tooth brushing ritual taught by a "dentist." By the late twentieth century, a host of different marketing and advertising groups were embracing Miner's idea to look at consumers. Sometimes people trained as anthropologists were employed to this end.[3] However, non-anthropologists embraced the concept of ethnography too. This trend made some academics uncomfortable; they complained that the nonacademic research was so shallow that it undermined the discipline. However, the new business ethnographers retorted—quite correctly—that the trend was giving the discipline new relevance and fostering some unexpected innovation around the concept of "fieldwork."

The Bad Babysitter group was a prime example of this trend. Back in the days of Malinowski and Mead, anthropologists mostly observed people with the naked eye; face-to-face observation was a defining trait of the discipline. However Kinney worked with Hal Phillips, a multimedia storyteller, to do so-called video ethnography, using a camera to film everything so that interactions could be reviewed and re-reviewed later. This enabled researchers to use another tool to see what was often unseen—and study the entire picture, in order to complement Big Data. "Every business problem is a human problem and every data point represents some human behavior at its core," Kinney explained.[4]

Kinney and Phillips rolled out this strategy for Primrose. They started by recruiting a dozen American families, including existing and potential Primrose parents, based in two locations. The average age of the parents was thirty-three and annual household income was above $50,000. Then the researchers sent each family "workbooks," which asked open-ended questions, such as how the parents might describe choosing a preschool if it was a sport (some likened it to scuba diving because of the risk they might drown). Armed with that, the researchers tracked the families, with a video camera, during their daily routines in school, stores, play areas, and around the home. They also went on parent tours of a Primrose School and videotaped how would-be parents reacted after the tours, when they got into their cars.

The footage revealed an important point that helped to solve the mystery around Primrose: the concept of childcare had different webs of meaning for the parents and teachers. The issue at stake was partly generational. The top managers at Primrose were mostly from so-called Generation X, or people born before 1975 who had absorbed the values of late twentieth-century America. They had grown up in an era when experts were respected and when it was assumed that parents who used childcare did so because they actively *wanted* to work and were looking for educational achievements for their tots, such as learning to read.

However the parents lived in the twenty-first century, were between the age of twenty-five and forty-five, and had different attitudes. "These happen to be the most educated cohort ever in the U.S. They also happen to be employed in an era of flat wages, more hours at work, and school debt," Kinney noted. "This cohort is at the forefront of parenting in the so-called 'attention economy'—an age of decreased attention spans, increased stress, and demand for personalization . . . [and] these young parents are raising children in an internet-first world."[5] These parents were often called "millennials," although Kinney herself avoided that tag. They felt a much deeper sense of moral conflict around childcare than their predecessors: although they used nurseries because both parents needed to work for economic reasons, they also knew that "policymakers, business, and working parents [continually] stressed the critical role of early children experiences." That created guilt and fear. They also had a different view from teachers of the role of early education. Teachers stressed educational milestones. The parents wanted to build character, curiosity, self-expression, and resilience in their children, which would prepare them for diverse social interactions, because they fretted about an uncertain future where their children would have to get along with different humans and AI-enabled machines. "Culturally, there is a shift away from the reassured child (e.g., participation trophies) towards the resilient child," Kinney noted. "Being adaptive is a Twenty-first-century skill."

The other area of difference was that the parents did not respect vertical hierarchies of authority, e.g., assume that "experts" like scientists, teachers, CEOs—or Primrose executives—were always the best source of advice; instead they were shaped by "horizontal" or "distributed" trust, to use the phases posited by the social scientist Rachel Botsman, because they put more emphasis on information from their peers.[6] They did not see "experts" as a source of authority or a reason to pay for preschool care. This was significant because the company's marketing literature extolled its "experts" and took an authoritative "one to many" tone.

The Bad Babysitters presented their study to the Primrose C-suite. The executives were startled. "This was something we had not experienced before," Paul Thaxton, vice president of brand management, Primrose Schools, told Kinney. To their credit, the schools changed strategy: they changed the brand tagline from "America's leader in Early Education and Childcare" to "We believe that who children become is as important as what they know." They also changed the digital content to downplay statistics, academic research, and advice from experts, and instead adopted a more approachable tone. Phrases such as "we believe" were used instead of "studies show"; school directors were encouraged to trade a formal script in favor of active listening. To build a sense of lateral community, the school directors also embraced another core tenet of anthropology: rituals and symbols. Since they realized that the parents' decision to enroll was as much about joining a community as anything else, they used cultural devices to reinforce this, handing out "first day of school" backpacks and staging ceremonies around an "Erwin the Dog" puppet who teaches friendship.

It worked. In the year after the study finished, there was a 4 percent growth in parent enrollment, an 18 percent increase in inquiries, a 24 percent increase in engagement (with social media metrics)—and the company went from fourth place to top place in the sector in terms of public awareness. The improvement was not a revolution. But it was progress.

To understand why Big Data alone cannot explain consumer culture it pays to look at a set of ideas about the "weird" nature of Westerners developed by Joseph Henrich, a professor of evolutionary biology at Harvard University. Henrich started his career as an aeronautical engineer before moving into anthropology, where he studied the interaction between culture, human biology, and the environment (or a blend of physical and cultural anthropology.)* As part of that, he did extensive fieldwork among the Mapuche people in Chile. However Henrich's findings ended up revealing less about the Mapuche per se—and more about the nature of the *Western* psychology profession.[7] This profession has flourished in the twentieth and twenty-first centuries by offering useful insights about how human brains function (or do not). But there is a catch, Henrich notes: psychologists have created many of their theories by studying the subjects they have closest to hand—student volunteers, who are typically Western, highly educated, and in their late teens or early twenties. Thus

*Although physical and cultural anthropology diverged into distinct branches in the early twentieth century, some anthropologists continue to analyze culture by looking at biology and the physical environment, and this approach has become increasingly popular in recent years due to the bestselling books of Jared Diamond, such as *Guns, Germs, and Steel: The Fates of Human Societies* (New York: W. W. Norton, 1999). Henrich's work is in a similar vein. So is that of Robin Dunbar, the evolutionary biologist whose work explores how brain size affects the structure and scale of social groups.

while psychology research purports to present universal findings, what it actually shows is how *Western*-educated brains work. When Henrich did the same experiments on the Mapuche, he got different results.

These differences fall into several broad buckets. One is the degree to which a brain solves problems and absorbs information through *sequential* reasoning (A leads to B leads to C) and highly selective observation, instead of looking at an *entire* situation in a holistic way. The former is associated with Western Enlightenment–era thought and reinforced by the pervasive habit of reading with an alphabet—or what Western students (hopefully) do all day. Thus when Henrich showed American students pictures of situations and asked them to interpret these, the students tended to "zero in on and track the center of attention [in a picture] while ignoring the context and background."[8] Logical analysis—and tunnel vision—ruled. However the second, holistic approach is often found in cultures without writing, like the Mapuche: they used "contextually appropriate holistic relationships to support their choices." When Henrich did similar experiments elsewhere, he noticed that the populations of other countries fell into two buckets, albeit on a spectrum (and with differences inside countries, as well as between them). Analytical thinking was more dominant in the Netherlands, Finland, Sweden, Ireland, New Zealand, Germany, the United States, and the UK. Holistic thought was more widespread in Serbia, Bolivia, the Philippines, the Dominican Republic, Romania, and Thailand.

A second realm of difference was identity. When Henrich asked people "Who am I?" he found that Americans and Europeans tended to answer with *personal* attributes (like job), while non-Western people such as the Samburu, Kenyans, or Cook Islanders defined themselves in relation to family and talked about kinship and community roles. "Focusing on one's attributes and achievements over one's roles and relationships is a key element in a psychological package that I'll clump together as the individualism complex," he wrote.[9] A third point was morality:

when Henrich asked whether it would be acceptable to lie or cheat for a family member, in Western societies people usually said no, since they assumed that morals and rules should be universally applied; however. non-Western groups tended to say yes, since it was presumed that rules could change according to context.[10] Henrich cited a startling natural experiment that occurred with New York parking tickets. Until 2002, diplomats to the United Nations enjoyed immunity if they received a city parking ticket. Despite there being no penalty for parking in the wrong place, "diplomats from the UK, Sweden, Canada, Australia and a few other countries got a total of zero tickets" in this period since they obeyed the rules even if there was no cost to breaking them. But "diplomats from Egypt, Chad, [and] Bulgaria accumulat[ed] over 100" tickets for each person; for them, morality was more context-dependent.

Westerners might react to this by criticizing non-Western cultures as "strange." But Henrich argues that it is actually the attitudes of American and European societies that are "strange" since "throughout most of human history, people grew up enmeshed in dense family networks. . . . In these regulated relational worlds, people's survival, identity, security, marriages and success depended on the health and prosperity of kin-based networks." Western societies are outliers since "people tend to be highly individualistic, self-obsessed, control-orientated, nonconformist and analytical . . . and see ourselves as unique beings . . . and prefer a sense of control and making our own choices."[11] He describes these traits as WEIRD—Western, Educated, Individualistic, Rich, and Democratic.

This distinction matters if you want to understand consumer culture. WEIRD cultures tend to assume that the individual is at the center of their world;* society is the derivative of the individual, not the other

*I use the word "tend" since it should be stressed that Henrich's framework describes a behavioral pattern seen in all societies to varying degrees, on a spectrum. There is obviously huge variation even within WEIRD societies, such as America.

way around, and individuals are presumed to have choice about their destiny and identity. Indeed, in the twenty-first century that concept has been extended to a once-unimaginable degree since digital technologies foster the idea that consumers can fashion the world around them to their desires, customizing music choices, food, coffee, media, or almost anything. We all live in our version of the movie *The Matrix*. Or, if you prefer, in the era of "Gen C"—or Generation Customization.

That creates the impression that Western consumers are driven by individual choice, hence the frequent employment of the insights of psychology and Big Data to show (respectively) how human brains function and what individuals are doing online. But there is a catch: although consumers think their decisions are driven by entirely rational, independent choices—in line with WEIRD ideals—this is rarely true. Consumers define their identity using symbols and rituals inherited from their surroundings. They are shaped by group loyalties and social relations. They operate in spatial patterns partly created by others. The ideas they absorb from their environment can be deeply contradictory and multilayered. However, they may not admit this—either to themselves or others—precisely because they have a WEIRD presumption that problems can or should be solved with logical, sequential thought—and tunnel vision. Thus while modern consumer culture arose out of WEIRD values, it cannot be understood *just* by using a WEIRD mode of thought. Western consumers are more complex and contradictory than they realize.

Mars, the gigantic company that produces everything from chocolate to pet food, is one company that knows the contradictions in consumer culture only too well. The group is best known among the public for selling confectionary, such as the iconic Mars bar. But in the 1930s it also started to sell pet food. This business line was initially modest. But by the end of the century this sector was growing fast. That reflected a bigger growth in the market, particularly in America: whereas just 56 percent of American households owned dogs and cats in 1988, by 2012 this had jumped to 62 percent.[12] And while Americans spent $17 billion on pet food in 1994, by 2011 this amount had more than tripled, to $53 billion.

In 2009, the executives at Mars decided that the sector was so attractive they wanted to expand market share. But it was not clear which marketing messages might be most effective. After all, the entire Western premise around pet food is very odd, or it is if you take a broader—anthropological—perspective. Until the twentieth century in the West, pets were usually just fed with table scraps (and in many parts of the world they still are). However, by the early twenty-first century, pet owners in America had become convinced that pets needed special food. But what was not clear was: *Why?* How did a shopper judge whether pet food was good? After all, the recipient itself—the dog—could not talk.

An anthropologist named Maryann McCabe was asked to conduct a study. A mild-mannered female academic who is skilled at blending into the background, she had started her career in the world of academic anthropology at New York University in the 1980s, doing a study of child sexual abuse, kinship, and the law in America. But she then gravitated into consumer research, where she learned the same lesson that Bell and Anderson had learned at Intel: when companies wanted some anthropological insight, they did not want to get this in the way that academic anthropologists did their research (i.e., with long, patient observation and studies of single communities, using analytical frameworks steeped in cross-cultural comparisons and theories); instead, they wanted studies of short duration across networks—not single communities. This frustrated some academics. But it could still be illuminating, since it offered three-dimensional microanalysis that was a good counterpoint to large statistical data sets.

The Mars executives identified two regions for her research: Philadelphia and Nashville. McCabe duly selected twelve families that owned pets and asked them to create photo diaries and collages that explained what owning pets meant to them. That was similar to what the Nestlé executives, say, had once done in relation to Kit Kat in Japan. The idea was to prompt dog owners to ponder their pooch, but in a nondirected manner. Then McCabe and a fellow anthropologist observed the families and dogs in their houses and went on shopping trips with them to buy pet food, encouraging them to talk about their feelings in a stream-of-consciousness way. McCabe sometimes asked the marketing team from Mars to accompany her, since she reckoned that one of the most useful services she could offer was not just writing a report—but teaching executives to look differently at the world, or to think more like an anthropologist.

The results were striking. After watching the families, McCabe could see that they did not regard their pets as just animals, or samples of the natural kingdom. Instead, "people who have pets speak of them in kinship terms," she noted in a report. "Respondents state that their cats and dogs are 'like blood' and members of the family." To American families, such imagery seemed normal. By the standards of global history and many other societies, however, the statements about "blood" and "family" were bizarre. In most societies that have been studied by anthropologists, animals sit in a different mental and cultural category from humans. When the anthropologist Claude Lévi-Strauss did research in Brazil, he noted that humans often defined themselves *in opposition* to animals. In a different context, the Lakota Native Americans also presume that animals are outside human or family circles. "[The Lakota] traditionally don't own animals. . . . People feed the dogs and care for them, but the dogs remain living outside and are free to be their own beings," note two senior academics from the Oglala Sioux tribe.[13] Thus, in many cultures it would sound nonsensical to depict pets as part of a human family, particularly since "kinship is the foundational concept organizing social relations" among most non-WEIRD societies, as Henrich observes and kinship bonds are imposed on people, not chosen.

However, WEIRD cultures tend to celebrate the concept of individual choice, even when people are defining their family. Adding a dog into a family is thus an extension of this sense of consumer agency: people are deciding to remodel their definition of "family," based on how they personally feel, rather than just accepting the "family" they inherit. (The dog itself does not have a choice, but that is another matter.) Why would a human *want* to exercise that choice by adding a dog to the family? McCabe suggested the reason was to strengthen human bonds. That might sound even more perverse. However, the issue at stake is another consequence of WEIRD values: *precisely* because family is seen as something that people actively choose to uphold (or not), Western consumers who value the idea of family are keen to find devices to uphold it—not least because they feel that there are other factors that put it under threat, such as digital distractions (e.g., cell phones). In a culture where nobody can take family bonds entirely for granted, animals are used to reinforce these.

"Pets are resources for communication," McCabe suggested, describing how parents and children take them to the dog park, dress them up for Halloween, talk endlessly about them, share silly stories—and create joint experiences as a result. Or, as the mother of one family remarked: "Not a day goes by in our house without discussion of our pets, like how cute they are or the silly things they do." The sensory nature of pets reinforces this sense of bonding since "when human family members hear, see, touch, and smell their dogs and cats while playing with them and tending to their needs, they become closer and develop memories."[14]

This finding had implications for how Mars should sell pet food, McCabe suggested. Until then the market messages had been created on the basis of animal health and science: it was assumed that it was the biology of an animal that mattered most to its owners. But McCabe suggested the company would do better to focus on human-to-human relations around pets, *not* just the animal itself—or even the animal-to-human link. The Mars executives listened. Their advertisements had previously depicted a lone animal, or an individual with their animal. But after 2008 they changed these images to feature happy families playing with animals and talking to each other, creating memories and bonds. The animals were depicted in a more "human" manner, sometimes even cracking jokes with one another. The emphasis was on group dynamics and a sense that "family" was being created by *choice*. Inside the company, a new conversation also got underway among the Mars executives about what pet food was supposed to mean to consumers. Indeed, the marketing campaigns were so successful—and Americans' interest in their pets kept swelling to such a striking degree—that by 2020 Mars was actually earning more revenue by selling pet food than chocolate. Few would have predicted that two decades before. But—like the tale of green Kit Kats—it was another example of the curiously unpredictable twists of culture.

McCabe did similar research for a wide range of other consumer goods companies. She teamed up with another anthropologist named Tim Malefyt to study how American mothers viewed food preparation, in a project commissioned by Campbell Soup.[15] This was an area where attitudes were as contradictory as those toward dogs. When asked about meal preparation in *structured* interviews (when faced with directed questions), mothers defined cooking as a chore. Thus Campbell Soup advertised its products around the concept of convenience. However, when McCabe and Malefyt repeated the same exercise they had done for Mars—namely *un*structured observation—they noticed that when mothers also talked about food preparation, they expressed pride in their creativity, and delight around the social bonds that eating forged. Food, like dogs, was perceived as a tool which people could use to create family, as an active choice. Hence another feature of twenty-first-century middle-class Western culture: a reverence for kitchen design, healthy recipes, and "home-cooked" food among many consumers. So McCabe and Malefyt suggested that Campbell Soup should produce marketing messages that celebrated creativity—not just convenience.

Laundry was similar.[16] In the late twentieth century and early twenty-first century, consumer goods companies tried to sell detergent to consumers by stressing the power (or agency) of laundry powder to remove dirt with science. This seemed logical given that when consumer goods companies conducted surveys that used directed (or predetermined) questions about laundry, these usually show that shoppers considered this to be a "chore"—like cooking. But in 2011 Procter & Gamble, the consumer group, asked McCabe to study laundry rituals. When she talked to mothers with *un*structured questions, she received messages that were similar to those around food. On the one hand, "participants spoke of the laundry as a boring and repetitious process that never ends," she noted.[17] But on the other hand, many women were reluctant to give the task to somebody *else*. (At the request of P&G, the study was focused on mothers, as the Campbell Soup project had been.) "I hate doing the laundry, but I can't stand it when someone else does it" was a common refrain. The reason, McCabe concluded, was that laundry was another way that consumers could choose to reinforce family bonds. "Amy, mother of three preschool children, talked about dirty baby bibs and remembered her six-month-old baby spitting out the green vegetable puree that she tried feeding her and dirt-stained clothes her other two children wore when they were making mud pies in the backyard," McCabe noted. "When mothers touch, smell, hear and see dirty clothes in the process of becoming clean, they connect past, present and future. Through mnemonics and remembering social occasions when dirty clothes were worn in the past and imagining drawers full of clean clothes to be used for cultivating subjectivity in the future, mothers place themselves in the ambit of passing time."[18] So McCabe suggested to P&G and its advertising agency, Saatchi and Saatchi, that they should try to sell their products in terms of not just science, but the celebration, maintenance, and display of social ties.

By the end of the second decade of the twenty-first century, the type of analysis done by McCabe had become prolific. So much so that when EPIC—the industry body for applied anthropology—held its annual meetings, tickets sold out within a few hours. The frenzy was a startling contrast to a decade earlier and partly reflected a scramble among well-funded tech companies, such as Intel, Facebook, Uber, Amazon, and Google, to embrace ethnography for user research in the digital sphere. However, anthropologists were also observing almost every other conceivable aspect of consumer behavior: they studied Japan Airlines and Boeing to see how disabled passengers experienced flying;[19] they explored the American Girl doll brand to see how these dolls might become more empowering for girls;[20] and an anthropologist named Grant McCracken observed how consumers watched Netflix television (which led him to suggest that the company should talk about "feasting" on shows, not "bingeing," since that had more positive connotations of control).[21] Sometimes the anthropologists just wrote reports about the cultural patterns they saw.[22] However some tried to change their clients' mindsets too. An anthropologist named Simon Roberts, for example, who ran a consultancy called Stripe Partners, told company executives that they needed to embrace the experience of participant observation themselves. He argued that it was a big mistake for anybody to presume that consumer behavior could simply be understood with WEIRD intellectual reasoning, since "embodied" physical experiences, habits, and rituals mattered deeply too. "In psychology, which has a disproportionate influence on consumer research, the idea is that most of what we want to know is in our heads and we just need to find ways that we can get into the minds of the consumer," he said. "[But] embodied knowledge is powerful." To explain that to the Duracell company he insisted on taking the executives camping in a park close to the Mexican border, to force them to experience how campers used batteries in the wild. The embodied lesson prompted Duracell to shift its advertising campaigns.[23]

There was one area of consumer experience, however, that remained—oddly—neglected: money. In the aftermath of the Great Financial Crisis, anthropologists had studied how people interacted with financial markets. But they tended to focus on what financiers sometimes describe as "wholesale" finance, or what happened in financial companies, such as banks or insurance companies, and in financial markets. A few anthropologists at Intel studied consumers' experience with finance and Bill Maurer, a professor at the University of California, Irvine, created a research institute to study money and financial technology, funded by a grant from the Bill & Melinda Gates Foundation.[24] However, what was striking was that few banks, insurance companies, or asset managers seemed interested in ethnography—in sharp contrast to the tech and consumer goods sector. One rare exception, however, existed in Denmark, where the consultancy ReD Associates was keen to explore this world. The group had emerged in Denmark soon after the turn of the century to do ethnographic and social research for the Lego toy company, helping the group to "understand children's play and know how to reconnect with kids," as Jørgen Vig Knudstorp, the former Lego CEO, said. The insights were later credited by Knudstorp as a key factor that helped revive the Danish company.[25] On the back of that, ReD expanded into other consumer sectors such as healthcare, fashion, and cars, and did a project on consumer attitudes for a medium-sized Scandinavian financial group called Danica.

The ReD researchers were not generally academic-style anthropologists. One, Mikkel Rasmussen, was an economist who had worked for the Danish government, creating complex macroeconomic models. Another, Martin Gronemann, was a political scientist. They—like Kinney—had gravitated toward anthropology late in their careers, when they realized the limits of using analytical tools that ignored context and started to embrace cultural analysis. Rasmussen, for example, fell in love with ethnography because the macroeconomic models he had been developing for the Danish government appeared to exclude so many variables that mattered, like the social context. He and Gronemann were very baffled that so few anthropologists were trying to see money from the vantage point of consumers. So they decided to launch a study. It turned out to be an arena where WEIRD attitudes were most weird of all.

Linda, a fifty-four-year-old event consultant, sat at a table in early 2016 and spread out fourteen separate credit cards onto a table. She explained that these were the tools she used in her daily life to make purchases and handle money. But that was not the whole tale: she also possessed cash, several mortgages, half a dozen insurance policies, and numerous pensions, she explained, looking embarrassed.

Across the room, the ReD research team listened. They had spent weeks moving around households in Germany, Britain, and America talking to people about banks, insurance companies, and pensions, and observing transactions. In theory, these should have been simple conversations. Money "makes the world go round," as the popular tag claims, and the discipline of Western economics often assumes humans are self-interested creatures driven by profit maximization. It is assumed in financial models that people's incentives and actions are so consistent that they can be predicted with frameworks taken from Newtonian physics. It is also assumed that money is fungible, which is why it is a store of value and medium of exchange.

Yet, the consumers that Gronemann and Rasmussen spoke with did not behave as if the concept of money was consistent at all. *Some* elements of the money conversation were easy: consumers were happy to explain how they used mobile phones to pay for things, say, and excited about the convenience of that technology. However, when it came to discussing savings, insurance, or lending and investment products, there was confusion, silence, or embarrassment.[26] "It's easier for a lot of Westerners to talk about sex than money," observed Gronemann. "It's a taboo."[27] Why? One issue was a moral paradox: Americans and Europeans are constantly told that they should strive to gain money; however, most religions and Western cultures claim people should not be driven by "the love of money" since it is "the root of all evil," to cite the Christian tag. But the other problem was cognitive dissonance: Western consumers know that money *should* be something that is viewed in a consistent, rational manner, in line with WEIRD ideals, but this is not how they actually live. Instead the families observed by Rasmussen and Gronemann amassed numerous credit cards they hardly used; had retirement accounts they forgot about; obsessively tracked and controlled some pots of money—but ignored others. "What often happened was that people would spend a huge amount of time talking to us about one tiny part of their finances, like a few sustainable investments that they had made, or their credit card or house," Gronemann said. "But then they totally forgot to mention something much more significant in their overall asset position, like a retirement account." Or as Christian, a sixty-eight-year-old astrophysicist, told the team: "I might be good at nuclear and atomic physics but I simply do not understand my pension."[28]

Why? One explanation might be found in individual brains, or psychology: as the psychologist Daniel Kahneman has shown, human brains have biases that affect our views toward money: we remember financial losses more than gains, say, or have different modes of decision-making that are either driven by "fast" impulses or "slow" reasoning.[29] Such psychological insights have helped to spawn an entire school of behavioral finance and economics. However, Rasmussen and Gronemann were interested in more than psychology: they wanted to explore the cultural webs of meaning that groups of people were constructing around money. After listening to consumers, they suggested that a crucial point about the cultural frame was that most consumers did not regard money as a single "thing." Western economists tend to presume that money is fungible; this is at the core of any economic model. However, anthropologists have described numerous societies that have different symbolic categories of money and realms of exchange.[30] When Rasmussen and Gronemann reviewed their fieldnotes they realized that their interviewees were using a sense of compartmentalization too when they visualized twenty-first-century money. To describe this split, the ReD team borrowed Kahneman's "fast" and "slow" labels.

The money that consumers considered to be fast money was the money used for everyday payments. Consumers talked about that without secrecy or shame, since they thought it was something they could control, and were thrilled with anything that enhanced that control and efficiency. "[My current account] is like electricity; it just comes out of the socket," Anita, a forty-five-year-old mother of two and lawyer at a publishing firm in Munich, observed. "I want my money to come out of the machine when I need it—that is it." However, other money was "slow money," or money that was used as a store of value. Attitudes around this were different: consumers often ignored slow money or lied to themselves about it, or expressed fear. Alice, a twenty-eight-year-old senior healthcare manager from London, who earned £80,000 a year, was typical. "She found it very easy to spend all the money on her credit card on nights out but diligently transferred money to her parents for safekeeping each month," Gronemann wrote in the report. She saw her pension as a "backup" plan, but did not trust it—yet presumed that her home was a reliable store of wealth, even though there had been turmoil in house prices a few years before. "For Alice, her mortgage was useful, productive debt, but her credit facility was negligent, indulgent debt."

This finding had a wider implication for public policy, Rasmussen and Gronemann argued. Because so many consumers found it difficult to talk about "slow" money, they could not tell if they were using financial services effectively—and were vulnerable to being exploited. The 2008 crisis illustrated this risk. However, the pattern also had implications for finance itself. Financial companies were unlikely to win much love from customers if they hated slow money. What made the pattern worse was that the industry itself was very fragmented: different companies gave consumers different products, and different departments in the same institution served consumers too. That just reinforced the fast-slow split. Some companies were pouring huge effort into using technology to offer slick fast money products, but the consumer was handling slow money in a different way.

Could this change? Danica, the life insurance and pension group that had worked with ReD, decided to try. Until 2013, the company executives had not devoted much time to studying its consumers. "The life and pension business is probably the only consumer business where companies hardly seem aware they have consumers—we think we have insurance policies instead," explained John Glottrup, head of business development at Danica. "Why? Because the activities we have today will only show in the book in five to ten years and there is so much inertia that you can get it wrong. And people in this industry are all trained to use numbers, almost exclusively, since they are actuaries and economists." As a result, he added, there is a "core belief which has shaped our industry . . . that a pension, a life insurance product, is of low interest for consumers—nobody cares—so you talk to consumers maybe once or twice in their lives but then it is better to leave people alone."[31] Life insurance, in other words, was treated as if it had nothing to do with culture; even though the act of making a financial bet on how long someone will live is actually rooted in distinctive Western cultural ideas that look odd to other cultures (e.g., that it is possible to predict how long someone will live with a model, and morally acceptable to make a bet about that).[32]

There was another reason why life insurance and pension executives often ignored consumers: when they *did* ask their customers what shaped their decisions, they heard messages that were so bizarre they seemed easy to discount with WEIRD logic. "We can ask a consumer what's most important for them when they pick out an insurance policy, and people will give us the standard answers: it's the cost, the expected return, the service, that people are friendly, and all of that," Glottrup said. "But when we pose the second line of questioning—what did you pay in costs last year, what was your return, when was the last time you actually used our service?—people will go blank. They will have no answer [so] these things simply cannot be the reason."

The ReD team suggested that the Danica executives try an experiment: recognize that consumers view pensions as "slow" money, i.e., existing in a category that sparks fear and confusion, and then seek ways to make this "slow" money seem more attractive. That meant giving customers the features associated with "fast" money: a sense of real-time transparency, control, and choice. So Danica created a "traffic light" dashboard that consumers could download, electronically, to monitor their slow money investments in real time, on their own electronic devices. Then, contrary to its prior practice, it reached out to its customers, asking them to activate the dashboard and talk about goals. The innovation increased consumer retention, Glottrup said. It also changed attitudes inside the company. No, the actuaries did not abandon their beloved models and Big Data sets. However, they realized that Big Data and macro-level statistics could be interpreted more effectively alongside micro-level cultural observations. It was the same lesson that health officials had learned while tackling the Ebola pandemic, or that the Bad Babysitter team had stressed to the Primrose nursery executives: computer, medical, and social science worked best in combination. That applied in any location, be that "familiar" or "strange."

PART THREE

LISTENING TO SOCIAL SILENCE

The gist: We live in a world of constant noise. The power of anthropology is that it can help us listen to social silence, and, above all, see what is hidden in plain sight. To listen this way, it helps to embrace tools from ethnography about being an insider-outsider and borrow ideas such as habitus, reciprocity, sense-making, and lateral vision. When we employ this frame of analysis, we get a different lens on politics, economics, tech—as well as on the humdrum question of what makes offices work and the startling rise of the "sustainability" movement.

SEVEN

"BIGLY"

(OR WHAT DID WE MISS ABOUT TRUMP AND TEENAGERS?)

"The most successful ideological effects are those which have no need for words, and ask no more than complicitous silence."

—Pierre Bourdieu

The mood in the hotel dining room in Davos, high in the Swiss mountains, was exuberant. The date was January 2014. Five years had passed since the worst of the panic unleashed by the 2008 financial collapse—and seven years since I had gone to the World Economic Forum meeting and warned about the dangers looming in credit derivatives. The dangers posed by the submerged pieces of the financial "iceberg"—all those CDOs, CDSs, and other newfangled pieces of financial innovation—had become clear to everyone. The sector had finally been given a *name*, which had propelled it onto the front pages of the newspapers and enabled it to be imagined and discussed: "shadow banking." Starting in 2009, regulators had introduced reforms to make the financial system safer. In Davos, where the annual meeting of the World Economic Forum—an elite gathering of global business, finance, and political leaders—took place each January, there had been endless handwringing on panels about shadow banking.

In January 2014, the chatter in the elite WEF village had changed:

I could see that discussions about finance were moving off the agenda. That was not because the financial system was entirely "fixed." Big problems still lurked, particularly in parts of that shadow banking world. But finance had started to heal. The global economy was recovering. People were getting bored of discussing those CDOs. So was I. Other themes seemed more exciting, like the tech innovation emerging from companies such as Facebook, Google, and Amazon. I was keen to widen the lens.

"It occurred to me that I [should] make sure you knew about danah boyd [*sic*]," Craig Calhoun, the head of the London School of Economics (and an anthropologist himself) suggested to me in an email in early January that year, just before I went to Davos. Boyd, he explained, had been doing research sponsored by Microsoft about social media and Big Data which drew on a training in anthropology; Calhoun wanted us to meet since he thought boyd's approach to tech echoed my experience on Wall Street and in the City of London.

I was intrigued. I headed to a dinner held at a shabby—but wildly overpriced—Swiss hotel near the Davos Dorf train station. Boyd was on a podium there, with other representatives from tech companies. Like the academic anthropologists I had once studied among, she looked defiantly scruffy, with a mop of curly hair, peeking from an odd fuzzy hat, and large boots. She insisted, I later learned, on writing her name in lowercase as a protest against unnecessary Western cultural norms; like many anthropologists, she was instinctively antiestablishment and countercultural. But her badge designated her as one of the Davos elite: a so-called "Young Global Leader." She often fretted about that paradox.

"I have been doing research on teenagers and their cell phones," she told the crowd, as they sat around tables covered with stiff white linen and china plates of stodgy Swiss meat and potatoes. I perked up. My own daughters were going to be teenagers in a few years, and I had already read multiple articles about how addictive and damaging cell phones could be. The writer Nicholas Carr had written a bestselling book that warned that "the internet, by design, subverts patience and concentration. When the brain is overloaded with stimuli, as it usually is when we are peering into a network-connected computer screen, attention splinters, thinking becomes superficial and memory suffers," he wrote. "We become less reflective and more impulsive. Far from enhancing intelligence, I argue, the internet degrades it."[1] Tristan Harris, a former engineer at Google, was even more scathing. As he would later explain, with fury, engineers at tech companies were deliberately using "persuasion" techniques to design games and apps to be as addictive as possible, often targeting children and teens. "What cell phones and apps are doing is creating a hook that goes straight into your brain, from the moment you wake up to the moment you go to sleep," he told the FT. Having helped create these products as an engineer at Google, he now wanted to expose and stop them.[2]

So how could a parent—or policy maker—mitigate this? Boyd's answer was not what I had expected. She started by telling the dinner crowd that she had spent the previous years crisscrossing America, conducting ethnographic research into how teenagers used their cell phones. As with the work that anthropologists were doing for tech companies and consumer groups, this was not quite the type of anthropology that Malinowski or Boas had done, since boyd did not place herself in one single community. Instead she spoke to multiple teenagers in different locations.[3] The shift was an inevitable consequence of a changing world. In Malinowski's day it made sense to sit on one island. In an era shaped by cyberspace, being on an island—or in just one physical location—made less sense. So anthropologists such as boyd were increasingly studying networks, talking to people in different places, who were not a single physical community, but nonetheless connected. Boyd had spent hours sitting with teenagers in their bedrooms or homes, hearing what they said about their cell phones and watching them use these. She observed them at teenage events like a high school football game, and hung out with them at malls. The idea—as ever—was to ask unstructured questions, observe everything she could, and ponder more than just those pesky phones.

As boyd sat in teenage bedrooms, she realized that the teenage middle-class American kids had striking attitudes toward time and space. A teenager called Maya in a middle-class suburb of Florida was typical. "Usually my mom will have things scheduled for me to do. So I really don't have much choice in what I am doing Friday nights," she told boyd, listing her extracurricular events: track, Czech lessons, orchestra, and working in a nursery. "I haven't had a free weekend in so long. I cannot even remember the last time I got to choose what I wanted to do over the weekend." A white sixteen-year-old named Nicholas, from Kansas, echoed this idea: he said he was not allowed to socialize with friends because his parents had packed his schedule full of sports. Jordan, a mixed-race fifteen-year-old living in a suburb of Austin, said she was barely allowed out of the house due to stranger danger. "My mom's from Mexico and she thinks I will get kidnapped," she explained. Natalie, a white fifteen-year-old in Seattle, told boyd that her parents would not let her walk anywhere. Amy, a biracial sixteen-year-old from Seattle, observed that "my Mom doesn't let me out of the house very often, so that's pretty much all I do . . . talk to people and text on the phone, 'cause my Mom's always got some crazy reason to keep me in the house." The parents backed this up. "Bottom line is that we live in a society of fear . . . as a parent I admit that I protect my daughter immensely and won't let my daughter go out to areas where I can't see her," said Enrique, a parent in Austin. "Am I being overprotective? Maybe. But it is the way it is. . . . We keep her very busy without making it depressing."

The parents and teenagers considered these controls to be so normal that they barely commented on them—unless asked. But boyd knew that in earlier generations in America teenagers had been able to congregate with friends, collide with acquaintances, and physically travel out of the house. As a teenager herself in 1980s Philadelphia boyd hung out at the local mall with other teenagers. Now the mall operators—and parents—were banning that. Teenagers were being excluded from other public places, such as parks or street corners, if they tried to congregate there in large groups. The contrast with even earlier eras was even more stark: in the mid-twentieth century it had been normal for teenagers to walk or cycle to school, congregate in fields, take part in "sock hops," stroll around town, travel between venues by themselves for jobs, or simply congregate in large groups on a street corner or in a field. "In 1969, 48 percent of all children in grades kindergarten through eighth grade walked or biked to school compared to 12 percent who were driven by a family member," boyd noted. "By 2009, those numbers had reversed: 13 percent walked or bicycled while 45 percent were driven." Boyd does not make any moral judgments about these new constraints (although she does note that there is scant evidence that stranger danger has increased in recent years). But she told the Davos dinner that if you wanted to understand why teenagers used cell phones, it was *not* sufficient to just look at phones or cyberspace. That was how parents and policy makers discussed the issue. So did the engineers when they designed phones; to them the physical real world of life outside a phone seemed less important than what happened inside it.

But while parents, policy makers, and techies ignored these real-world, physical—non-phone—issues, they mattered. The reason was that controls in the tangible world made "roaming" online doubly appealing; cyberspace was becoming the *only* place where teenagers could explore, wander, congregate with friends and acquaintances in large groups—or do what teenagers had always done in the real world—with freedom. Indeed, it was almost the *only* place where teenagers could push the boundaries, test limits, reshape their identity without "helicopter" parents watching them or the need to schedule an appointment into their busy schedules.

That did not absolve tech companies of responsibility in relation to digital addiction: boyd knew that clever engineers were using "persuasion" technology to make apps appeal to people's brains. But it did mean that parents (or anybody else) had to acknowledge these physical controls if they wanted to understand why teens seemed addicted to their phones. Most people treated cyberspace as if it were a disembodied place and so they ignored the physical world. That was as much of a mistake as ignoring derivatives in finance before 2007. *It's just like the financial iceberg*, I thought to myself.

I left Davos with two pledges. One was to ensure that my own kids had plenty of chance to roam physically in the world. The second was to keep reminding myself to think about blind spots. I had to listen to social silence in all arenas, as I had done with finance. It was easy to forget to do that, and I often did: the media, like much of modern life, is a place that is dominated by noise, created by journalists and everyone else. There is such intense competition to get the "story," and track what others are talking about, that listening to silence seems self-indulgent. Yet if my dance with credit derivatives had taught me anything, it was that the media is at its best when journalists focus on the silence, rather than just the noise. Especially in an era when politicians are becoming increasingly "noisy."

Two and a half years later, on the evening of September 26, 2016, I was at the news desk in the FT office in New York. The American election was in full swing, and the monitors above the news desk displayed shots of Donald Trump participating in the first official debate on television with Hillary Clinton. Halfway through the discussion, Trump used an odd word: "bigly." Chuckles erupted on the news desk. I laughed too. Trump later insisted he said "big league," not "bigly," and was misheard. Either way, the word sounded odd; it was not the type of "proper" English of the sort that presidents were supposed to use or that journalists employed every day.

But as I heard myself laugh, a stray thought flashed into my mind:

Am I forgetting my training—yet again? Laughter, after all, is never neutral or irrelevant—or not to anthropologists. We tend to ignore it, since it seems like just an inevitable piece of social interaction or a psychological safety valve. But laughter inadvertently defines social groups since you have to have a shared cultural base to "get" a joke. Insiders know when to laugh, even instinctively; outsiders do not "get it." That merriment also does something else: it helps a community to address, at least in part, the numerous ambiguities and contradictions in their everyday lives. This mattered—and matters—as the work of Daniel Souleles, another anthropologist, shows. Between 2012 and 2014 Souleles studied Wall Street's private equity industry, employing the same methods to study this that I had used to look at CDOs: attending bank conferences and then decoding the rituals and symbolism he saw. He was struck by how often the private equity executives engaged in ritualistic bouts of laughter. He started collecting these jokes, with the same voracious attention to detail and sense of wonder as Lévi-Strauss, say, had used when he gathered myths among the tribes of the Amazon jungle. As he later explained in a paper with the catchy title "Don't Mix Paxil, Viagra, and Xanax: What Financiers' Jokes Say About Inequality," these jokes were not neutral or irrelevant.[4]

That financiers cracked them at conferences reinforced the sense that there was an in group of elite dealmakers. It also helped them handle the potential contradictions in their founding creed. By 2012, in the wake of the Great Financial Crash, the private equity executives knew they were under attack from politicians and social activists. They were keen to defend themselves—and had concocted a powerful rhetoric (or narrative) about the way that private equity was allegedly making the American economy more efficient and vibrant. However, as with the creation myth that had been concocted by derivatives traders I saw on the Riviera in 2005, the private equity rhetoric contained plenty of intellectual contradictions which the financiers did not want to address. Cracking inside jokes was one way to bond around a sense of shared ambivalence.

Journalists also used jokes in this way. When they chuckled at Trump's use of the word "bigly," they sometimes did so because they scornfully assumed that his seeming (mis)use of language showed he was unfit for office. Such open dislike and conscious scorn was the visible "noise." The reason why "bigly" sounded so funny, though, also rested in an area of social "silence" that few in the media wished to acknowledge. Most journalists took it for granted that to set the agenda of public life you needed to talk "properly," using the words and phrases that were typically instilled in educated people. A command of language was one of the few forms of publicly acceptable elitism and snobbery in America because it implied a sense of meritocracy, due to personal educational achievement. This assumption was reinforced every day in the public sphere since the people who controlled the television screens, newspapers, radio shows—and many other arenas of influence—did so by wielding words. Command of language and education was seen as a prerequisite for gaining power; *not* having command of language, conversely, was something that kept you out.

But not everyone in America felt they had command of words, let alone money or power. Most did not. That had created an epistemological split that elites were often only dimly aware of. I had learned this the hard way because of a mistake I had made myself. In the summer of 2016 I had called the British vote on Brexit wrong: since I personally hated the idea of leaving the European Union (partly because my own identity was wrapped up in a sense of globalization and European affiliation), I had extrapolated my own feelings onto everyone else, and wrongly assumed that the British public would vote to stay in the European Union. The result shocked me. Chastened, I then resolved to do a better job with the US election, and in subsequent months I made a point of trying to listen to as many different Americans as I could encounter, with as open a mind as possible, to hear what people were saying and what they did *not* say. That approach left me convinced that there was a far greater level of hostility toward Clinton than was recognized and that many people were hungry for disruption and unusually ready to take a risk to achieve this disruption.

It also left me convinced of something else: the way that educated elites (like journalists) looked at Trump relied on a sense of epistemology that was different from the cultural framework that many voters were using. One way to describe this distinction was with the phrase memorably coined by Salena Zito, the journalist: while the elite took Trump "literally but not seriously," many of his voters did the reverse—and took him seriously but not literally.[5] Or to use the framework outlined by Henrich that I cited in the last chapter, around WEIRD cultures: the "educated" groups in America were interpreting Trump's words through the type of sequential logic that WEIRD education taught people, namely one-directional reasoning, and thus thought that Trump's comments did not "make sense." But, as Henrich had always stressed, WEIRD thinking operated on a spectrum, and even inside a WEIRD country like America, there were variants. Some voters did not use this one-directional reasoning and logic, I realized, but were reacting to a holistic vision of Trump and his overarching brand. People like me might laugh at the word "bigly" because it was not part of a logical sentence; others just heard it as a sign that he was not elite—and cheered.

There was another way of framing what was going on which an anthropologist like Geertz might have championed: to think about performance, symbols, and rituals. Early in Trump's presidential campaign, a friend called Joshua who had grown up in a poor rural region of Upstate New York and then North Carolina told me that "if you really want to understand Trump, you should go to a wrestling match." The reason, he explained, was that while middle-class viewers knew Trump best from shows like *The Apprentice*, working-class viewers were as much (if not more) familiar with his brand because of wrestling matches. That was because Trump had invested in the World Wrestling Entertainment, and then appeared in those contests, on TV, and wrestling was wildly popular among many working-class Americans—albeit largely ignored by the elite. "Pro wrestling might be largely invisible as a cultural force to most liberal voters, but WWE generates close to a billion dollars in annual revenue," points out Naomi Klein, the social activist.

I went to a match in midtown Manhattan, and was struck by the parallels I saw between the event and Trump's election rallies and campaign. That was no accident. As Klein also notes, wrestling matches are driven by a clearly defined sense of ritual performance.[6] Contestants are given nicknames "like "Lil' John." They make displays of excessive aggression designed to whip up the crowds, and engage in dramatic bouts of manufactured conflict. The crowds cheer this on, knowing full well that the dramas are artificial. By design or instinct, in 2016 Trump was deploying much of the same performative pattern in his own campaign: he threw out nicknames for his opponent, engaged in equally manufacturered bouts of political melodrama, delivered displays of extreme aggression, and whipped up the crowds.* His supporters often acted in that political arena as if they were still at a wrestling match; through symbolism and speech, the performance style of wrestling had been transposed into a political campaign. Or as Klein observed: "His carefully nurtured feuds with other candidates were pure pro wrestling . . . [as well as] the way he handed out insulting nicknames ('Little Marco,' 'Lyin' Ted') . . . and played ringmaster at his rallies, complete with over-the-top insult-chants."

That had two important implications. First, Trump supporters

*It is worth pointing out that this type of ritualistic drama, with performative signaling, is widely studied in other cultures by anthropologists. One of the most famous examples of this is a study that Clifford Geertz did of Balinese cockfighting, where he highlighted the role of "deep play" (Clifford Geertz, *The Interpretation of Cultures.*) However, as Ed Liebow notes, Geertz's sense of "deep play" viewed theatrical performance as partly separate from "real" life, Trump's use of WWE-style performative signaling overwhelmed real-world American politics, for a period.

did not treat his actions and utterances as if they were literal policy documents—but as pieces of performative signaling. That was different from how they were interpreted by the "educated" elite; hence that "literally" and "seriously" split identified by Zito. Second, most of the elite could not see this profound epistemological split. That was partly because they did not watch as much wrestling, so were in no position to spot the parallels. But it was also due to that pesky matter of words. Educated people took it so thoroughly for granted that education should frame the way that people would talk and think—and define what was valuable—that they did not even notice other modes of thought or consider them important. People completely dominated by a WEIRD mode of thought and assumptions tended to ignore other mental patterns. And it was hard to appreciate the gap in epistemology until you sat in a wrestling ring and were physically "embodied" in the experience of watching, with a crowd, to use the frame of the anthropologist Roberts.[7] "[There is] a lesson that journalists, social scientists, writers and anyone who studies others for a living needs to remember: namely, that we are all creatures of our own cultural environment, prone to lazy assumptions and biases," I observed in a column in October 2016, ahead of the election, that lamented how the media was misreading the Trump voter. The only solution, I argued, was for the media to borrow a leaf from anthropology and think about what the discipline sometimes calls the "dirty lens" problem, or the point that journalists do not act like microscopes on top of a petri dish, i.e., neutral, consistent tools of observation. Instead, they have bias—dirt—on their mental lens. That meant, I argued, that journalists needed to take four steps: First, "recognize that our lenses are dirty. Second, to consciously note our biases. Third, to attempt to offset these biases by trying to see the world from different perspectives . . . [and] last but not least, to remember that our personal lens will never be perfectly clean, even if we take the first three steps."[8] Instead of laughing, we—I— needed to listen to social silence.

It was, and is, temptingly easy to forget this lesson about the dirty lens, as I know only too well from the mistakes I have made in my own intellectual journey. I misread the Brexit vote in the early summer of 2016. And while I took Trump's candidacy more seriously than many other journalists later that year (writing columns about the election that turned out to be prescient),[9] I still instinctively chuckled on the news desk that autumn when I heard him utter the word "bigly." I was a creature of my own environment too. Similarly, while I might have spotted the social silences in finance in 2005 and 2006, I could be very blind to other types of silences. Tech was a case in point. A year after I had first met boyd at Davos, I went to a think tank called Data and Society that she had created in midtown Manhattan with fellow social scientists—funded by tech companies such as Microsoft, where she had worked—to look at the digital economy through the lens of anthropology. We discussed teenagers and their cell phones. One of her colleagues asked me if I had ever tried to draw a sketch in my own mind of how the internet worked. I had not. If I thought about cyberspace, I visualized it as a vague gigantic cloud or series of pixels whizzing through the air which somehow landed on plastic devices around me. I had no idea of how those connections worked, even though I depended on the internet for almost every aspect of my daily life. So Ingrid Burrington, an artist and social scientist who was one of boyd's colleagues, showed me a model that they had created to explain the three "layers" that made the internet work: the "surface" layer (which was the only part that most users ever cared about or saw), which was made of digital features such as apps; the middle layer of networks that enabled machines to talk to one another; then the bottom layer of routers, cables, and satellites that connected the supposedly disembodied net in an all-too-physical sense. I did not even know where this bottom layer existed.

"It's all around you in New York!" I was told: the pavements (or sidewalks) were painted with symbols that showed where the cables that connected the internet lay. I walked over those sidewalks every day but had never noticed the symbols before at all; my brain was trained to screen them out. Like anyone raised in a WEIRD world, I had grown up looking at my environment in a highly selective way, rather than in a holistic manner, and considered this so normal that I did not notice how fragmented my vision was apt to be.

To counter that, Burrington published a so-called "illustrated field guide to urban internet infrastructure" for New York that showed readers how to see these half-hidden networks in Manhattan and interpret the symbols they usually ignored just under their noses, on the streets. This, she stressed, was not an atlas but a tool to "help people make their own maps" of what they usually ignored. She also arranged walking tours in New York and cities such as Chicago, which not only explained the workings of the internet to people, but also changed how they see the world. "Whenever we start talking about technology, computation and networks we are really just talking about power," she explained. "When this stuff stays really opaque it is easier [for elites] to retain power. There is this assumption that this is just how things are."[10]

To understand that, try looking down at the sidewalk of a Western city yourself, the next time you walk on a street. You will almost certainly find strange symbols there that you too have never noticed before. It is a daily reminder of just how little we really see or understand about the structures that shape our lives, be they related to money, medicine, the internet, or anything. Unless, that is, we start to look at not-so-empty spaces and actively listen to social silence.

EIGHT

CAMBRIDGE ANALYTICA

(OR WHY DO ECONOMISTS STRUGGLE IN CYBERSPACE?)

> "The universe is a vast system of exchange. Every artery of it is in motion, throbbing with reciprocity."
>
> —Edwin Hubbel Chapin

In the spring of 2016, half a year before Donald Trump won the US election, I bumped into a man named Robert Murtfeld who worked for a data science group named Cambridge Analytica.[1] We were at a seminar in New York. I had never heard of his company, but I was happy to chat since I (wrongly) assumed that the company was linked to my alma mater of Cambridge University. Murtfeld was eager to have lunch. He knew I had trained in anthropology, and the company's founders considered themselves experts on behavioral science, using work from sociologists, psychologists, anthropologists, and others. So on May 26 I sat in a Japanese restaurant in downtown Manhattan, at a table laden with bento boxes, next to Murtfeld, a jolly German, and a thin, intense British man named Alex Taylor, who ran their research.

I had no idea that what was about to unfold would provide a powerful lesson showing why techies, economists—and journalists—need to listen to social silence. But Taylor opened a laminated plastic booklet that displayed maps of America, overlaid by complex charts with bright colors. I later realized this diagram referred to a psychological model named OCEAN that had become fashionable in the latter parts of the twentieth century because it divided people up according to different personality traits, depending on each person's Openness (to experience), Conscientiousness, Extraversion, Agreeableness, and Neuroticism (hence OCEAN). Taylor explained that the charts predicted what voters might do in an election.

That is really weird. Are they mad? I wondered. The chart did not look like any business anthropology I knew; this was data analysis. But Taylor and Murtfeld retorted that this was a *new* version of social science; instead of trying to understand human nature by eyeballing a few people intensively in a holistic way, to extrapolate from micro-level observations to the macro level, their models collected a massive data set about the intricate details of millions of people's lives to get holistic snapshots of people on a massive scale. I asked them how they collected the data; did they pay for it?

"It varies," one said. Some came from data brokers, a new breed of twenty-frst-century company which harvests the digital traces that consumers leave when they use credit cards, online shopping services, or any other platform, and repackage this information for sale. Cambridge Analytica also got data from other sources, such as social media, "for free."

Free? The word stuck in my mind since it sounded odd. After years of covering financial markets, I tended to assume that the definition of modern capitalism was that everything had a monetary price. But as we sat with our bento boxes and chopsticks that day, I did not press them about what "free" meant, since I was so distracted by the noise in the media around the political outlook. The Cambridge Analytica officials indicated that they were working for Donald Trump's 2016 presidential campaign, although nothing had been announced publicly yet. I was eager to know if they thought Trump might win. We stayed in touch, as

I was keen to track the presidential race. But I did not bother to write anything about the OCEAN diagrams, since they seemed so odd.

It was a big mistake. Many months later, I realized that I should have paid far more attention to those strange charts—and the word "free." That autumn Trump won the election, sparking public fury from his opponents. When they investigated his team's tactics, the furor intensified: it turned out that Cambridge Analytica had created these charts by harvesting data from sites such as Facebook to track voter sentiment and develop influence campaigns.[2] Chris Wiley, a then pink-haired data scientist who had worked with Cambridge Analytica (but later became a self-styled whistleblower), described this as a "mindf*ck!," claiming that the company had a plot to "break the world" by manipulating voter sentiment with misinformation.[3] Cambridge Analytica staff vehemently denied this. But an outcry erupted about privacy breaches and unsavory political tactics. The company collapsed.[4]

That was shocking. But the headline-grabbing noise about political manipulation concealed a second, potentially even more interesting arena of social silence: the questions raised by the word "free." When the Facebook scandal broke, critics declared that personal data had been stolen. But that was untrue: Cambridge Analytica had acquired most of the data with exchanges; data had been swapped for services. "Probably about half of our data was gathered without paying any money," Julian Wheatland, the jovial former chief financial officer (and final chief executive officer) of the group, later told me.[5]

There is no easy word to describe this data-service exchange, or not one that indicates its proper weight. Using the word "free" expresses the situation in terms of a negative (i.e., the *absence* of money). This means it tends to be ignored in a world obsessed with money. Labeling something as "free" for economists is thus the financial equivalent of putting the "empty" label on the oil drums that Whorf wrote about in the 1930s:

affixing a cultural tag that is tantamount to "nil" and thus so boring it is easy to ignore. However, one word that could be used to describe these exchanges is "barter." Techies almost never use those two syllables themselves, since the word tends to evoke images of prehistoric tribes swapping berries and beads, rather than computing bytes. Nor do economists; ever since the days of the economist Adam Smith, the word "barter" has been scorned as a primitive practice.[6] But while economists and techies might shun the word "barter," these exchanges are central to how Silicon Valley works. And until policy makers start discussing barter in an explicit manner, it will be difficult to create a tech sector that feels ethical to consumers or to combat political misinformation—or even just get an accurate vision of how the economy works and how to value tech companies. For that reason, it pays to take an anthropologist's lens to the story of Cambridge Analytica and look not just at the noisy political scandals but also at the social silences embedded around barter and economics, particularly since one irony in this tale is that the company itself partly emerged from the anthropology world.

To understand why economists (and techies) need to pay more attention to barter, a good place to start is to think about the roots of the English word "data." Techies rarely ask where this word hails from. If they did, they might guess that it is linked to something to do with numbers, or digits. "Is it the same root as digital? Or date?" one room of Silicon Valley luminaries asked when I asked them to guess. It is not. Etymologists link the word's origins to the latin verb *dare*, meaning "to give," expressed in its passive past form. "As the Latin root tells us, 'data' means the thing that is given," observes Kadija Ferryman, a medical anthropologist who studies data and biomedical research. And, she adds, a "thing that is given" is quite literally "a gift."[7]

To internet users this might seem bizarre. "The modern ideal of the gift [is] . . . an impossible mirror of market behavior: an act of pure generosity untrammeled by any thought of personal gain," observes David Graeber, another anthropologist.[8] Data collection, of the sort Cambridge Analytica was involved in, does not look charitable. And precisely because "gifts" are usually considered to be the mirror of market—or commercial—behavior, they tend to be excluded from economists' models of the economy. However, anthropologists have always had a much broader vision of "economics" than the one used by most economists: instead of just tracking "markets" and exchanges that are mediated with money, they study how exchanges bind societies together in the *widest* possible sense. "Economics is a creature of its Western environment," argues the anthropologist Stephen Gudeman.[9] "In the places where anthropologists work, there are many spheres of the economy—household economies, for example, are crucial [too]."[10] One key theme that influences this study of exchanges is a set of ideas advanced by Marcel Mauss, the French intellectual.[11] Mauss argued that gift-giving is endemic to societies around the world, and has three parts: an obligation to give, to receive, and most crucially, to reciprocate. Sometimes there is immediate bilateral reciprocity (people swap presents). But reciprocity is usually delayed, creating a social "debt" (if I get a birthday present from you, I will give you one later). Reciprocity can be "bilateral" (in the sense that if I get a present I must give one back to you, and no one else). But it can also be "generalized" (I can repay my debt to the entire social group). Either way, the point is that "gifts" create trailing debts that bind people together.

This pattern of reciprocity might seem removed from the modern vision of a market economy. But if you take a wider lens, you can see that we are surrounded by all manner of exchanges that do not carry monetary tags or end in a neat, bounded manner, as economic models might imply. Just think of how the gigantic student loan industry in America, say, is embedded in family obligations and relations which cannot be captured just by a trillion-dollar number: as the anthropologist Zaloom notes, these financial flows are about money but they also involve far more than finance, since they are rooted in kinship structures and trailing patterns of reciprocity.[12] And the existence of these numerous types of exchange is one reason why talking about "barter" in the twenty-first century might not be as odd as it seems. Economists often assume that societies only used barter in the past because they did not have money or credit—which implies that once modern finance was invented, barter disappeared. However, "our standard account of monetary history is precisely backward," points out Graeber. Instead of humans using barter first, then "evolving" to adopt money and credit, "it happened precisely the other way round." This might seem hard to believe. But there is no evidence that ancient societies operated as Smith imagined. "No example of a barter economy, pure and simple, has ever been described, let alone the emergence from it of money; all available ethnography suggests that there never has been one," observes Humphrey, my former professor at Cambridge.[13] Instead, communities without money often have extensive and complex "credit" systems since households create social and economic debts.

What should really make us rethink lazy assumptions about economic "evolution," though, is the fact that barter is not dead in the modern world. Far from it. In Silicon Valley information is constantly being "given up" in exchange for the "gift" of free services. A purist might quibble that this is not exactly a "barter" trade in the sense of being struck with deliberate negotiation. Fair point: many of the participants in this "barter" are not explicitly aware that they are involved in a barter at all. However, since there is no other readily available word in English to describe this trade, describing this as "barter" is probably the least bad option. The word does, after all, help us see what is normally unseen. We cannot hope to improve our tech world until we see it clearly. Hence the reason why economists need to widen the lens to talk not just about "economics" but "exchanges." Looking at the controversial tale of Cambridge Analytica is one way to start.

In November 2015 an intense blond-haired young man, wearing a neat blue-and-white striped shirt, gave a speech to social and computational scientists at the office of ASI, a consulting entity in London. His name was Jack Hansom, and he had done a master's in experimental physics at London University, followed by a PhD in "experimental quantum information" at Cambridge University. A decade earlier, that educational background might have driven him to the City of London, if he wanted to seek riches. But after the 2008 financial crisis, the City lost (some of) its allure, and brilliant geeks who had once moved into derivatives were entering a new sphere: "ad tech," or the field of marketing and advertising that used complex algorithms to track data to help marketing and ad companies dispatch messages more effectively. The skills needed for this were surprisingly similar to those needed for crafting CDOs.

"I would like to start with a question: Could you fall in love with a computer?" Hansom asked the audience.[14] Behind him, a PowerPoint displayed a picture from the science fiction movie *Her*, starring Joaquin Phoenix and the voice of Scarlett Johansson, in which a computer enabled with artificial intelligence is so adept at reading the signals that a lonely man admits that they have a romance. "To fall in love with a computer you need a computer to fall in love with you. Can we use tools from data science and machine learning to allow a computer to understand and predict your personality?"

The audience chuckled. Hansom explained that he had recently started working with colleagues at Cambridge Analytica to use Facebook data to track the personality of voters, based on the OCEAN psychology frame that I saw over bento in the New York restaurant. "For a consultancy [like us] it is extremely important to understand the electorate. If we can understand the personality of the electorate on an individual level, we can really design a message which resonates with each person. I want to use the Facebook likes to be able to predict [people]'s personalities." The predictive power of such "likes" could be startling, he claimed. "Liking the New Orleans Saints [on Facebook] means you are less likely to be conscientious. Liking the Energizer bunny means you are more likely to be neurotic." Hansom put up a photograph of an office on the board. "With [this] model and Facebook likes, I can predict how conscientious or neurotic you are, better than your coworkers! . . . In fact one day your computer will know you well enough to be able to fall in love with it!" The audience laughed—and clapped.

Almost nobody outside that room saw the presentation at the time; if they had, they might have reacted like me: *This is nuts.* But behind Hansom's story there was a bigger tale about the use—and potential abuse—of social and data science. The roots of Cambridge Analytica stemmed from a company named Strategic Communications Laboratories Ltd. that had been created by an upper-crust British advertising executive named Nigel Oakes. He worked with the agency Saatchi and Saatchi back in the 1980s. When Oakes started his career, "creatives" dominated advertising. These people, immortalized in the television show *Mad Men*, presumed that the best way to reach consumers was with their "gut" or marketing genius. But Oakes thought there was a more rigorous way to do this. "We looked at anthropology and social psychology and semiotics and structural analysis to see how we could bridge social science and creative communication," he recalls.[15] This echoes a theme about embracing the science of "persuasion" that has been present in advertising since the mid 1950s.[16] He peeled off to create a consultancy in Switzerland, partly funded with money from an Estée Lauder executive, hoping to serve corporate clients. But there was limited demand for that. So he focused on the one group of clients who did seem interested in the ideas: politicians in emerging markets, such as Indonesia or South Africa, who wanted to employ behavioral science to win elections. Nelson Mandela's team was one client.

In 2004, Oakes rebased SCL to London and persuaded an old friend,

Alexander Nix, to join him. By then, Oakes had decided to stop selling his services to emerging markets' political campaigns. "It was a very unpleasant business—most people ended up not paying us," he recalls. Instead Nix and Oakes pitched their services to the Western military, arguing that behavioral science could combat Islamic extremism in places such as Iraq and Afghanistan. "I told them it's about using science to save lives. If we can persuade the enemy to bugger off [due to] an information campaign, it is better than shooting them," he explains. "The question is how can you persuade an enemy group to change behavior? Is it a reward? Talking to a religious leader? Or what? You need to understand culture."

He won a stream of business. "We didn't work in theater [of war]. But [we] became the lead supplier to NATO," he recalls. To get the cultural analysis he needed, Oakes discreetly hired academics to help. "We mostly chose people with PhDs from Oxford and Cambridge because we were applying genuine social science—experimental psychologists and anthropologists." This tactic was not novel: American anthropologists such as Ruth Benedict and her British counterpart E. E. Evans-Pritchard had helped the Allied forces understand different cultures in World War Two, and the US military subsequently used anthropologists in the Korean and Vietnam Wars. It was wildly controversial in the anthropology world, since many academics hated the idea of helping a government's military strategy.* Oakes, however, insisted he was engaged in a humanitarian mission. "It was about saving lives. Think about Iraq—did you

*The idea of anthropologists working for the military has sparked endless angst inside the discipline. Bitter internal fights erupted in America during the Vietnam War and then in the twenty-first century when it emerged that the US military had created a so-called Human Terrain System Project and was using anthropologists for cultural analysis in Afghanistan and Iraq. The US military says this has improved operations. However, in 2007 the American Anthropological Association issued a statement decrying HTS for overturning the ethics of the discipline: https://www.americananthro.org/ConnectWithAAA/Content.aspx?ItemNumber=1952.

really need to bomb the crap out of the country and spend a trillion dollars there? Or could you have done it with strategic communications? Using persuasion makes far more sense."

In the second decade of the twenty-first century, Oakes and Nix separated. Nix wanted to return to the political election business that Oakes disliked and became enamored with data science. No expert in data, he had studied art history at college. However, in the early years of the new decade Nix ran into Silicon Valley luminaries who were excited about the idea that they could understand human behavior by tracking individuals' online footprints. Oakes thought this was ridiculous, since these digital traces were often poor quality. In any case, he doubted whether fragmented pieces of *individual* digital activity were a good guide to cultural patterns; instead, he believed—like most anthropologists—that behavior was shaped by *group* sentiment as well, which could not be tracked by fragmented, individual data points. (This was the same argument that drove the work of the anthropologists and ethnographers doing consumer research described in Chapter Six.) "If I say on Facebook that I like someone's hat that doesn't mean I necessarily like the actual hat—I like *them*. I say that to preserve a social relationship. But collecting data on likes doesn't show that."

But Nix was entranced—and all the more so when he met a brilliant American hedge fund manager named Robert Mercer, and his daughter, Rebekkah. The Mercers, archconservatives, had been horrified by Barack Obama's victories in the 2008 and 2012 elections. Since they believed that Obama's team had won through the superior mastery of digital tech, they wanted to fight back by creating their own digital consultancy. So, on the advice of their friend Steve Bannon, a far-right activist, the Mercers invested $15 million into a new company that Nix created out of a subsidiary of SCL, and they christened it, on Bannon's advice, "Cambridge Analytica," to boost the credibility of its brand. (It worked: the reason I agreed to have lunch with the company representatives was due to the "Cambridge" tag.) Nix wanted to grab whatever revenue he could find—and the Mercers needed to find compliant data scientists who were not part of the Democrat-leaning Silicon Valley group. "The Republicans were where the gap in the market was," Wheatland observed. "That is why we went there."

The Facebook connection started in a convoluted way. As he built the group. Nix tapped the services of a twenty-four-year old Canadian data scientist named Chris Wylie, who had previously worked in liberal politics in Canada. Wylie knew that Cambridge University academics had been doing some cutting-edge psychology experiments by collecting data from social media platforms, seemingly with the tech companies' permission. He suggested working with one, Alexandr Kogan, who had started a project in which he offered Facebook users a "free" quiz that they could complete if they clicked a button giving Kogan permission to use their data, and those of their friends, also for "free." Kogan viewed this game as a tool which enabled his research. It might also be described as barter.

As it happened, barter was not the only mechanism the company used: it also paid for reams of data, with money, from data brokers. But barter was an effective method and was used for more than just the acquisition of Facebook data. Company officials went to schools, universities, hospitals, churches, and political groups, offering to help these entities create models using any data they held that would enable them to spot trends and thus get better insight for their work. Cambridge Analytica promised to do this for free if they could keep the data. Many institutions happily agreed, since they lacked the funds to pay for expensive data analytics services. Such tactics were commonplace, since hordes of entrepreneurs were entering this space too, and racing to use barter and cash to get as much data as they could. Gigantic companies such as Palantir and WPP were rushing into the field of data analytics too. Indeed, activity was so frenetic that insiders likened it to a new gold rush.

The image was apt: not only were there profits to be made and cutthroat competition, but it was a regulatory Wild West, since regulators had not yet updated their frameworks to cover this new innovation. It was difficult for government to track what was going on because data scientists were hopping across borders, out of the reach of national laws. But while this space was crowded, Nix and Taylor thought they had several advantages: Nix was well connected to powerful people; he had powerful financial backers in the Mercers; and his data models were using barter in a seemingly innovative way, combining the Facebook material with the OCEAN psychology framework.

Not everyone agreed this worked—or should command value. "The OCEAN methodology and Facebook data was bollocks. Total bollocks!" Oakes later argued. But Nix thought this data was so valuable that he was willing to go to enormous lengths to protect it. In 2015, for example, he found that some employees at a separate company that Wylie had created, named Eunoia, were pitching services to the Trump organization. Nix was furious: Wylie had left Cambridge Analytica in 2014, and Nix feared that Wylie had taken its intellectual property with him, the models and Facebook data. He threatened to sue Wylic—until Wylie signed a deal promising not to use the data or models.[17] (Wylie denied wrongdoing, and his lawyers subsequently told me that Wylie signed this simply "to avoid protracted legal proceedings and because he had no intention of using any CA IP or to work for the American Alt-right again, his main interest being in fashion trend forecasting.")[18] Since Wylie presented himself as a vociferous critic of both Cambridge Analytica and Trump, the pitch to the Trump group was an embarrassing twist of history. However, as these complex competitive battles rumbled on, the key point was this: the bitter fights showed just how precious the activity based on barter trade was becoming. The data sets being amassed by Cambridge Analytica did not have an obvious monetary value. Economists were not tracking the type of exchanges that Kogan had organized. Nobody could easily measure the commercial implications of the numerous tussles for market share that were erupting in this murky world. However, there was extensive "value" there, not just at Cambridge Analytica but at numerous other companies in Silicon Valley and beyond. That illustrated another, even more important point: although the financial community measured the value of companies in the twentieth century by looking at "tangible" assets, which could be tracked with monetary units (such as sales of goods or investment into machinery), so-called intangible assets, which were harder to measure with money, were becoming very important. So much so that, by 2018, intangibles were calculated to represent a stunning 84 percent of all enterprise value for the S&P 500.[19] In 1975, the ratio had been a paltry 17 percent.*

By the time I met Murtfeld and Taylor in the New York Japanese restaurant in May 2016, the company was on a roll. With the Mercers' backing, it had won business running digital campaigns for conservative candidates such as John Bolton (later national security advisor) and Ted Cruz (a presidential candidate), and then grabbed digital work for the Trump presidential campaign. Since Brad Parscale, Trump's digital campaign manager, lived in San Antonio, Texas, this work—code-name "Project Alamo"—was based down there and run by a genial, low-key American computer scientist named Matt Oczkowski. He operated from a cheap rented office in an unprepossessing corner of San Antonio, next to a La-Z-Boy furniture store and a multilane highway along which

*Data is not the only intangible asset; brand, IP, talent, and access to environmental resources can be considered as intangible assets too. But the problem with measuring these is similar to the issue around the use of the word "free": because "intangible" is expressed in terms of a negative (i.e., not being tangible) it is easy to ignore and systems for studying it are weakly developed.

traffic constantly thundered.[20] "We stayed under the radar," Oczkowski liked to say. He hired a team of data scientists who set about analyzing voter trends with all the data they could find—and then dispatching targeted messages to them on social media platforms. Facebook sent an "embed"—or embedded official—to help them to do this. The tech group usually offered this service to large corporate clients, and reckoned it made sense to help the Democrats and Republicans in this way too. However, the Democrats' digital campaign was so vast and bureaucratic that the Facebook embed there did not have much impact on the overall strategy. In San Antonio, however, the operation was run like a scrappy, freewheeling entrepreneurial start-up, and the group was hungry to test every possible idea they could find, using all the freedom that their anonymity—and odd location—offered. Since Oczkowski disliked Nix, his team kept him at a distance. In any case, American election law barred non-Americans—like Nix—from direct involvement with presidential campaigns. However, up in Cambridge Analytica's office in Washington, Wheatland and others kept an eye on the battle. They did not really think that Trump could possibly win the presidency. So on the morning of the US election, November 8, they rang the FT office in Washington to tell us that Hillary Clinton would triumph, narrowly. (They did that since the Cambridge Analytica managers wanted to spin the expected loss as a quasi victory for the data analytics company, since they were proud of how much progress Trump had made in terms of amassing votes, even though he had started out as a contender with very low odds of victory.)

However, on November 8, Trump won the election, shocking not just liberal pundits and the Democratic Party, but Nix and Wheatland too. Suddenly, everything changed. As the news leaked out, Nix triumphantly declared in a blog post that the election results validated the models that Cambridge Analytica had used. Work poured in for the group, not just from a range of corporate clients but other political campaigns around the world too.* Inside the company, euphoria mounted. "We thought that we were going to ride this success to an IPO or maybe sell ourselves to WPP," Wheatland says. "It was classic tech start-up dream—have a brilliant idea, build it up, sell up, get rich, and then go and sit on a beach."

As Trump's rivals licked their wounds from their unexpected loss they started to scrutinize Project Alamo. Until that point, there had been remarkably little debate in public about what was happening in the ad tech world: like the derivatives sector a decade earlier, this sphere was regarded as a place where geeks worked, and something that was so complex that it was easy to ignore. It was—yet again—a classic area of social silence. But revelations about the 2016 campaign began to tumble out. It transpired that the Russian intelligence services had been active on social media in a bid to manipulate the campaign in favor of Donald Trump. It also emerged that parts of the Cambridge Analytica group had used aggressive tactics in the past to manipulate voters in emerging market countries such Kenya and Trinidad and Tobago.[21] Nix was caught on camera by an undercover reporter boasting that he knew ways to blackmail politicians by sending "some girls around to the candidate's house," and explaining that Ukrainian girls "are very beautiful, I find that works very well." The *Guardian* newspaper in Britain published whistleblowing allegations from the (then pink-haired) Wylie which declared

*The *Financial Times* was briefly one corporate client. So was the *Economist.* When this detail emerged in 2018, there was speculation about how the FT work arose. To clarify: in 2016, Murtfeld asked me for a contact name in the FT commercial department, to pitch data projects. I supplied a name, stressed that editorial was separate from commercial, and had no more involvement or knowledge about what work was ever done. According to a FT spokesman, a pilot "market research project" took place, but was quickly terminated. Details on this controversy can be seen at https://bylinetimes.com/2020/10/23/dark-ironies-the-financial-times-and-cambridge-analytica.

that "we exploited Facebook to harvest millions of people's profiles. And built models to exploit what we knew about them and target their inner demons. . . . That was the basis the entire company was built on."[22] Nix and Wheatland argued that these allegations were driven by malice; Wiley was simply taking revenge for having lost the battle for the company's intellectual property, they said. Wylie retorted that he was fighting to protect Democracy. Either way, a full-blown scandal exploded. By the summer of 2018 the company was bankrupt.

That was not the end of the story. For the next two years, political and regulatory investigations rumbled on, as politicians expressed fury about the apparent breach of consumer privacy and threat to democracy from the alleged manipulation campaigns. Regulators on both sides of the Atlantic imposed fines on Facebook, amid a welter of criticism.[23] British regulators tried to impose similar big fines on the former Cambridge Analytica group, but ultimately backed away from this since it was hard to prove that the company had actually broken any rules; precisely because laws in this digital Wild West were so incomplete, just like in the early days of financial derivatives, say, behavior that the public might consider to be unethical was not necessarily illegal.[24] But away from the media furor, something striking happened: almost all the employees found jobs in other areas of data science. Hansom—the intense experimental physicist who thought the OCEAN models could "know you better than your own spouse"—became chief data scientist at a wellness company named Verv. Oczkowski—the man who had run Project Alamo—created a consultancy that advised companies in the consumer goods, logistics, and finance sectors. Trucking companies were a key client. Other Cambridge Analytica staff joined the data science campaigns run by American political candidates such as Michael Bloomberg, worked as consultants for Middle Eastern and Indian families, and advised Wall Street banks. Wheatland then took a job running a fintech group in London. In some senses, this trend seemed surprising, given the political furor around the company. In another sense, though, it was not. Yet another irony of the drama was that it had advertised the power of data science to such a degree that it made other companies and political campaigns far *more*—not less—eager to harness these tools. That left a big question hanging: Was there any way to create a world that used these barter trades in a more ethical manner? Or for economists to start seeing what they had missed?

In November 2018—or just as the Cambridge Analytica company was being wound down—I flew to Washington to take part in a conference at the headquarters of the International Monetary Fund. It was presided over by Christine Lagarde, the IMF president, who exuded her famously chic style: a cream-and-beige jacket with zigzags, and matching slacks. But the audience was anything but glamorous: dozens of economists and statisticians from government agencies, multilateral organizations, and companies; the event was entitled *The IMF Sixth Statistical Forum: Measuring Economic Welfare in the Digital Age: What and How?*[25]

By a curious twist of fate, the group sat across the street from the main American headquarters of the Cambridge Analytica office. The data company had been based in a warehouse in a cheap-but-trendy suburb of DC when it first entered America. But after its seeming triumph in the 2016 election campaign the company had attracted so much business that it moved to a prestigious location in central DC, not far from the White House. "I could pretty much see the IMF from the window," Wheatland later told me, describing the company's last, grand office in Washington.

None of the economists and statisticians at the IMF forum would have known about that twist of geography—or cared if they did. By the autumn of 2018 the Cambridge Analytica scandal had been defined in the media and public debate as a story about tech and politics, not economics. But as I walked through the lobby of the IMF building for the "Sixth Statistical Forum," it occurred to me that the collision of locations was appropriate. The reason why IMF officials had convened the event was that its economists were worried about how they measured the economy. Ever since the IMF had been founded after World War Two, its staff had used statistical tools that had been developed in the early twentieth century, such as gross domestic product calculations. These tools measured things like how much companies spent on new equipment, what stocks of raw materials they held, how many people they employed, what consumers were buying. That worked fairly well in an industrial age. But it did not easily capture the type of thing Cambridge Analytica had done, since GDP could not capture the value of ideas, amorphous data, or exchanges that occurred without money—"for free."

Did this matter? Some economists thought not. After all, they pointed out, the GDP data had always excluded some parts of the economy, such as household work, but was still very useful.[26] However, what worried some of the IMF staff was not just the size and rapid growth in the tech world, but a separate issue too: the signals in some official economic statistics seemed increasingly odd. Productivity was a case in point. Ever since the Great Financial Crisis of 2008, Silicon Valley had churned out innovations that appeared to enhance consumer and corporate productivity. However, the GDP data suggested that productivity had collapsed in America and Europe. The Princeton University economist Alan Blinder, for example, reckoned that between 1995 and 2010 annual productivity growth in the United States had been around 2.6 percent (and even higher before then). After 2010 it fell to a quarter, or less, of that.[27] One possible explanation for this was a time lag effect (companies were adopting these new digital tools at such an uneven, slow pace that they were not yet appearing in the data). But another was the word that had stuck in my mind when I first had that bento lunch with officials from Cambridge Analytica: "free." The twentieth-century economic metrics that measured activity in monetary terms did not have an obvious way to track activity without money.

Could this be fixed? Economists were trying, by making guesses about the putative value of digital. In the spring of 2018 the tech platform Recode surveyed Facebook users, and the results suggested that 41 percent of consumers were willing to pay $1 to $5 a month to get Facebook, while a quarter would pay $6 to $10 month (compared to the $9 a month which Facebook was estimated to be harvesting from each user by using data to sell advertising services).[28] Other economists reckoned that the value of Facebook to consumers was nearer to $48 each month, or more than $500 a year—while the equivalent yearly sums for YouTube and search engines such as Google were $1,173 and $17,530 respectively.[29] A paper from economists inside the Federal Reserve argued that tech "innovations boost consumer surplus by nearly $1,800 (2017 dollars) per connected user per year for the full period of this study (1987 to 2017) and contributed more than ½ percentage point to US real GDP growth during the last ten [years]." They concluded that "all told, our more complete accounting of innovations is (conservatively) estimated to have moderated the post-2007 GDP growth slowdown by nearly .3 percentage points per year."[30] Separately, some economists were trying to look at these issues by calculating the advertising revenues that tech companies amassed from services based on user data; that was the point at which the nonmonetary data started to gain monetary value. But these were just guesses. Thus the really crucial question, Lagarde solemnly told the crowd in the IMF hall, in her charmingly measured address, was this: How could anyone visualize and track "the economy" in a digital world?

"We should talk about barter," I suggested.[31] I had been invited to speak at the IMF podium to offer an "outsider" (non-statistician) view. Some economists looked nonplussed since they had been reared on Adam Smith's presumption that "barter" was a hopelessly old-fashioned concept. I tried to counter that. "Barter is a pillar of the modern tech economy, even though most of us never notice or think about it. It is at the heart of the smartphone ecosystem and many of our transactions in cyberspace." Failure to recognize that meant that the official productivity statistics were probably undercounting how much activity was actually occurring in the economy, I suggested. It might also shed light on why some tech companies were attracting sky-high valuations even though they had few assets on their balance sheet: barter trades were one of the intangible items that were so hard to measure with twentieth-century corporate finance tools (even though intangibles now accounted for four-fifths of the value of the S&P 500 sector).[32]

There were big antitrust implications too. Back in 1978 Robert Bork, the former solicitor general of the United States, decreed that the best way to decide whether or not a company was abusing a monopoly position was to watch what happened with consumer prices: if prices rose, that indicated an absence of competition; if not, no monopoly problem existed. This so-called Bork principle had defined the government's antitrust policies ever since. "[But] while this principle is often useful, it is hard to see how it can (or cannot) be applied if we are dealing with barter—a situation where there are no prices at all," I told the IMF group. By the autumn of 2018, many consumers and politicians felt that the current situation around data collection was "unfair"—if not abusive—since the tech companies dominated the platforms to such a startling degree that they appeared to wield excessive power. But it was impossible to prove that there was any abuse since there were no consumer prices to track. One solution to that might have been to create consumer prices by ensuring that these exchanges were mediated with money. This was precisely what some techies thought should happen. After Cambridge Analytica collapsed, one of its former employees, Britney Kaiser, launched an initiative called OwnYourOwnData, which was committed to building a site where consumers could get "possession" of their personal information and decide whether or not to sell it.[33] "It's the only way to create property rights for consumers and ordinary people!"

enthused Kaiser, who was so evangelical about the idea that she always wore a lump of metal around her neck inscribed with "#ownyourdata." Many other young techies agreed. "At its core, data ownership is not a privacy issue—it's an economic issue," argued Jennifer Zhu Scott, a Silicon Valley entrepreneur.[34]

By the time of the IMF event, innovative experiments were even offering ways to turn barter trades into monetary transactions. Facebook had launched a new platform named "Study," which promised to pay users who engaged in market research. But the survey from Recode showed that only 23 percent of Americans were willing to pay money to get a Facebook that didn't have advertisements and didn't harvest their data; 77 percent of Americans preferred to get the platform "for free," i.e., they liked an arrangement that was an implicit barter trade.[35] "People always say they want privacy, but it is not clear they want to pay for it," Randall Stephenson, the chief executive of AT&T, had pointed out to me a couple of years earlier, noting that when his telecoms giant had offered its own consumers the chance of paying a modest fee each month to ensure that they could watch videos on a platform that would not grab their data, only a small minority chose this option.[36]

Why? Privacy campaigners blamed the preference for barter on consumer ignorance and/or the duplicity of tech groups. I suspected that something else explained the pattern too: digital innovation had made barter so convenient and easy that consumers found these exchanges more efficient than those mediated with money. "People might be angry about the abuse of data or political manipulation; they might feel that the terms of the trade are 'unfair' or that the system of trust that tends to be created by any gift relationship has been abused," I told the IMF. "But they like getting 'free' cyber services and are addicted to customization." That reflected yet another bitter irony that swathed the tech world: "Barter is more efficient in the Amazon economy than the Amazon jungle precisely because of the digital links. Modern technology. . . has made it easier to revive a seemingly 'ancient' practice." It was a complete inversion of the evolutionary framework Adam Smith had once used, not to mention his intellectual descendants, which dominated the halls of banks, finance ministers, asset managers, and institutions such as the IMF.

Acknowledging the role of barter did not mean, I stressed, that we needed to accept that the current status quo was "good." Far from it. I thought—and think—reform is urgently needed. There needs to be more scrutiny of tech companies. Regulators need to revise their concept of monopoly power. The terms of the barter trade need to be improved for consumers by making these terms more transparent. Consumers need to be able to shop for alternatives, control the time span of barter trades, and understand how data will be used. Above all else, governments need to force companies to make data portable, and thus make it as easy for consumers to switch providers as it is for people using banks to open and close accounts. The onus should lie on the companies, not consumers, to ensure that users can easily make a switch; this, after all, is what is required for financial services and other utility businesses to preserve the principle of market competition. Or to put it more starkly, even if barter remains dominant, the terms of trade around the barter trade need to be modified.

Yet there was little hope that this could be achieved, I observed, until regulators, politicians, consumers, and techies took a crucial first step: *acknowledging the existence of barter in the first place*. Instead of just focusing on the noise of political scandal, hacking, and democracy threats, policy makers had to look at the social silence. That was, and is, the only way to update the tools of economics for the twenty-first century, and to build a better tech world.

NINE

WFH

(OR WHY DO WE NEED AN OFFICE?)

"Intelligence is the ability to adapt to change."

—Stephen Hawking

In the summer of 2020, Daniel Beunza, a voluble Spanish social scientist management professor who taught at Cass Business School in London, organized a stream of video calls with a dozen senior bankers he knew in America and Europe. Some of these financiers were sitting in elegant second homes in American enclaves such as the Hamptons or Aspen; others were in the Caribbean, fashionable holiday haunts in Continental Europe, or the leafy Cotswolds of England. A couple were still at smart addresses in London or Manhattan. What unified them was that they had taken shelter at "home" during the COVID-19 lockdown and were trying to run their financial business from there. Beunza wanted to know how they had handled this "working from home" (WFH). Could you run a trading desk with WFH? Did finance require flesh-and-blood humans?

He had studied bank trading floors for two long decades—long before COVID-19—using the same type of anthropological fieldwork techniques that Bell had used at Intel or Briody at General Motors. That left him fascinated by a paradox. On the one hand, digital technologies had entered finance in the late twentieth century in a manner that pushed markets into cyberspace and enabled most financial "work" to be done away from the office—in theory. "For $1,400 a month you can have the [Bloomberg] machine at home. You can have the best information, access to all the data at your disposal," Beunza was told back in 2000 by the head of one Wall Street trading desk, whom he christened "Bob." On the other hand, the digital revolution had not caused banks' offices and financial trading rooms to disappear. "The tendency is precisely the reverse," Bob had also observed in 2000. "Banks are building bigger and bigger trading rooms."[1]

Why? Beunza had spent years watching financiers like Bob seek the answer. Now, during the COVID-19 lockdown, many corporate executives—and human resources departments—were asking that question too. But Beunza thought they were focused on the wrong debate. For companies embracing WFH this discussion tended to be focused on questions such as these: Would employees burn out from stress? Have access to information? Still feel part of a team? Be able to communicate with colleagues? However, Beunza thought they should ask questions like this too: How do people act as *groups*? How do they use rituals and symbols to forge a common worldview? How do they share ideas to navigate the world? There were two key anthropological ideas that could help financiers, or any other executive, to frame this, he argued. One was the concept of habitus developed by Bourdieu, or the idea that we are all creatures of our social and physical patterns, and these two elements reinforce each other. The other was "sense-making," or the idea that office workers (and everyone else) make decisions not just by using models, manuals, or rational, sequential logic—but by pulling in information, as groups, from multiple sources that they react to. That is why the rituals, symbols, and space linked to habitus matter. "What we do in offices is not usually what people think we do," Beunza chuckled. "It is about how we navigate the world."[2] Sense-making is utterly crucial, whether on Wall Street, in Silicon Valley, or elsewhere in our modern digital economy.

The geeks who first created the internet have always recognized that flesh-and-blood humans—and their rituals—matter, even when dealing with cyberspace. Back in the 1970s, for example, when a group of idealistic engineers who were (mostly) based in Silicon Valley created the World Wide Web, they also created an entity known as the "Internet Engineering Technical Forum" (IETF) to provide a forum for them to meet and collectively design the architecture of the Web. They decided to make their decisions about design by using "rough consensus" since they believed that the net should be an egalitarian community where anybody could participate on an equal footing, without a hierarchy or coercion from any government bureaucrat, the United Nations, or a corporation. "We reject: kings, presidents and voting. We believe in: rough consensus and running code" was (and is) their mantra. "[The IETF] is supposed not to be run by a 'majority rule' philosophy," insists Pete Resnick, a computer scientist at the American company Qualcomm.[3] Instead, it does its technical work "through a consensus process, taking into account the different views among IETF participants and coming to (at least rough) consensus."

To cultivate "rough consensus" the geeks devised a distinctive ritual: humming. When they needed to make a crucial decision, the group asked everyone to hum to indicate "yay" or "nay"—and proceeded on the basis of which was loudest. The engineers considered this less divisive than voting. "Many Internet standards, such as TCP, IP, HTTP, and DNS, have been developed by the IETF in this surprisingly informal manner [with humming]," observes Niels ten Oever, a Dutch computing professor. "But do not be fooled: the decisions they make significantly influence the Internet—and the multibillion-dollar industry attached to it."[4]

A meeting that took place in a bland room of the Hilton Metropole in London's Edgware Road in March 2018, with representatives from Google, Intel, Amazon, Qualcomm, and SAP, to name but a few, illustrates the significance of this ritual. A controversial issue at this particular gathering of the IETF was whether the computer scientists should adopt an innovation dubbed the "draft-rhrd-tls-tls13-visibility-01" protocol. To anybody outside the room that protocol sounded as much like gobbledygook as credit derivatives. But the protocol was important: engineers were introducing online measures to make it harder for hackers to attack crucial infrastructure such as utility networks, healthcare systems, and retail groups, and what the proposed "visibility" protocol would do was signal to users whether or not anti-hacking tools had been installed. This was a mounting concern since cyber hackers, seemingly from Russia, had just shut down the Ukrainian power system. "I don't know how you would detect [cyber attack] threats with the US server port just announced for the US utility industry," a blond-haired American woman named Kathleen told the room, wearing a flowery shirt over her jeans. "Unless there is a mechanism put in place for detection [of cyber threats], something is needed. Otherwise we may not have power in the US."[5]

For an hour the engineers debated the protocol. Some opposed telling users if this tool had been installed, in case it made it easier for hackers to circumvent controls; others insisted on it. "There are privacy issues," one computer scientist told the meeting. "It's about nation states," another argued. "We cannot do this without consensus." So a man named Sean Turner—who looked like a garden gnome, with a long, snowy-white beard, bald head, glasses, and checked lumberjack shirt—invoked the IETF ritual.

"We are going to hum," he declared. "Please hum now if you support adoption as a working group item."* A moan erupted, akin to a Tibetan

*Some readers might find it hard to imagine that this description of the IETF's process and humming rituals is actually true. But to see a demonstration of the humming see https://hackcur.io/please-hum-now/, or for the entire debate see https://rb.gy/oe6g8o.

chant, bouncing off the walls of the Metropole. "Thanks. Please hum now if you oppose." There was a much louder collective hum. "So at this point there is no consensus to adopt this," Turner declared. The protocol had been put on ice.

Few people ever knew that this potentially crucial decision had been made. Most do not even know that the IETF exists, much less that the computer engineers design the web by humming. You are probably among them. That is not because the IETF hides its work. On the contrary, its meetings are open to anyone and posted online.[6] But phrases like "draft-rhrd-tls-tls1.3" are such gobbledygook that when most journalists and politicians see this string of letters and numbers they instinctively look away, just as they did with derivatives before the 2008 financial crisis. And, as with finance, this lack of external scrutiny—and understanding—is alarming, particularly given the accelerating impact of innovations such as AI. "Our society has effectively outsourced the building of software that makes our world possible to a small group of engineers in an isolated corner of the country," as Alex Karp, the CEO of the data company Palantir, wrote in a filing letter to the SEC in August 2020.[7] Many of these engineers are well-meaning. But they—like financiers—are prone to tunnel vision and often fail to see that others may not share their mentality, let alone endorse it. "In a community of technological producers, the very process of designing, crafting, manufacturing and maintaining technology acts as a template and makes technology itself the lens through which the world is seen and defined," observes J. A. English-Lueck, an anthropologist who has studied Silicon Valley. "Technology permeates the metaphors used by people to describe their lives . . . 'useful,' 'efficient' and 'good' merge into a single moral concept."[8]

There is a second important issue raised by the humming ritual: what it reveals about how humans respond to digital machines. When the IETF members employ their humming ritual, they are reflecting and reinforcing a distinctive worldview—namely their desperate hope that the internet should remain egalitarian and inclusive, even in the face of mounting US-China rivalry. That is their creation myth. However, they are also inadvertently signaling something else: even in a world of computing, human contact and context matter, deeply. The humming rituals enable them to collectively demonstrate to themselves and one another the power of their founding myth. It also helps them navigate through the currents of shifting opinion in their tribe and make decisions by reading a range of signals taken from the intangible *and* real world. Humming is not something that anyone could put into a computer algorithm or spreadsheet; it does not sit easily with the way we imagine tech, or how engineers present themselves. However it highlights a crucial truth about how humans navigate the world of work, in offices, online, or anywhere else: even if we think we are rational, logical creatures, we make decisions in social groups by absorbing a wide range of signals. And the best way to frame this practice is to employ a term developed at Xerox and since used by Beunza (and others) on Wall Street: "sense-making."

John Seely Brown was one geek who helped develop the ideas around sense-making. Brown, or JSB as he is usually known, was not trained as an anthropologist. He did a computing degree in the 1960s—just as the internet was emerging—and then taught advanced computing science at the University of California. "I started out as a hard-core computer scientist and AI [artificial intelligence] junkie with a strong leaning towards cognitive modeling," he later explained.[9] But when he met some sociologists and anthropologists he became fascinated by the question of how social patterns influence the development of digital tools.

So he applied for a research post at the Xerox Palo Alto Research Center (PARC), a research arm created by the Connecticut-based company out in Silicon Valley. As *Fumbling the Future*, a book on Xerox history explains, the executives liked to think of themselves as a bastion of cutting-edge science and innovation. Xerox scientists were (in)famous for having developed the photocopy machine that was so successful it became a brand that defines an entire category. The group also produced numerous other digital innovations, including "the first computer ever designed and built for the dedicated use of a single person . . . first graphics-oriented monitor, the first hand-held 'mouse' inputting device that was simple enough for a child, the first word processing program for nonexpert users, the first local area communications network . . . and first laser printer."[10]

During his application process to join PARC JSB met with Jack Goldman, its chief scientist. The two men discussed Xerox R&D and its pioneering experiments with AI. Then JSB pointed to the chief scientist's desk. "Jack, why two phones?" he asked. The desk contained both a "simple" device and a more sophisticated—newer—model.

"Oh my God, who the hell can use this phone?" Goldman wailed. "I have it on my desk because everyone has to have one, but when real work gets done I've got to use a regular one." *That,* JSB declared, was what the scientists at Xerox also needed to study: how humans were (or were not) using the dazzling innovations that Silicon Valley companies kept creating. Having started life steeped in "hard" computing science, he realized that it paid to be a "softie," looking at social science;[11] or, to employ the buzzwords that were later popularized in Silicon Valley by the writer Scott Hartley, to be a techie *and* a "fuzzy."[12]

JSB joined PARC and put his new theories to work. The center had initially been dominated by scientists, but a collection of anthropologists, psychologists, and sociologists joined too (foreshadowing Intel's research team). An army veteran named Julian Orr was one such recruit. He had worked in the US Army as a technician repairing communications equipment and joined PARC in the Computer Science Lab, working primarily as a technician on the prototype printers that were in development there. But he then became fascinated by anthropology. He thought of doing fieldwork in Afghanistan, but this was cut short by the Soviet invasion. So he decided to look at the "tribe" of the technical repair teams in Xerox instead. It was not as glamorous as the Hindu Kush. However, just as Briody realized that union workers at GM represented a new frontier of research, Orr could see that the Xerox technicians were an unstudied yet important "tribe." By the late twentieth century, copy machines were a ubiquitous artifact in offices. Work could collapse if a photocopy machine broke down. Thus Xerox employed numerous people whose only job was to travel between offices, servicing and fixing machines. Yet these workers were routinely ignored, partly because the Xerox managers assumed they knew what the technicians did. Orr and JSB suspected this was a big mistake on the part of the Xerox managers, since it seemed that the technicians did not always think or behave as their bosses thought they should.

JSB first noticed it early in his time at Xerox when he met a repairman known as "Mr. Troubleshooter," who "threw out a challenge" to the elite scientist: "Well Mr. PhD, suppose this photocopier sitting here had an intermittent image quality fault, how would you go about troubleshooting it?"[13]

JSB knew there was an "official" answer in the office handbook: technicians were supposed to "print out 1,000 copies, sort through the output, find a few bad ones, and compare them to the diagnostic." It sounded logical—to an engineer. "Here is what I do," the "master" told JSB with a "disgusted" look on his face. "I walk to the trash can sitting here by the copier, tip it upside down, and sort through its contents looking at all copies that have been thrown away. The trash can is a filter between good copies and bad ones—people keep the good copies and throw the bad ones away. So just go to the trash can . . . and from scanning all the bad ones interpret what connects them all." What the engineers were doing, in other words, was ignoring the office protocol and using a solution that worked—but was "invisible . . . and outside [the] cognitive modeling lens" of the people running the Xerox company, JSB ruefully concluded. It echoed what Briody had seen at General Motors when workers hid parts in their lockers.

But was this subversive pattern ubiquitous? Orr set off to find out, employing participant observation. He first enrolled in technical training school. Then he shadowed the repair teams. "Observing the technicians involved going with them to customer sites on service calls or courtesy calls, going to the Parts Drop to pick up spare parts, eating lunch and hanging out at local restaurants with other technicians when there was little work to do, and occasionally going to the branch, or District Office, for meetings, paperwork, or to consult with the technical specialists," he later explained.[14] "All of my observations were made on the job or between calls; I did not do structured interviews. . . . I made audio tapes of our conversations; I also took copious field notes." The fact that he had worked as a technician himself helped in some respects: the repair crews welcomed him in. However, it also created a trap: he sometimes had the same blind spots as the people he was studying. "I had a tendency to regard certain phenomena as unremarkable which are not really so to outsiders," he remembers. He had to perform mental gymnastics to make "familiar" seem "strange." So, like many other anthropologists before him, he tried to get that sense of distance by looking at the group rituals, symbols, and spatial patterns that the technicians used in their everyday life.

Orr quickly realized that many of the most important interactions took place in diners. Those cheap restaurants were not something that senior managers ever thought about when they considered the work of repair teams (insofar as they ever bothered to reflect on that). Xerox managers usually assumed that the repair crew did their jobs fixing machines *inside* client offices, or back at their base in the Xerox office. Time spent in diners between office visits seemed like "dead" or wasted time; it was defined in negative terms (i.e., not working) and thus seemed as uninteresting as words such as "empty" and "free." But it was not. "I drive across the valley to meet the members of the CST [Customer Support Team] for breakfast at a chain restaurant in a small city on the east side," Orr observed in one section of his field notes.[15] Later he observes: "Alice has a problem: Her machine reports a self-test error, but she does not quite believe it. So many of the parts of the control system in this particular machine have failed that she suspects there is some other problem that is producing the failure . . . [so] we are going to lunch at a restaurant where many of [Alice's] colleagues eat to try to persuade Fred, the most experienced [technician], to go to look at the machine with her."[16]

The notes continue: "There are many inexpensive restaurants scattered around Silicon Valley; this has been adopted by the technicians as a place to hang out. Fred tells her there is another component that she needs to change according to his interpretation of the logs." What the repair teams were doing in diners, in other words, was collective problem solving over their coffee, using a rich body of shared narrative about the Xerox machines, and almost every other part of their lives. Their "gossip" was weaving a wide tapestry of group knowledge, and tapping into the collective views of the group—like the IETF humming.

This knowledge mattered. The company protocols assumed that "the work of technicians was the rote repair of identical broken machines," as Lucy Suchman, another anthropologist at PARC, who supervised Orr's PhD, noted.[17] But that was a fallacy: even if the machines seemed identical when they emerged from the Xerox factory, by the time that repairmen encountered the machines they had histories—shaped by humans. "Frank and I are heading for the first call of the day, but he is having trouble finding the building," Orr's notes continue. "The users reported problems with the RDH ["recirculating document handler," an input device which automatically positions a stack of originals one by one on the glass for copying] . . . which does not surprise him. Nobody has worked on the machine for a month and a half and things will get dusty."[18] What engineers shared at the diner was this history and context. "Diagnosis is a narrative process," Orr explained. Managers did not care about dust. Repairmen did.

The same point about group dynamics applied *inside* companies too. While Orr was studying the repairmen, his colleague Suchman was looking at how office workers reacted to photocopy machines, or how humans and machines communicated (or, most important, did not).[19] The Xerox managers had received feedback that suggested many customers considered some of the photocopiers too complicated to use. A machine called the 8200 photocopier sparked particular angst. That seemed odd since the 8200 device had (supposedly) been designed for easy use. "The machine was a relatively large, feature-rich photocopier that had just been 'launched,' mainly as a placeholder to establish the company's presence in a particular market niche," Suchman later explained. "The machine was advertised with a figure dressed in the white lab coat of a scientist/engineer . . . reassuring the viewer that all that was required to activate the machine's extensive functionality was to 'press the green [start] button.' " The engineers were particularly proud of that green button; they thought this made the machine foolproof.

Researchers at PARC who were trained in cognitive and computer science set about studying what had gone wrong, and Suchman decided to inject some cultural analysis. She conducted some ethnography, observing how the 8200 photocopier was used in customer offices. Then a 8200 machine was brought into the PARC laboratory, combined with an "intelligent interactive interface" system as a prototype, and Suchman encouraged her own colleagues to use it, filming the result. It was not what computer scientists had expected. When the machine was switched on, it issued instructions like "User may want to change job description," "Making two-sided copies from a bound document," and "Instructions for copying a bound document."[20] The humans were supposed to follow these sequentially. But what actually happened were conversations like this:

> **A:** Okay, we've done what we're supposed to do. Now let's put this [handle] down. Let's see if it makes a difference. . . . It did something."
>
> **B:** "Good grief."
>
> **A:** "Oh, it's still telling us we need to do a bound document. And we don't need to do a bound document because we've done that. Maybe we ought to go back to the beginning, and erase that thing about the bound document."
>
> **B:** "Okay, that's a good idea."
>
> **A:** "Then it says 'Is it bound?' Just put no."
>
> **B:** "Not anymore."[21]

That revealed several key points. First, even if users wanted to follow the instructions correctly—and sequentially—they encountered ambiguity where they had to make judgments using reasoning which was not in the instruction manual. Second, users did not always think—or act—in a bounded, sequential manner, even though this was the basis of the manual and computer programs. Third, the users who were trying to interpret machines were not uniform, isolated beings, but had their own social dynamics. As another PARC researcher Jeanette Blomberg (later at IBM) pointed out, when groups of office workers respond to an unfamiliar machine someone tends to emerge as a de facto instructor or leader and influences the group. Social dynamics matter. Computer scientists tended to ignore such dynamics. Suchman, however, thought that the human-computer interaction would work better if the design took these social factors into account.

To help explain this, Suchman invoked a classic anthropology technique: crosscultural comparison. In this case, her example was taken from the Trukese people in the Micronesian Islands in the South Pacific. These had been studied with brilliant insight by another anthropologist, Edwin Hutchins, who had previously worked in the American Navy and was an expert on naval navigation. That background enabled Hutchins to see that although the Trukese are excellent sailors who are adept at traversing vast distances, they do not do this using the modern scientific tools that Western navigators (and the US Navy) rely on, such as compasses, GPS, and sextants. Nor do they follow a preset course.[22] Instead, the Trukese navigate by responding, as a group, to conditions as they arise: reading the winds, waves, tides, currents, fauna, stars, and clouds, listening to the sound of water on the boat, and smelling the air. "Although the objective of the Trukese navigator is clear from the outset, his actual course is contingent on unique circumstances that he cannot anticipate from the outset," Suchman explained in a memo published by PARC.[23] "European culture favors abstract, analytical thinking, the ideal being to reason from general principles to particular instances. The Trukese, in contrast, having no such ideological commitments, learn a cumulative range of concrete embodied responses, guided by the wisdom of memory and experience." That meant, Hutchins explained: "Human cognition is not just influenced by culture and society, but it is in a very fundamental sense a cultural and social process."[24]

By the time that PARC grappled with the 8200 photocopier, Hutchins's ideas about were starting to be embraced in the sphere of management science.[25] However, Suchman thought they could and should be applied to engineering and computer science too. "The view of action exemplified by the European navigator is now being reified in the design of intelligent machines," Suchman warned. "[However] we ignore the Trukese navigator at our peril." To design effective AI systems, the engineers needed to acknowledge the role of sense-making.

The Xerox scientists eventually listened to the anthropologists—to some degree. The advertising for the machine with the "intelligent interactive system" was changed, and the patronizing white-coated scientist no longer told users they could understand everything with one green button. After Orr issued his report on the technicians, the company introduced systems to make it easier for repair people to talk to one another in the field and share knowledge—even away from diners. "Julian realized that what was called for was a social technology—a two-way radio (like the early Motorola phones with the push-to-talk button) so each tech rep in a region could easily tap the collective expertise of others in his community," JSB said.[26] Xerox later supplemented these radios with a rudimentary messaging platform on the internet known as Eureka, where technicians could share tips. JSB viewed this as "an early model for social media platforms."

As the PARC team experimented, other Silicon Valley entrepreneurs became increasingly fascinated by what they were doing and tried to emulate their ideas. Steve Jobs, the founder of Apple, for example, toured PARC in 1979, saw the group's efforts to build a personal computer, and then developed something similar at Apple, hiring away a key PARC researcher. Other ideas that emerged at PARC were echoed at Apple and other Silicon Valley companies. However, one irony of the PARC story is that Xerox itself was remarkably ineffective at turning some of these brilliant ideas into lucrative gadgets, and in subsequent decades its corporate fortunes ailed.[27] That was partly because the company culture was conservative and slow-moving, but also because PARC was based on the West Coast, but the Xerox headquarters were in Connecticut—and the main engineering and manufacturing groups were in Rochester, New York. Good ideas often fell between the cracks, to the frustration of PARC staff.

However, the PARC staff could take comfort in something else: as the years passed, their ideas had a big impact on social science and Silicon Valley. Their work helped to spawn the development of the "user experience" (USX) movement, prodding companies such as Microsoft and Intel to create similar teams. Their ideas about "sense-making" spread into the consumer goods world, embraced by ethnographers there.[28] Then the concept of sense-making" entered another unlikely sphere—Wall Street.

A social scientist named Patricia Ensworth was one of the first to use sense-making in finance. In 2005 she received an urgent message from a managing director at an institution that Ensworth described as "Megabling" (a pseudonym she chose to describe "one of the world's top five largest investment banks").[29] "We need a consultant to help us get some projects back on track!" the IT manager said. Ensworth was used to such appeals: by then she had spent more than a decade quietly borrowing the techniques that Orr, Suchman, and Seely Brown had pioneered to study how finance and tech intersected with humans.

Like many in the field, she had moved into this uncharted territory in an unplanned way. She had started her career in the 1980s, as an administrative assistant working on the so-called Wang networked computer system, because she needed to grab a paycheck to finance her graduate studies in anthropology. Since women had traditionally been associated with the skill of typing, "people who had been administrative assistants got their hands on word processing programs, spreadsheets, and document management software early and were the first office automation consultants," she recalls.[30] Then, after completing her degree, she took a job as an office automation analyst and Help Desk call center operator at Merrill Lynch in 1985, while plotting how to use her social science credentials. She eventually realized the best research material was sitting under her nose: stand-alone personal computers were just appearing in the Western business world and MS-DOS coders were challenging the data processing hierarchies that had been ruled by mainframe mandarins. An entire community was in flux. She decided to use social science to help explain why IT issues tended to generate such angst in finance.

Her research quickly showed that the issues were social and cultural, as much as technical. In one early project, for example, she found that American software coders were completely baffled that their internally developed software programs kept malfunctioning—until she explained that office work customs in other locations were different. In the early 1990s Ensworth joined Moody's Investors Service, where she eventually became director of quality assurance for its IT systems. It sounded like a technical job. However, her key role was pulling together different tribes—software coders, IT infrastructure technicians, analysts, salespeople, and external customers. Then she formed a consultancy to advise on "project management, risk analysis, quality assurance and other business issues," combining cultural awareness with engineering.

The "Megabling" project was typical. Like most of its ilk, this investment bank had been racing to move its operations online. But by 2005 its capital markets team faced a crisis. Before 2000 Megabling traders had outsourced much of the IT platform to vendors in India, since they were cheaper than IT experts in America. But while the suppliers' coders and testers were skilled at handling traditional investment products, like stocks, bonds, and options, the Indian teams struggled to cope with a new derivatives business that Megabling was building since the Indian coders had formal, bureaucratic engineering methods. So Megabling started to use other suppliers, in Kiev, Ukraine, and Toronto, Canada, who had a more flexible style and were used to collaborating with creative mathematicians. But that made the problems even worse: deadlines were missed, defects emerged, and expensive disputes erupted.

"In the New York Megabling office, tensions were running high between the onsite employees of rival outsourcing vendors," Ensworth later wrote. "The pivot point occurred when a fight broke out: a male Canadian tester insulted a female Indian tester with X-rated profanity and she threw hot coffee in his face. Since this legally constituted a workplace assault, the female tester was immediately fired and deported. Debates about the fairness of the punishment divided the office . . . [and] at the same time risk management auditors uncovered some serious operational and security violations in the outsourced IT infrastructures and processes."[31]

Many employees of Megabling blamed the issues on an interethnic clashes. But Ensworth suspected another, more subtle problem. Almost all the computer coders at Megabling, whether they were in India, Manhattan, Kiev, or Toronto, had been trained to think in one-directional frameworks, driven by sequential logic, without much lateral vision. In that sense, they were similar to the Xerox engineers who created AI programs for copiers. The binary nature of the software they developed, which fundamentally translates all experience into electronic on-off, hexadecimal 0-1 switches, also meant that they tended to use an "I'm-right-you're-wrong mentality." That also shaped how they created their IT systems: although the coders could produce algorithms that solved *specific* problems, they struggled to see the whole picture or collaborate to adapt the framework as conditions changed. The problem was similar to the one dogging Xerox copy machines: just as dust could make once identical machines perform in different ways, when bankers used IT systems and put new products onto these, this changed how the code worked. "The [coders] document their research in the form of use cases, flowcharts and system architecture designs," Ensworth observed. "These documents work well enough for version 1.0 because the cyberspace model matches the user community's lived experience. But over time, the model and the reality increasingly diverge."

The coders often seemed unaware of the gap between their initial plan and subsequent reality, or concealed it from embarrassment.

Could this be fixed? Ensworth tried to address it by attempting to instill a sense of lateral vision into the coders. She persuaded the suppliers in India to add training material for their staff about American office rules and customs and tried to teach the suppliers in the Ukraine and Canada about the dangers of taking an excessively freewheeling approach to IT. She showed videos to coders that demonstrated the noisy and chaotic conditions on bank trading floors; that was a shock since IT coders typically toiled in library-like silence and calm. She explained to Megabling managers that coders felt angry that they could not access important proprietary databases and tools. She also reassured the coders with a bureaucratic bent that they were appreciated in the company—even if the bankers themselves sounded angry.[32] The goal was to teach all "sides" to copy the most basic precept of anthropology: seeing the world from another point of view.

When the financial crisis erupted in 2008, the project was wound down, and Ensworth moved on to work for other banks, often focused around the fast-swelling threats of cybersecurity. That cut the experiment short. But Ensworth hoped that some of the anthropology lessons stuck. "Delivery schedules and error rates were occasionally troublesome but no longer a constant, pervasive worry," she later wrote.[33] Better still, the IT workers stopped throwing coffee at the bankers.

In another corner of Wall Street, Beunza was using the sense-making concept too—but among financial traders. In 1999 he walked onto the equities trading floor of a company he dubbed "International Securities" that was based in "an imposing corporate skyscraper in Lower Manhattan." The head of equities trading—"Bob"—had agreed to let Beunza shadow traders, hoping to get some free management ideas and feedback from him. But the study did not go to plan. Beunza wanted to study how trader yelling affected the markets. "I had watched Oliver Stone's *Wall Street* and was moved by the drama of corporate takeovers. I had read Tom Wolfe's *The Bonfire of the Vanities* and imagined the trading rooms of Wall Street to be overcrowded and dominated by emotion and, as Wolfe wrote, full of "young men . . . sweating early in the morning and shouting,"[34] he later explained.

But when he finally arrived at International Securities, he had a shock: the trading room was silent. Beunza was dismayed. "Why don't your traders act like in the movies?" he asked. The answer was simple: in the previous years trading in equities had mostly moved "online," and was no longer executed over a phone or in person, at a securities exchange trading "pit." The drama happened on a computer screen.

Beunza was even more baffled: if everything can be done online, why did banks even bother to use trading floors? "Understanding each other," Bob replied. "When I have something complicated to explain to someone else I hate to do it on the telephone, because I need to know if the other guy is getting what I say. The trading room . . . is a social place. You can overhear other people's conversation. The market sometimes doesn't move. You get bored. You like to have contact with the other guys." Indeed Bob considered this social interaction to be so important that he spent a vast amount of time pondering the seemingly old-fashioned question of where to seat the traders. "I rotate people as much as I can. They resist. My rule of thumb is that they only talk to people around them . . . [so] they can complain about me and get to know each other in doing so. . . . The trick is to put people who don't know each other together just long enough for them to get to know each other but not so long that they are at each other's throats."

The reason, Bob added, was that "once two traders have been sitting together, even if they don't like each other, they'll cooperate. Like roommates." So he rotated every trader, every six months. He also insisted on keeping "the PCs at a low level so that they can see the rest of the room" and sat on the desk with the rest of the financiers so that he could watch them.

Bob presented this strategy as common sense. (And Beunza later concluded that Bob was one of the best managers he ever saw on Wall Street.) But Beunza was still baffled. The financiers were supposed to make investment decisions with the benefit of financial models based on science and complex math, particularly since they were using "quantitative" finance strategies. So why did it matter where they sat? The answer, he concluded, was best framed in terms of "sense-making." Traders "navigating" markets were essentially deploying two modes of thought. Sometimes they used models to chart and follow a preset course, like a twenty-first-century sailor might use GPS. However, they also "navigated" the markets by absorbing a vast range of other signals and information. Sense-making took place when traders huddled together around a whiteboard, or assembled at bars. But it also occurred when traders overheard one another's conversations or simply bantered with whoever sat next to them. Just as Orr had realized that the "diagnosis is a narrative process" for Xerox technicians, Beunza decided that the "gossip" on a bank trading floor created "a social system that equipped traders to better confront the uncertainty inherent in the use of financial models." It was the bankers' equivalent of technicians talking about dust.

This mattered because the models—just like those Xerox machines—did not behave in uniform ways when humans interacted with them. Financiers often talk about models as if they are a "camera" on the markets, capturing what is going on, and then using that supposedly neutral snapshot to forecast the future. However that is illusory. As the financial sociologist Donald MacKenzie has observed, models are not so much a "camera" as an "engine" of markets, since people trade on the back of them, thus moving prices.[35] Models change the very thing they are supposed to track. Moreover, models are not used the same way by everyone, since their use is influenced by local "material" factors.[36] When MacKenzie watched bankers in London and New York, he discovered that different desks used the same model to produce different values for securities.

That was why narratives mattered, both for diagnosis of past events *and* for forecasts of the future. The same point applied to policy makers. When another anthropologist, Douglas Holmes, studied central bankers at institutions such as the Bank of England, Riksbank, and the Bank of New Zealand, he realized that verbal interventions by central bankers—and their own reactions to the stories they heard about the economy—played a crucial role in how monetary policy "worked."[37] Financiers and policy makers might try to depict their craft in terms of science, devising models to track the price of money; but Newtonian physics did not work in the world of money because protagonists constantly reacted to one another—with words. Individual and group psychology mattered.[38] Hence the importance of what the economist Robert Shiller calls "narrative economics," or what anthropologists might call sense-making.[39]

These narratives and interactions also meant that the geography of trading desks was very important, for reasons that were good *and* bad. Managers such as Bob believed that when the right traders sat next to each other, they were more likely to outperform, even when trading on electronic screens. However, the geography of a trading desk could also create tribalism and tunnel vision, since excessively close-knit teams might not communicate with other teams. Physical and social patterns tended to reflect and reinforce each other, creating a habitus, to use Bourdieu's term. That could foster groupthink inside teams. There was also a big split between the "front," "middle," and "back" offices, or the teams who devised trades and those who then actually executed them in a logistical sense. "The boundaries between front, middle and back offices describe social hierarchies," observed Ho. "Front-office and back-office workers do not socialize with each other even during work hours (the tiered elevators make this rather difficult.)"[40] This split felt so normal to the financiers that they rarely questioned it because physical and social geography was entwined. But it created all manner of risks: traders who did not have a holistic sense of a trade could become more cavalier about infrastructure issues, or about the consequences of the trades they made. That bred what Beunza described as "model based moral disengagement": once the traders had executed a trade with their models, they did not feel the need to consider the real-world logistics of how that trade would be executed, or the impact on the "real" economy (and "real" people, as I noted in Chapter Four).

Smart managers such as Bob instinctively recognized these risks. That was why he constantly tried to shuffle the traders around in the seating plan, spending vast sums in the process. Bob also tried to foster interaction between teams, to create what sociologists call "incidental information exchange," or the type of flow of ideas that can occur when people bump into each other. This helped to break down the ever-present tendency for the traders to sink into echo chambers, or herd behavior, in particular asset classes. There was no way to measure the tangible value of this in monetary terms. Bob could never prove that the vast sums he spent regularly rewiring the trading desk as his teams shuffled around was worth it. Yet Beunza understood why Bob did it: even in a digital financial market, humans needed to interact to get that all-important lateral vision and sense-making.

That, of course, begged a question: What would happen if humans were suddenly *prevented* from working face-to-face? As he hovered, like a fly on the wall of trading rooms on Wall Street and in the City of London in the early years of the twenty-first century, Beunza often asked himself that question. He thought he had no way to know. However, in the spring of 2020, he was unexpectedly presented with a natural experiment: as COVID-19 spread, financial institutions suddenly did what Bob had said they never would or could—they sent traders home with their Bloomberg terminals. So during the course of the summer, Beunza contacted his old Wall Street contacts to ask a key question: What happened?

It was not easy to do the research. Anthropology had emerged as a discipline that prized face-to-face observations. Conducting research by Zoom seemed to fly in the face of that. "As an ethnographer and user researcher in industry a lot of my work depends on speaking to people face to face, understanding how they live their lives on their own terms and in their own spaces," explained Chloe Evans, an anthropologist at Spotify, in an EPIC debate that was convened in 2020 to discuss the challenge. "Being in the same space is vital for us to understand how people use products and services for the companies we work for."[41] However, ethnographers realized there were benefits to the new world too: they reach people around the world on a more equal footing, and—on occasion—with more intimacy. "We see people in contexts not available to us in lab situations," observed an ethnographer named Stuart Henshall, who was doing research among poor communities in India. Before the COVID-19 lockdown most of the Indians he interviewed were so ashamed of their domestic spaces that they preferred to meet in a research office, he explained. But after lockdown, his interviewees started talking to him via video phones from their homes and rickshaws, which enabled him to gain insight into a whole *new* aspect of their lives. "Participants are simply more comfortable at home in their environment. They feel more in control," he observed. It was a new of type of ethnography.[42]

When Beunza interviewed bankers by computer link, he found echoes of this rickshaw pattern: respondents were more eager to engage with him from home than in the office, and it felt more intimate. The financiers told him that they had found it relatively simple to transfer some functions into cyberspace, at least in the short term. WFH was easy if you were writing computer code or scanning legal documents. Teams that had already been working together for a long time also could interact well through video links. The really big problem, though, was incidental information exchange. "The bit that's very hard to replicate is the information you didn't know you needed," observed Charles Bristow, a senior trader at JPMorgan.[43] "[It's] where you hear some noise from a desk a corridor away, or you hear a word that triggers a thought. If you're working from home, you don't know that you need that information." WFH also made it hard to teach younger bankers how to think and behave; physical experiences were crucial for conveying the habits—and *habitus*—of finance through being an apprentice. "The best way to set the tone for conduct in financial services is through observation and senior leadership setting the message," Bristow added. "In a distributed [pattern] it becomes much harder."

Given this, Beunza was not surprised to hear that the financiers were eager to get traders back to the office as soon as they could, nor that most had quietly kept some teams working in the office throughout the lockdown. Nor was he surprised that when banks such as JPMorgan started to bring some banking teams back in—initially at 50 percent capacity—they spent a huge amount of time devising systems to "rotate" people; the trick at places such as JPMorgan seemed to be not bringing in entire teams, but people from *different* groups. This was the most effective way to get the all-important incidental information exchange that managers such as Bristow valued when the office was half-full. But one of the most revealing details from Beunza's lockdown interviews was around the question of performance. When he asked the financiers at the biggest Wall Street and European banks how they had fared during a bout of wild market turmoil that erupted in the spring of 2020, "the bankers said that their trading teams which were in the office did much, much better than those which were at home," Beunza told me in the autumn of 2020. "The Wall Street banks kept more teams in the office, so they seem to have done a lot better than Europeans." That may have been due to malfunctions on home-based tech platforms. But Beunza attributed it to something else: in-person teams had more incidental information exchange and sense-making, and at times of stress this sense-making seemed doubly important.

The bankers that Beunza observed were not the only ones to realize the value of physical. The same pattern was playing out with the internet geeks at the IETF, even though these were the professionals who arguably had most expertise of all about cyberspace. When COVID-19 hit in the spring of 2020, the IETF organizers decided to replace their normal in-person conventions with virtual summits. A few months later they conducted a poll among almost 600 of the IETF members to see how they felt about this switch to digital.[44] Over half of the engineers said that they considered the online meetings *less* productive than the in-person version, and a mere 7 percent of them preferred meeting in cyberspace. That distaste for virtual gatherings was not because they found it hard to do the technical business, such as writing code, online. The key problem was that the engineers missed the peripheral vision and incidental information exchange that happened with in-person meetings. "[Online] doesn't work. In person is NOT just about the meeting sessions—it is about meeting people outside the meetings, at social events," complained one IETF member. "The lack of hallway, serendipitous meetings and chats is a significant difference," said another. Or as a third respondent explained: "We need to meet in person to get meaningful work done."

They also missed their humming rituals. As the meetings moved into cyberspace two-thirds of the respondents said they wanted to explore ways to create rough consensus in cyberspace. "We need to figure out how to 'hum' online," declared one member. So the IETF organizers experimented with holding online polls. But the IETF members complained that virtual polls were too crude and one-dimensional; they craved a more nuanced, three-dimensional way to judge the mood of their tribe. "The most important thing to me about a hum is some idea of how many people present hummed at all, or how loudly. Exact numbers don't matter, proportionality does," said one. Or as another complained: "[We] can't replace in-person humming." A Silicon Valley veteran might have described this as a case of techies craving some "fuzzy" connections, to use Hartley's metaphor.[45] Anthropologists would depict this as a search for sense-making. Either way, the key point was (and is) this: the pandemic forced workers into cyberspace and made them more digitally adept; but it also exposed a social silence, namely the role of human interactions and rituals. We forget this at our peril, with or without a pandemic.

TEN

MORAL MONEY

(OR WHAT REALLY DRIVES SUSTAINABILITY?)

> "Markets have well-known inherent inefficiencies [such as] whoever's making the decisions doesn't pay attention to what are called externalities, effect on others."
>
> —Noam Chomsky[1]

In the summer of 2020 I met Bernard Looney, chief executive of BP. The word "met," however, was a figure of speech. Since we were in the midst of the COVID-19 lockdown, I was sitting in my scruffy spare bedroom in New York; he was talking on a cyber link from a smart home office in West London, with chic bookshelves in the background. This created an odd illusion of intimacy. Instead of staring at Looney's face across a desk in a conference room, I could see his craggy demeanor pixel by pixel. He oozed self-deprecating charm, with a lilting Irish accent.

He also had a good story to tell. A few months earlier, he had become chief executive of BP and surprised investors by announcing a pivot. The company had been a fossil fuel behemoth for decades. Until 1998, its name had been "British Petroleum." But Looney seemed determined to move away from that "petroleum" past and had pledged to go "carbon neutral" by 2050, or earlier, which implied the company would reduce its investment in oil and gas wells, emphasizing renewable energy, such as solar power.[2] That did not satisfy environmental activists such as Greta Thunberg who wanted oil and gas companies to cease drilling immediately. BP was unwilling to do so, not least because it insisted that it needed the revenues from fossil fuel to fund a transition to clean energy. But for BP the pivot was startling, and different from the stance taken by other groups such as Exxon. Doubly notable was how Looney framed this. As he liked to tell the tale, he had been influenced by an event a year earlier when he attended the Annual General Meeting of BP in Aberdeen and encountered someone from a radically different social tribe—an environmental activist.

Like others of their ilk, BP executives were used to having protestors show up to these annual rituals, seeking to grab as much attention as they could. This AGM was no different. As it got underway in Aberdeen, a group were scaling BP's London headquarters. Up in Aberdeen, climate activists stood outside the building wielding placards that depicted BP's normal yellow-and-green sun logo as a bleeding and burning orb. Some smuggled themselves into the meeting so they could shout protests (before being dragged out by security men). Others tossed questions at the BP management during the AGM; since they owned shares, they had a right to speak and always aimed to do so. The BP executives usually tried to answer these questions but did not usually engage too deeply. To the executives who had spent years enmeshed in the hard-charging world of energy extraction, activists seemed a completely alien tribe.

But that day, as Looney listened to the protests and questions at the AGM, he was struck by how articulate one protestor seemed. He asked to meet her since he wanted to find out what drove her criticism, and see the world through her eyes, even for a moment. "My mum always told me that you have got one mouth and two ears and you have to use them in that proportion. I wanted to hear what the protestors had to say," he told me. "So we quietly met up, over lunch, and I asked her to explain why she hated us. I just listened. It wasn't screeching at each other. She laid out a case. I didn't agree with most of it. But she said things that I had not thought about before. I learned a lot."[3]

"What type of things?" I asked.

"Lots of it was criticism of us. I had heard this before. But then she asked me: 'Why don't you have pictures of oil and gas rigs in your adverts? Why do you just have pictures of renewables? Are you ashamed of the oil and gas? If so why?" It got me thinking." He adamantly refused to tell me the name of the protestor "because if I did, that would make it harder for her to do her work. I don't want that." But he subsequently met up with her about half a dozen times, to try to listen. "I don't agree with all or most of what she says. But I do want to hear her, to see the world through her eyes. She has definitely changed some of my views."

I was surprised. During my career as a journalist I had interviewed numerous business executives, many of whom had come under fire. Most had reacted to criticism by being defensive. Almost none had gone out of their way to listen to people who hate them. When I had worked on the Lex column in 2004, I spoke with energy companies who dismissed protestors as hippies. In 2009 I listened to the men (and they were almost exclusively men) who ran City and Wall Street banks heap scorn on protest movements such as Occupy Wall Street. In 2016 I heard Silicon Valley titans rail against the "techlash." (When Mark Zuckerberg, the head of Facebook, announced in 2017 that he wanted to embark on a "listening tour" among ordinary people, it attracted attention because the gesture seemed so rare; in any case, it was far from clear that Zuckerberg was open to hearing criticism.)[4] Looney, however, was claiming that he genuinely wanted to listen. It sounded as if he had just swallowed a textbook on social anthropology: he was trying to think himself into the mind of the strange "other" to get another point of view.

"Did you ever study any anthropology?" I asked. His shook his head on my computer screen and explained that he had studied engineering in Dublin. He attributed his desire to listen to his mother—and the fact that he had been a mediocre student at college and had consequently never felt confident enough to ignore the views of others. He also seemed to have been influenced by the fact that he had used therapy in his personal life and, unlike most CEOs, was willing to admit this to remove the stigma this had sometimes attracted in the corporate sphere. "I have always believed you have to listen. It's just good management."

I could not tell whether he really meant this. Like any newly installed CEO, Looney had a strong incentive to go on a charm campaign. His predecessor at BP, Bob Dudley, had been criticized by investors for seeming aloof and the BP board had selected Looney for the job partly because they were keen to change the company's image. Looney had yet to turn this bold rhetoric into tangible action plans. Would those plans even work if he did deliver real action?* I did not know. But the sheer fact that he was using this language was striking. For one thing it showed that it was possible for a CEO to adopt some of the mentality and thought process of an anthropologist—albeit without ever actually using that word or having adopted it from the discipline per se. Looney framed this as mere good "management." But it was astonishing that so few corporate leaders appeared to actively adopt it in a volatile world.

The second striking point was how the wider environment was influencing Looney. He wanted to tell me—and the outside world—that he was engaging with environmental activists because the zeitgeist was changing faster than almost anyone had ever expected. Not only were companies such as BP under attack from people such as Thunberg, but they were also under pressure from more mainstream investors. In the

*This account is not intended to provide a full accounting of whether BP is, or is not, doing enough to combat climate change. Supporters note that BP's promised measures are potentially more radical than most rivals, which may reflect the fact that the company has a more risk-taking culture than others. Critics point out that there are elements of its planned reforms that do not seem particularly "green" (it is selling its dirty assets to less scrupulous producers, for example). In truth, it will take time for the verdict on BP's reforms to become clear.

year before we met, the BP share price had almost dropped by half, as had the stock price of other energy companies. The economic pain of the wider COVID-19 lockdown accounted for some of that drop. However, investors were shunning fossil oil and gas stocks because they feared that the sector would not be as profitable in the future as it had been in the past, because governments were clamping down on the use of fossil fuel, and consumers were agitating over climate change. That had created rising anxiety about "stranded assets," a shorthand for the idea that the oil and gas reserves that fossil fuel companies owned might turn out to be worthless, making the company less valuable than investors had assumed. Or to put it another way, issues such as the environment had previously seemed to sit outside investors' and economists' models. They were called "externalities" and often ignored. Now the externalities were threatening to become so important that they were overturning the models. The idea of keeping them "external" from the line of sight looked increasingly ridiculous—as any anthropologist knew it was.

The way that most investors framed this dramatic shift in attitude was in terms of the rise of the "sustainability" movement or "green finance"—or with reference to the acronym "ESG," short for "environmental, social, and governance" principles. Another frame that was also used was "stakeholderism," or the idea that the people running companies should not simply aim to produce returns for shareholders—as men such as Milton Friedman, the University of Chicago economist, had once argued—but protect the interests of all stakeholders: employees, the wider society, suppliers, and so on. But as I listened to Looney speak, it occurred to me that there was another—simpler—way to frame what was, and is, going on: corporate and financial leaders were moving away from tunnel vision to embrace lateral vision. The vision of companies that Friedman had laid out in the 1970s was focused, bounded, and streamlined: CEOs were expected to just chase one target (shareholder returns) and ignore almost everything else; or, more accurately, let governments and philanthropic groups worry about "externalities." Critics argued that this was myopic and selfish. "If you're in a system where you must make profit in order to survive, you are compelled to ignore negative externalities," as Noam Chomsky complained.[5] But most business leaders and free market economists retorted that focusing on shareholder profits enabled companies to be vibrant and thus boost growth.

However, as Looney looked at me on the video screen, he faced a world where investors were demanding more than returns; they were suddenly focusing on the context of companies and the consequences of what companies did. Or to put it another way, it was not just Looney who was acting as if he had somehow swallowed a beginners' course in anthropology; investors were acting that way too. Which raises an intriguing question: Why had so many investors started to adopt a more lateral—anthropological—vision at this precise point in history?

The link between ESG and anthropology was not always visible to me. I stumbled on it—as so often in my career—as much by mistake as design. This tale started in the summer of 2017. At that time I was running the editorial operations of the *Financial Times* in America, a role which required me to monitor finance, business, and politics. I was constantly bombarded with emails from the public relations teams of large companies and institutions, who were eager to pitch us stories. As I scrolled through the bottomless black pit of my email box one day, it occurred to me that the words "sustainability," "green," "socially responsible," and "ESG" kept appearing in email headers. I usually ignored or deleted these. From a personal perspective, I sympathized with initiatives that addressed climate change or inequality. But my training as a journalist had made me instinctively suspicious of anyone working in PR with a story to pitch that depicted companies in a flattering light. I was doubly cynical since I had read studies by anthropologists (and others) describing how the concept of "charity" can sometimes become a smoke screen for activities and social patterns that may not be beneficial. (A masterful study of the Hershey Foundation in Pennsylvania, to name just one example, illustrated the contradictions that can arise around corporate "charity.")[6]

"ESG should really stand for eye-roll, sneer, and groan," I joked to myself. In any case, in the spring of 2017 there was another issue grabbing my attention: Donald Trump and his incessant, colorful tweets from the White House. But one day, as I pressed the delete button on my computer, I suddenly wondered: *Am I repeating the same mistake?* Many years earlier, when I joined the FT, prejudice had initially made me shy away from economics because it seemed boring. So too when I first encountered derivatives and other complex financial instruments. Was my "eye-roll, sneer, and groan" joke just another blind spot? I set about doing an experiment that was not dissimilar to what I had done a dozen years before with CDOs: for several weeks I tried to hear, without sneering, what people said about ESG. I read the emails I kept receiving. I asked executives and financiers why they kept talking about sustainability; I attended some conferences—and listened. Slowly, several points began to crystallize in my mind. The first was that this shift in the zeitgeist was occurring not in one place—but three. One was the C-suite, or the corporate executive sphere, where business leaders were starting to talk about "purpose" and "sustainability," instead of just profits. The second was in the financial sector, where investors and the financial companies that served them were tracking how they made returns. The third—less noticed—sphere sat at the intersection of the policy making and philanthropic worlds: governments were running out of taxpayer money to fulfill their policy goals and needed to tap into private sector resources, along with philanthropists.

These three focal points for change reinforced one another: companies were seeking a broader purpose; investors wanted to finance this; and governments and philanthropists wanted to coordinate firepower.

"We are rethinking what philanthropy means these days," Darren Walker, head of the mighty Ford Foundation, told me. "It's not just the 5 percent of your money you give away that matters. What you do with the other 95 percent is almost more important."[7] That affected how companies approached environmental issues. But it was also sparking a new conversation around social reforms (such as fighting income inequality or gender exclusions) and corporate governance. While the "E"—environment—tended to grab most attention, due to the eye-catching campaigns of activists such as Thunberg, all three were interrelated. "You cannot easily pull the 'E' or 'S' out of ESG—and everything revolves around the 'G,'" Axel Weber, chairman of the mighty UBS bank, told me; his bank was keen to present itself as a champion of the new movement.

But do people like Weber really believe this stuff? I wondered. My curiosity was wrestling with cynicism. Banks such as UBS were profit-seeking entities that had played a central role in the mania that occurred during the run-up to the 2008 credit bubble. The top executives were still paying themselves salaries that looked extraordinarily high to ordinary mortals, and financing activity which was far from "green." The idea that banks were selling ESG products seemed a little like priests in the medieval Catholic church selling "indulgences," or tokens that were supposed to offset sins, for themselves and others. My joke about "eye-roll, sneer, and groan" kept popping into my mind. However, as I forced myself to keep listening, I realized that I was confronted with another version of the "iceberg problem" I had seen with derivatives; once again, the noise in the system was concealing a more important arena of silence.

The issue at stake revolved around risk management. If you listened to the noise around ESG, it seemed that the movement was all about activism: vocal campaigners were calling for social and environmental change, and companies and financial groups were shouting about what they were doing to support this (and sending all those emails I had deleted). But if you looked more closely at ESG, with an anthropologist's lens, it was clear that there was a second factor at work that was less openly discussed: self-interest. A growing number of business and financial leaders were using ESG as a tool to protect *themselves*. The activists who had initially launched the ESG movement a decade or two earlier did not usually want to admit this. Those campaigners had championed sustainability issues because they had a genuine, noisy—and laudable—desire to improve the world with finance; they often presented this in terms of "impact investing," i.e., investing to drive social change, and the exclusion of "sin" stocks from portfolios. "That's the nuns, Danish pension funds, and American trust fund kids!" I sometimes joked to my colleagues (a group of nuns had become outspoken shareholder activists, pressuring companies to clean up their act, while some wealthy American heirs and heiresses, such as Liesel Pritzker Simmons, were championing "impact investing").

But while activists who wanted proactively to *change* the world had started the ESG movement, by 2017 it seemed that many investors had the less ambitious goal of simply avoiding doing any *harm* to the wider world. "That's the sustainability crew," I told colleagues. Then there was a bigger—and even less ambitious—cohort who were primarily interested in ESG because they wanted to *avoid doing harm to themselves*. That category included asset managers who did not want to lose money on fossil fuel stranded assets, or invest in companies that faced reputation risks, be that around sexual abuse inside the office (of the sort that had erupted around the #metoo movement), or human rights abuse in the supply chain, or racial issues (of the type exposed by the BlackLivesMatter protests). Similarly, corporate boards did not want to be tripped up by nasty surprises, or see shareholders flee or scandals erupt that might cause executives to lose their jobs. Nor did they want to see their employees (and customers) walk out of the door because they were angry about these issues. Conversely, investors did not want to miss out on the new opportunities that the shifting zeitgeist might create, such as a shift toward "green" technologies. Nor did companies.

Did this make the whole venture hypocritical? Many journalists thought so. However, I saw it as a victory of sorts for the original founders of the movement. History shows that when a revolution takes place, it tends to succeed *not* when a tiny minority of committed activists embrace a cause, but when a silent majority decide that it is too dangerous or pointless to resist change. ESG was nearing this tipping point since the mainstream of the investing and business world was starting to be pulled along by the tide, even if they did not define themselves as activists at all.

That begged another question: Why had this occurred in 2017 rather than, say, in 2007, 1997, or 1987? Few ESG activists seemed to know. But I suspected it was because of a rising sense of uncertainty and instability among corporate leaders. The annual meetings of the World Economic Forum in Davos were a good barometer of this. Back in early 2007, when I had attended my first Davos meeting—and been criticized for writing negative pieces about credit derivatives—I had been struck by the mood of sunny optimism among the global elite. The fall of the Berlin Wall and the implosion of the Soviet Union had left the Davos elites embracing "a holy trinity of ideas," I later wrote in the FT. There was reverence for innovation, faith that capitalism was good, an assumption that globalization was beneficial and unstoppable, and confidence that the twenty-first century would be "an era when capitalism, innovation and globalization would rule—and develop in a straight line."[8]

But by 2017 the Davos elite had realized that progress could also go into reverse; or, more accurately, that historical trends move in pendulum swings. The Great Financial Crisis of 2008 had smashed apart the idea that "innovation" was always a good thing, at least in finance. It had also undermined the argument that free-market capitalism could solve all problems; governments were meddling in the financial system and other parts of the economy too. Globalization had retreated in all manner of areas. Democracy seemed under attack. The status and credibility of Western governments had crumbled in many other parts of the world, particularly Asia. China had become more assertive—and less willing to embrace Western ideas. Political upheaval had also erupted inside Western countries with the 2016 Brexit vote and the surprise result from America's election. Protectionism, populism, and protest seemed to be everywhere. The net result was a world beset with intensifying "VUCA," or volatility, uncertainty, complexity, and ambiguity, to use the term beloved by the US military.[9]

That instability and volatility was subtly shaking the elite's assumptions. It also made them fear the potential risks that might be created if they ignored social issues, income inequality, vulnerabilities in their supply chains, the future impact of climate change, and so on. This, in turn, was making some of Friedman's ideas—namely that businesses should just focus on shareholders to the exclusion of everything else—seem less attractive. Perhaps that was no surprise. After all, Friedman was also a creature of his own environment: when he developed his theories about shareholder value in the middle of the twentieth century, he was operating at a time when faith in the efficacy of government, innovation, scientific progress, and free markets was generally high in the Anglo-Saxon world. He was also reacting to the fact that previous generations of business leaders had often acted in an unaccountable manner. As ever, the *context* of Friedman's ideas needed to be understood—not least because by 2017 that context had radically changed. In a VUCA world, neither business executives (nor voters) felt much confidence that governments in the Anglo-Saxon world could fix problems such as climate change or inequality. On the contrary, surveys conducted by the Edelman public relations firm suggested that faith in government had crumbled in most Western countries after the 2008 financial crisis. Trust in business also fell in the years after the crisis, with a particularly stark (but unsurprising) decline recorded for the banking sector. What was noticeable, however. was that the trends left government looking little better than business, and the pattern did not significantly change in subsequent years. Indeed, by 2020 the polls indicated that the public trusted business leaders more than government leaders, in terms of solving problems, in eighteen of the twenty-seven countries that Edelman surveyed. Surprisingly, business was also trusted more than nongovernmental institutions. (The latter were regarded as slightly more ethical than business, but less competent, while governments were viewed as unethical and incompetent.)[10]

These trends created a positive reason for company leaders to embrace ESG, argued Richard Edelman, head of the company that carried his name. However, there was a more negative, less-discussed incentive too: a fear of metaphorical pitchforks. As protest rose, company leaders realized they had to do something to reform capitalism and make it look more acceptable, or face a rising risk that the public backlash would depose them. Activism, self-interest, and self-preservation were mingling, albeit in a manner few executives wished to discuss openly.

In 2018 I suggested to my FT colleagues that we should launch a dedicated section of the website to track ESG. I reckoned there might be a gap in the market, since interest was clearly swelling, but there was precious little coverage in the mainstream media, with reports found only on specialist news sites. It echoed the patterns of information flow that I had seen around securitization and credit derivatives a decade earlier. Once again, journalists faced a story that was developing in a slow-moving, elliptical trend that did not easily fit the cultural definitions of a good "story." Yet again, it was hard to "sell" this story because clunky acronyms and technical jargon alienated outsiders. The ESG sector was also opaque and fragmented, since it had been run in a cottage-industry style: different innovators kept coming up with different product ideas, each with its own label and standards. It was tough to get an overarching picture of what was underway. The media coverage reflected this: in early 2019, FT researchers tried to measure how many stories the FT website was running about ESG issues and discovered that it was difficult to monitor this since the internal tagging system used more than a dozen different linguistic "tags" for this content and thus put the stories into different topic buckets. ESG was everywhere but nowhere. That created an information gap. "The state of ESG now is very similar to what the venture capital industry was like when I started four decades ago," Ronald Cohen, a man dubbed the "father of venture capital" in Europe, told me. He had started his career as a red-blooded capitalist, cofounding the Apax venture capital group. By the twenty-first century he had become an ESG evangelist, working with Harvard Business school to develop "impact" accounting metrics.[11] Or as Marisa Drew, a senior financier at Credit Suisse (who later ended up as chief sustainability officer for that bank), observed: "I started my career doing leveraged loans and other structured finance in the 1990s and early years of the twenty-first century, and what I see with ESG is very similar. It's what happens with any sector at an early stage of innovation before it matures."

So in the summer of 2019, the FT launched a newsletter named "Moral Money."[12] I suggested the name *not* to imply any religious link, but simply because we were hunting for a catchy tag free of acronyms. I was keenly aware of how hard it had been to make CDOs, CDSs, and so on sound exciting before the 2008 financial crisis, because of all the acronyms and jargon. "Moral Money" seemed easy to remember. Better still, it invoked the framework of Adam Smith, the eighteenth-century intellectual. He was often considered a founding father of free market capitalism because his 1776 book *The Wealth of Nations* celebrates competition as a source of innovation and growth. However, a second book that Smith wrote in 1759, *The Theory of Moral Sentiments*, argued that commerce and markets could only work with a shared moral and social foundation. The ESG movement seemed to reunite these two books: "moral" sentiments were being introduced to make markets and capitalism more durable and effective.

Our timing was fortuitous. In August 2019, two months after the start of "Moral Money," America's Business Roundtable (BRT)—an elite grouping of the chief executive officers of two hundred of America's largest companies—issued a formal statement which declared that it was embracing a "stakeholder" vision of capitalism. In previous decades the BRT had backed Friedman's mantra, i.e., focused on shareholder returns. But the BRT was now pledging to look after the interests of employees, the wider society, the environment, and suppliers. Almost all of the BRT's two-hundred-odd members signed the statement.[13]

"What does that actually mean?" my colleagues at the FT asked. Cynicism was rife. That was not surprising: on a micro-level, it was not clear how much practical impact the BRT statement might have. When the "Moral Money" team contacted CEOs, some insisted that their company had always respected stakeholders; many were vague about how they did (or did not) plan to make changes to adhere to this new mantra. Then Lucian Bebchuk, a Harvard professor who was a self-pronounced skeptic of ESG, conducted research into the BRT signatories with a colleague. He found that almost none of the CEOs involved had contacted their board before they signed, which prompted Bebchuk and his co-researcher Roberto Tallarita to conclude that the BRT statement was just a piece of empty PR. "The most plausible explanation for the lack of board approval is that CEOs didn't regard the statement as a commitment to make a major change in how their companies treat stakeholders," they suggested.[14] That "eyeroll, sneer, and groan" factor had not disappeared.

Yet, from the perspective of an anthropologist, the symbolism of the BRT announcement still looked striking. Years earlier, in Tajikistan, I had learned that rituals matter, even if the message they impart seems to be at odds with "real" life. In the case of the BRT, the announcement showed that the contours of what was considered to be normal were shifting. As the anthropologist Bourdieu might have argued, the "doxa"—boundaries of debate and orthodoxy—had moved.[15] "The perspective of business, boards, investors is changing. It's about stakeholders now," observed

James Manyika, a senior executive from McKinsey, the American consulting firm. Money flows were changing too. By autumn of 2019 it was estimated that $32 trillion worth of money was already being invested according to a broad definition of ESG norms, double the level a decade ago. Others guesstimated an even higher number. "Global markets have seen some exponential growth in responsible investment inflows and a plethora of new fund launches this year, despite the rolling Covid-19 pandemic," a report from BNY Mellon, the American bank, observed in September 2020. "According to ratings specialist Morningstar, money flowing into global ESG funds rose by 72% in the first quarter of 2020 alone and, as of 30 June, assets allocated to ESG funds totaled US$106 trillion."[16] In early 2021 Anne Finucane, vice chair of Bank of America, estimated that 40 percent of all global investible assets were being managed according to some form of ESG criterion.[17]

Financiers such as Larry Fink, CEO of BlackRock, the world's largest private sector asset manager, predicted this would continue. At the start of 2020 Fink issued a missive to his investors and the companies that BlackRock invested in—via an annual missive he sent investors known as "Larry's Letter"—which declared that BlackRock would embed climate change analysis into all areas of its actively managed investment strategies (as opposed to passive strategies, which simply track a preselected index, on autopilot). "Climate change is investment risk, and once markets understand that there is a risk, even if it is in the future, they pull it forward," he told me that autumn.[18] "What we are seeing is a revolution. I think in the ten years' time sustainability will be the lens through which we see everything." Indeed, Fink suggested that the scale of zeitgeist shift was so striking—and its potential impact on financial markets so large—that it had only been paralleled once before on this scale in his career: when he had started out as a bond trader five decades earlier and spotted how securitization might transform the mortgage and corporate debt markets. ESG accounting systems were emerging with a new set of acronyms (such as TCFD, short for Task-Force for Climate Related Financial Disclosures, or SASB, the Sustainability Accounting Standards Board). Ratings services for ESG products had emerged too. Companies were creating a new role of "chief sustainability officer" and conducting internal audits to see how their performance measured up. "It's hard to find a single company right now that does not want to talk about ESG," Barry O'Byrne, global head of commercial banking at HSBC, told me in the summer of 2020, as the bank released a global survey of nine thousand of its corporate customers. This showed that 85 percent said that sustainability was a priority action, 65 percent wanted to increase or maintain their focus on it after the COVID-19 pandemic—and 91 percent said they wanted to build their operations on a better environmental footing.[19] "People are looking at supply chains, their environmental footprint, their dealings with the local community, their employee relations—everything." Strikingly, two-thirds of these companies said they were doing this *not* because of government regulation but due to pressure from their customers and own employees or investors.

Walmart was typical of the shifting zeitgeist. When the entrepreneur Sam Walton created the American retailer in Bentonville, Arkansas, in the 1950s, it epitomized both the spirit of small-town America *and* the type of capitalist dream that underpinned so much of America's public rhetoric. "Wal-Mart presents itself as a proud embodiment of American patriotism, democracy, Christian family values, consumer choice and free market principles," observed Nicholas Copeland and Christine Labuski, two anthropologists who studied the retailer, using participant observation, in the early years of the twenty-first century. "With the possible exception of McDonald's no other business represents America like Walmart," they added, citing a poll conducted by *Vanity Fair* in 2009, in which some 48 percent of respondents apparently cited the company as the one that "best symbolizes America today."[20]

However, as Copeland and Labuski also noted, by the early twenty-first century this all-American image was beset with contradictions. The symbols and rituals that Walmart used at its annual general meeting projected the folksy image associated with the company's creation story—or myth—linked to Sam Walton. However, the reason why the retailer could offer low prices to consumers was that the company also epitomized the equally all-American twentieth-century cult of ruthless corporate efficiency and shareholder returns. The retailer sourced a growing proportion of its goods cheaply from Chinese factories. It kept labor costs low partly because it banned unions and streamlined supply chains. That had enabled Walmart to expand, but critics complained that this strategy had crushed many other small retailers, contributing to the hollowing out of traditional towns. Environmental activists also criticized the company for using supply chains that were associated with alleged environmental damage and allegedly poor working conditions. Walmart denied this. However Copeland and Labuski argued that "Wal-Mart's success is directly related to its adaptability to a regulatory regime that privileges efficiency and profit maximization above all else," and noted that the retailer "has shown a remarkable ability to mask its externalities, fend off unions, avoid major lawsuits and unwanted regulations, and expand into new towns and countries."[21]

In 2005 the company shifted track: it started working with groups such as the Environment Defense Fund to find ways to reduce environmental damage inside the company. Some critics scoffed that it was another PR stunt, since the strategic shift initially seemed very limited in scale. However, Walmart subsequently created a dedicated sustainability unit, appointed a chief sustainability officer, and the reforms accelerated. In 2018 the company created a "Project Gigaton" initiative. This not only aimed to reduce carbon emissions *inside* Walmart—but also slash an entire gigaton of carbon emissions by 2030 from Walmart's wider supply chain. Some retailers in Europe, such as Tesco, were engaged in similar moves. By American standards, though, Walmart's moves made it a pioneer; or, at least, a symbol of the bigger mood shift. Not uncoincidentally, the CEO of Walmart, Doug McMillon, was also chair of the Business Roundtable, or the body that had issued the startling statement that repudiated Friedman's narrow "shareholder" focus.

"We embarked on Project Gigaton to reduce emissions in what people call 'scope three' [operations outside the main company]," Kathleen McLaughlin, the WalMart chief sustainability officer, told the FT's "Moral Money."[22] "We had made a commitment to science-based targets for our own operations, or what people call 'scope one and scope two': practical initiatives in renewable energy, energy efficiency, especially our long-haul fleet, refrigeration equipment . . . even air conditioning at our facilities. But like any other retailer, 90 to 95 percent of the emissions lie in our supply chain." The new scrutiny of green issues in the supply chain could soon spread into social issues too, she argued. "We're starting to see additional opportunities with social issues . . . [such as] responsible recruitment when it comes to the issue of forced labor and human trafficking." Activists hoped that this type of shift would be good for impoverished communities and the environment. Investors, however, seemed to see a new benefit too: by scrutinizing supply chains in this way, companies were also collecting the type of information that they needed to enable them to weather shocks such as COVID-19 and become more resilient. "Screening supply chains for ESG risks is about good management," argued HSBC's O'Byrne. "This is what investors now expect and reward."

This enhanced scrutiny was thus creating a snowball effect. The people pursuing a sustainability agenda were not just doing this in their own operations, but forcing others to embrace it too. A pension fund run by the Norges Bank Investment Management division of the Norwegian central bank showed how this played out. In 2020 Douglas Holmes, who had previously studied central banks, joined forces with a fellow anthropologist from Norway named Knut Myrhe to do a fly-on-the-wall study of NBIM.[23] The fund managers there prided themselves on pioneering a stakeholder mantra that championed ESG values: whenever they had meetings with the portfolio companies they invested in, they kept restating the stakeholder mantra, like a religious text. But Holmes and Myrhe noticed that the asset managers did not expect to chase those goals just by themselves; they expected that those portfolio companies would uphold the mantra too and evangelize it to others. Myrhe described this as a process of "productive incompleteness,"[24] in the sense that NBIM managers were coopting others to fill the gaps in their mission that they could not fill themselves. Holmes preferred to describe it as another case of "narrative" economics. The words around ESG were changing money flows—just as the words linked to monetary policy had changed markets around the sphere of central banking that he had earlier observed.

Would this last? I suspected it would, at least for the foreseeable future. The COVID-19 pandemic had shown the corporate and business world the dangers of tunnel vision, or why it was dangerous to look at the future through a narrow corporate financial or economic lens. That was sparking a desire for lateral vision. The pandemic had also reminded everyone that it is dangerous to ignore science—or news unfolding on the other side of the world, in seemingly strange places. The climate change challenge was linked to both these points: tackling it required lateral, not tunnel, vision and a sense of global connectivity. Meanwhile, the problems of volatility, uncertainty, complexity, and ambiguity remained—and remain—as real as ever. Insofar as the acronym ESG was a reaction to VUCA, it seemed likely to continue, along with the shift toward an outlook that sometimes echoed the perspective of anthropology. "An ethnographic conversation is the bridge to the moral," argued Holmes, as he continued his research into Norwegian sustainability.

"Listening is decisive."

CONCLUSION

AMAZON TO AMAZON

(OR WHAT IF WE ALL THOUGHT LIKE ANTHROPOLOGISTS?)

"The wise man doesn't give the right answers, he poses the right questions."

—Claude Lévi-Strauss

In 2018 a New York University professor named Kate Crawford, who runs a center dedicated to the study of artificial intelligence and society, published a chart describing the "black box" of an Amazon Echo device.[1] This gadget, laced with an artificial intelligence system known as "Alexa," is found in innumerable Western homes. Yet few users know how the magic in Alexa's "virtual assistant" AI platform works. Crawford thought they should.

The diagram that she and a colleague, Vladan Joler, eventually drew was so breathtakingly complex and intricate that it can only be viewed across several computer screens—or printed out on a vast piece of paper. It has a haunting beauty. So much so that the Museum of Modern Art in New York eventually bought the chart for its own display[2]—a move which might sound odd until you remember a point once made by Viktor Shklovsky, the Russian writer, that one goal of art is to make the "unseen" properly "seen" and promote "defamiliarization," to see what we normally miss.[3]

However, there is a twist. A casual observer of that piece of MoMA "art" might assume that the chart shows the mysteries of what sits *inside* the Alexa smart-speaker system. The topic of AI, after all, is a burning issue of our age, since it inspires fascination and awe in equal measure. Few people really know what lies within a smart device. But Crawford's chart actually depicted another mystery that we usually ignore: the *context* around Alexa, in the sense of all the processes needed to make an Echo device work. This context includes the labor of what Microsoft anthropologists call "ghost workers,"[4] or unseen low-paid humans who perform vital functions to support AI; the complex processes around mineral extraction; the energy that generates electricity for data centers; the convoluted chains of finance and trade. "In [a consumer's] fleeting moment of interaction [with Alexa], a vast matrix of capacities is invoked: interlaced chains of resource extraction, human labor and algorithmic processing across networks of mining, logistics, distribution, prediction and optimization," Crawford points out. "How can we begin to see it, to grasp its immensity and complexity as a connected form?" How indeed.

Crawford is not an anthropologist. Instead she trained as a lawyer, did a PhD in media studies, and then did research into the social impact of AI, absorbing lessons from anthropology along the way. But the chart illustrates the core message of this book: we find it hard to see what is really happening in the world around us today and need to change our vision. The twentieth century has bequeathed powerful analytical tools: economic models, medical science, financial forecasts, Big Data systems, and AI platforms like the one inside Alexa. That should be celebrated. But these tools are ineffective if we ignore context and culture, particularly when that context is changing. We need to see what we ignore. We need to appreciate how webs of meaning and culture shape how we perceive the world. Big Data tells us *what* is happening. It cannot tell us *why*, since correlation is not causation. Nor can an AI platform—like Alexa—tell us about the layers of contradictory meanings we inherit from our surroundings: how semiotic codes mutate, ideas move, and practices mingle. For that we need to embrace another form of "AI": "anthropology intelligence." Or, to use other metaphors, we urgently need to put our societies on the couch as a psychologist might, or use the analytical equivalent of an X-ray machine, to see all the half-hidden cultural biases that influence us for good and bad. Anthro-vision does not usually produce neat power points, hard scientific conclusions, or binding proofs; it is usually an interpretive discipline, not an empirical one. But, at its best, it combines qualitative and quantitative analyses to reveal what makes us human.

And sometimes the act of widening the lens in this way can even make the world better. After Crawford and Joler published their startling chart that made the unseen (slightly) more visible, Amazon announced it would no longer create quasi cages for the "ghost workers" in its fulfillment sites.[5] That was a tiny (badly needed) sign of progress for ghost workers. It was also a step forward for some Amazon executives too: they were getting a broader vision. Defamiliarization can drive change.

So how do we get anthro-vision? This book has laid out at least five ideas. First, we need to recognize that we are all creatures of our own environment, in an ecological, social, *and* cultural sense. Second, we must accept that there is no single "natural" cultural frame; human existence is a tale of diversity. Third, we should seek for ways to immerse ourselves—repeatedly, even if only briefly—in the minds and lives of others who are different to gain empathy for others. Fourth, we must look at our own world with the lens of an outsider to see ourselves clearly. Fifth, we must use that perspective to actively listen to social silence, ponder the rituals and symbols that shape our routines, and consider our practices through the lens of anthropology ideas such as habitus, sense-making, liminality, incidental information exchange, pollution, reciprocity, and exchange.

Or, if you need another tool to gain some anthro-vision, take a look at that chart of Alexa and try to imagine how it would look if *you* were at the center; what hidden flows, links, patterns, and dependencies might you see if you painted a picture of the system around you? As Shklovsky said, art can start a process of "defamiliarization" that can help you be an insider-outsider. So can travel. So can etymology, or the study of the words we unthinkingly toss around. In Chapter Eight I described the counter-intuitive roots of the English word "data." Other words in English also have odd, but revealing, roots. Consider "company," for example. This hails from *con panio*, or "with bread" in old Italian, because when medieval traders first created "companies" they ate together. That is not how investors and executives usually define "companies" today, since they focus on balance sheets. But the root should remind us that companies started life as social institutions—and ordinary workers would probably prefer it if companies remained that way.

The etymology of "bank" and "finance" is also striking: these words derive respectively from the Old Italian for *banca*, or the benches on which financiers once met customers, and the Old French *finer*, meaning "to finish," because finance first emerged to settle obligations or blood debts. This is not how bankers see "finance" now, since they tend to treat it as an end in itself, i.e., a ceaseless flow of disembodied liquidity. But most non-financiers prefer to view finance as a means to an end (i.e., a profession that serves real people) and that gap helps explain the sense of moral outrage many non-financiers feel about bankers. So too with "economics": the word hails from *oikonomia*, Greek for "household management" or "stewardship." This is also often at odds with the modern meaning of economics, i.e., complex math models. But the Greek meaning is more attractive to most non-economists. Every time we utter words like "data," "company," "finance," or "the economy," we have a fresh reminder of why it pays to see life from many dimensions and listen to social silence.

So what might happen if more people embraced some anthro-vision? The implications could be radical. Economists would broaden their lens beyond money and markets, to consider a wider range of exchanges, and pay more attention to issues once labeled as "externalities," such as the environment. The economic profession would see how the tribal patterns in their own discipline have encouraged tunnel vision.[6] (Some economists are trying to do that, and I salute them; but not enough.)[7] Similarly, if corporate executives adopted anthro-vision, they would pay more attention to social dynamics *inside* companies and recognize that social interactions, symbols, and rituals matter, even if they are not *con panio*. They would see that it is a mistake for human resources departments to only hire candidates that are a "good cultural fit" (i.e., the same as everyone else already there) and realize instead that embracing a diversity of mindsets creates dynamism. Corporate executives with anthro-vision would also pay more attention to the social and environmental footprint of a company on the world, and think about the *consequence* of what companies do, for good and bad.

So, too, in finance. If the people running banks and asset-management groups employed anthro-vision, they would see how their internal tribalism and pay structures exacerbate risk taking (as we saw in the 2008 financial crisis), and how "sense-making" shapes their interactions with markets (and vice versa).[8] They would recognize how their own social and professional environment fosters an obsession with "liquidity" and "efficiency" that is not (usually) shared by others, and how their reliance on abstract models can make them blind to the real-world consequences of their innovations.[9]

The same point applies to techies. As I have described in this book, many tech companies have hired anthropologists to study their customers in recent decades. This is laudable. But there is now an urgent need for techies to flip the lens and study *themselves*, to see how they (like bankers) have slipped into a mental frame that can seem amoral to others, with its reverence for efficiency, innovation, and Darwinian competition, and a tendency to borrow the language and imagery of computing to talk about people (say, by using phrases such as "the social graph" or "social nodes").[10] Anthro-vision would also force coders to recognize how computing programs can embed biases, such as racism, into systems in a manner that may be intensified by AI; or how digital technologies can exacerbate social and economic inequalities (say, when populations do not have equal access to education or infrastructure such as fast internet).[11] If the executives of tech companies had adopted anthro-vision in the past, in other words, they might not face techlash now. If they hope to counter this in the future, they urgently need a wider social lens. Similarly, if policy makers hope to create sensible rules around data privacy and AI, it will be crucial for them to adopt some anthro-vision.

Doctors would also benefit from anthro-vision: as we saw in the COVID-19 pandemic (and Ebola), battling a disease requires more than medical science. So would lawyers, given that contracts always come with trailing cultural assumptions that are all-too-often ignored.[12] If political pollsters listened to social silence, their analyses might be more accurate too. My own profession—the media—would also benefit by learning lessons from anthropology. The best journalism is done when reporters have the space, time, training, and incentives to ask questions like "What am I *not* seeing in these headlines?" "What is no one talking about" "What is wrapped up in this scary jargon we shy away from?" "Whose voice am I not listening to?" Journalists usually want to do that. But it is hard enough for us to pose such questions when resources are abundant. It is doubly hard when there are scant resources available to finance journalists' curiosity and the industry is so fragmented and crowded that there is a constant fight for attention. It is even harder when politics is polarized, information customized, and "audiences" will often only consume news that confirms their preexisting biases. Donald Trump's Twitter account in 2016 was the symptom—not the cause—of a bigger problem. The media needs to recognize this and address the issue of tribalism and social silences—in others *and* ourselves.* That mission is more important now than ever. Anthro-vision can help.

Which brings me to my last point: if policy makers and politicians would embrace lessons from anthropology, they would be better equipped to "build back better," to use the popular tag. Anthro-vison prompts people to think about climate change, inequity, social cohesion, racism, and exchanges in the widest possible sense (including barter). It encourages policy makers to ponder the rituals, symbols, and spatial patterns that shape public life. It enables bureaucrats and politicians to think about how their own biases and cultural patterns can hobble them, creating bad policy. It fosters an openness to learning lessons from elsewhere (starting with students in the education system). It recognizes that embracing diversity is not just the morally right thing to do, but the key to dynamism, creativity, and resilience. Or as the anthropologist Thomas Hylland Eriksen observed: "The single most important human insight to be gained from this [anthropological] way of comparing societies is perhaps the realization that everything could have been different in our own society—that the way we live is only one among innumerable ways of life which humans have adopted."[13] In times of stress, it is easy to forget the need to widen our lens. A lockdown and pandemic forces us—quite literally—to retreat to the safety of our own group and look inward. So

*How can journalists break down their own silos? That topic is worth a separate book, particularly given the degree to which trust in the media has declined. But one tactic I favor is what might be called a "domino" strategy, *not* in the sense of pieces toppling over in a chain reaction, but rather the principle of similarity and difference displayed in the actual dominos game. Think about it: in the game players match the number of one half of a domino with someone else's piece; however, the number on the second half is different. Matches are made, but difference retained too. That metaphor can work for reporting: a good story catches the audience's attention by offering something familiar, but a *better* story opens their eyes to something strange too, that they did not expect, like the second half of a domino. This helps to break mental and social bubbles.

does an economic recession. But that is precisely when we need to widen, not narrow, the lens, during and after a pandemic, however counter-intuitive this might feel.

Can this embrace of lateral vision, or anthro-vision, ever happen? Maybe. After all we live at a time of great flux, for bad *and* good. When I went to Tajikistan in 1990, as a British child of the Cold War, I felt as if I were going to a far-flung place that was remote and strange. As I finish this book, in early 2021, the world has become so interconnected that "familiar" and "strange" is colliding in new ways. One granddaughter of the family I lived with in Dushanbe, named Malika, is now studying for a PhD in history at Cambridge University herself. Her brother is a tech entrepreneur in Hong Kong. Another relative, Farangis, is composing award-winning music in Canada. Her grandmother Munira has created a foundation that highlights Tajikistan's role as a cultural crossroads, or bridge between East and West, along the ancient Silk Road.[14] Three decades earlier these far-flung connections would have seemed almost impossible to imagine, even for fairly elite families like this one. But when the Soviet Union crumbled in 1991, borders opened, flights started, scholarships appeared, and the internet suddenly linked cultures and communities in startling ways. Or to put it another way, when I flew to Central Asia in 1990, the region was best known as the site for a historical physical Silk Road where ideas and goods were exchanged on dusty caravans or markets in ancient cities like Samarkand. Today new silk roads exist around us in cyberspace and on planes, creating endless contagion for good and bad.

The world has also taken a surprising turn in terms of anthropological ideas, so much so that when I look back at my own life in the last three decades, it seems as if the different threads have almost come full circle. When I studied anthropology at Cambridge University in the 1980s, the students who worried about "culture," social justice—or the state of the Amazon rain forest—were a different social tribe from those who wanted to become accountants, lawyers, business executives, financiers, management consultants, or create companies such as Amazon; fans of the free market ethos of Margaret Thatcher and Ronald Reagan did not usually embrace the ideas advanced by Malinowksi, Geertz, or Radcliffe-Brown. Today the business and finance world is infused with a new sustainability movement that is driving conversations about not just the environment, but inequality, gender rights, prejudice, and diversity. The idea that Boas championed about the need to value *all* humans is being raised in corporate boards and investment committees, along with debates about "ghost workers," ecological damage, and human rights issues in corporate supply chains.

This has partly occurred because of a genuine sense of alarm about the dangers stalking our planet, particularly among millennials. But it also reflects self-preservation and risk-management in a world beset with VUCA. Or, to use a canoeing metaphor aptly invoked by John Seely Brown, the former scientist at PARC, ESG is a response to our "white water" world,[15] in which it is becoming harder to plot a course through life as if we were canoeing down a calm river with preset contours. We face rapids bubbling with confusing unseen currents that are constantly interacting with one another in dynamic ways, and networked AI could make feedback loops worse. Neat—bounded—models are poor navigation guides in this world; we need lateral, not tunnel, vision.

So when I think back today to that frightening night in Tajikistan three decades ago—when Marcus asked me "what the hell is the point" of anthropology—my answer today is this: we need anthro-vision to survive the half-hidden risks all around us; we also need it to thrive and seize the exciting opportunities created by cyber silk roads and innovation. At a time when AI is taking over our lives, we need to celebrate what makes us human. In an era when political and social polarization is surging, we need empathy. After a period when a pandemic has forced us online, we need to acknowledge our physical, "embodied" existence. When lockdowns made us look inward, we need to widen the lens. And since problems such as climate change, cyber risk and pandemics will threaten us for years, we need to embrace our shared humanity. Moreover, I think that the rise of the sustainability movement means that more people instinctively recognize those points, even if they never invoke the word "anthropology."

Therein lies a reason for hope.

POSTSCRIPT

A LETTER TO ANTHROPOLOGISTS

Diversity is our business.

—Ulf Hannerz[1]

This book was not written primarily for anthropologists. Instead, my main aim was to tell *non*-anthropologists about some of the valuable ideas that emanate from the little-known discipline that I tumbled into three decades ago and love. As a result, some academics might find my depiction of their prized concepts and methodology simplistic. If so: apologies, but I did this for a reason; I would love to see the ideas emanating from anthropology inserted more prominently into public debate—and I am sad that this has not happened to the degree that it has for economics, psychology, and history.

Why not? Part of the problem is that issue of communication: the discipline trains its adherents to see life in subtle shades of gray, which is admirable but means they sometimes struggle to explain their work to outsiders in easy terms. Another issue is personality and method: anthropologists are trained to hide in the metaphorical bushes to observe others and are thus often reluctant to push themselves into the limelight. People who become anthropologists often have an antiestablishment view (perhaps because once you have studied how power works in the political economy, it is hard to avoid feeling cynical and/or angry). All of this makes it harder for anthropologists to be plugged into the networks of influence.

Another issue is that when anthropologists moved from studying supposedly "simple" or "primitive" societies and started analyzing culture in industrialized Western contexts, they entered territory occupied by other disciplines and seemed unsure where they fit in: Should they collaborate with other fields? Import other observational and analytical tools? Let their methods seep into other disciplines, like user research, even if the word "anthropology" is lost in the process? Or should anthropologists stay aloof and stress their distinctive nature? How, in short, do they find a "mission"? Back in the nineteenth century colonial era, as Keith Hart notes, the goal was clear: Western elites used anthropology as an intellectual tool to justify empire and assert that nonwhite people were inferior; in the early to mid-twentieth century, there was an opposing mission: anthropologists were keen to undo the horrors of nineteenth-century imperialism and racism. But today? Anthropology is more valuable than ever in terms of defining our common humanity and celebrating diversity. It can impart lessons from around the world to governments, companies, and voters. It can help us see our own world afresh. But how does participant observation work among powerful elites? On the internet? Or when people are both linked and separate in cyberspace? Anthropologists are hotly debating these ideas, but they do not always have clear answers.[2]

I would—humbly—suggest that this means that anthropologists need to get more collaborative, ambitious, flexible, and imaginative. The revolutions in Big Data and cyberspace give social and computer scientists powerful new tools to watch people. But they also show why Big Data alone cannot explain the world. There is a desperate need to combine social and data science, and a dire shortage of people who can do this. That creates opportunities that anthropologists should grab. In a globalized world where semiotic codes keep changing we should value people who can navigate different cultures in the real world and cyberspace. And as contagion risks arise, policy makers, businesses, and nongovernmental groups need people who have the imagination to see dangers in a holistic way, be that in relation to pandemics, nuclear threats, the environment, or something similar. In short, the world would benefit if there were more anthropologists who can blend their perspectives with other disciplines such as computing, medicine, finance, law, and much else, or inject their vision into policy making.

Such blends do not always fit easily into university departments, which sometimes have a bureaucratic culture and borders that are almost as artificial (and unhelpful) as the boundaries that imperial administrators drew in their colonies. As Farmer lamented during the Ebola crisis, anthropology also sometimes suffers from a "guild" mentality (in terms of being suspicious of those working in other disciplines).[3] Academics sometimes spurn non-academics and vice versa. The human resources departments of private sector companies, nonprofit groups, or government agencies do not always know how to use people with anthropological skills. But as this book has shown, some people have managed to bring anthropological ideas into practical arenas in unlikely and powerful ways, whether it is the Data and Society group in New York (using anthropology to study cyberspace) or the PIH team (championing social medicine) or the research unit at Microsoft (exposing the plight of "ghost workers") or the institute run by Bell at Australia National University (studying AI), or the Santa Fe Institute (studying complexity), to name but a few. I salute them all and fervently hope these numbers proliferate and get wide support, drawing academics and nonacademics together. I also hope that non-Western, nonwhite anthropologists play a much bigger role in the field. The discipline started life as a European and North American intellectual enterprise and remains dominated by Western voices. It needs more diversity, but building that will require commitment and money.

Last but not least, I hope that anthropologists get better at hustling their ideas into the mainstream. Some are trying: the American Anthropological Association's 2020 meeting was titled *Raising Our Voices* to show intent. "The aim is to make anthropology more inclusive and accessible," explained Mayanthi Fernando, program chair.[4] Anthropology podcasts such as *This Anthro Life* are emerging, along with nonacademic online publications like *Sapiens*. Anthropologists are contributing to platforms like *The Conversation*. Some social scientists with a training in ethnography, if not anthropology, are entering public service too. As this book went to press in early 2021, the incoming administration of US president Joe Biden nominated Alondra Nelson, a sociologist and ethnographer, to be deputy head of the White House Office for Science and Technology Policy. In recent decades, (almost) no social scientist has held such a role, and what makes this appointment doubly notable is that Nelson's recent academic research has focused on the social aspects of tech. (She co-led an initiative, say, that tried to give social scientists access to the Facebook data sets to study issues such as political manipulation and misinformation.)* Her work, in other words, demonstrates how social science can tackle modern policy issues; I hope that her elevation signals that policy makers are becoming ready to embrace these skills.

But far more could and should be done to push insights from anthropology, ethnography, sociology, and other social sciences into the mainstream, and combine qualitative and quantitative analysis. A key message of this book is that if there was ever a time when the discipline's perspective is needed, it is now. The world might not always be ready to listen to what anthropologists have to say; their messages and mode of looking at the world often make people uncomfortable. But that is precisely why the messages of anthropology need to be heard, now. I hope this book will help.

*The initiative, known as Social Science One, which was subsequently run out of Harvard, did not achieve its initial aims. However, it marks a striking new venture and form of collaboration between the Social Science Research Council, then headed by Nelson, and a tech group. Full details can be seen at https://socialscience.one/blog/unprecedented-facebook-urls-dataset-now-available-research-through-social-science-one.

ACKNOWLEDGMENTS

This book is an intellectual tapestry woven from threads collected from numerous conversations with people over three decades. I am grateful to everyone who has wittingly and unwittingly supplied these threads.

I should start by thanking the people of Obi Safed who were so kind to a stranger who landed in their midst for a year in mid-1990, and were remarkably welcoming in spite of my numerous clumsy mistakes, questions, and bad dancing. Thanks also to Aziza Karimova at Dushanbe university and all the members of the Shahidi and Nurulla-Khodjaev(a) family in Dushanbe, particularly the indomitable Aya-Jon, who taught me so much about the resilience, cultural fusion, and poetry of Rumi that makes this corner of the Silk Road so vibrant.

I am very grateful to all the professors at Cambridge University who sparked my love for anthropology, particularly (the late) Ernest Gellner, Caroline Humphrey, Keith Hart, and Alan Macfarlane. Humphrey and James Laidlaw of Cambridge read parts of the book and commented. Keith Hart kindly provided a rich stream of ideas and challenges. More recently I have benefited enormously from conversations with American and British anthropologists linked to EPIC, Data and Society, the Business Anthropology Summit, Social Science Foo, and the American Anthropological Association; particular thanks in this respect should go to Ed Liebow, Elizabeth Briody, Patricia Ensworth, Grant McCracken, Robert Malefyte, (the late) Gitti Jordan, Caitlin Zaloom, Simon Roberts,

Melissa Fisher, Robert Morais, Greg Urban, and danah boyd. Many of these also offered very thoughtful comments on the manuscript. Danny Goroff and Christian Madsbjerg have also been great sources of inspiration. My colleagues at the FT have been fantastic friends and intellectual companions over the years; particular thanks should go to Andrew Edgecliffe Johnson, Emiliya Mychasuk, Ed Luce, Gwen Robinson, Alec Russell, Robert Shrimsley, and (more recently) the "Moral Money" team of Billy Nauman, Patrick Temple-West, Kristen Talman, and Tamami Shimizuishi. I am also very grateful to the Nikkei leadership, particularly for their support of "Moral Money," Lionel Barber (the former FT editor), and Roula Khalaf (his successor) and Patrick Jenkins (her deputy) for their support, as well as Martin Wolf, the FT's intellectual "rabbi."

In addition to those named above, Jim Swartz, Emily Kasriel, Jon Seely Brown, Kay Allaire, and Christian Madsbjerg also read the book and offered thoughtful comments. Useful comments on passages were also provided by Phil Surles, Dorotea Szekely, and FT colleagues Rana Faroohar, Andrew Edgecliffe-Johnson, Emiliya Mychasuk, Richard Waters, Jamil Anderlini, and Anjli Raval. Elodie Marran did timely fact-checking. My brother, Richard, has been a pillar of support. Thanks should go to my father, Peter, and his wife, Lorna, and I am deeply grateful to the Swartz family. I also received great support and (badly needed) laughter from friends including, in no particular order: Rana, Merryn, Vicky, Charlotte, Stephen, Aline, Carey, Tim, Gary, Richard, Jon, Holly, Zach, Ursie, Lucy, Amanda, Rolf, Afsun, Simon, Julie, Sophie, Kevin, Christiana, Paul, and Josh, to name but a few. My agent, Amanda Urban, backed the project, even when I (badly) struggled to explain why I wanted to write about the strange world of anthropology. Ben Loehnen is a wonderful and patient editor who improved the book dramatically, and Rowan Borchers offered valuable feedback too. If I have forgotten to thank anyone, I apologize; blame it on the pressure of book-writing during COVID-19 and political upheaval. Any mistakes are my own.

I want to acknowledge the role played by two amazing women who shaped my early life: Ruth Tett, my great aunt, and Joy Carley Read, my grandmother, who first inspired me to seek adventure. If they had been born fifty years later, with the opportunities I was lucky enough to have, they might have been anthropologists too. Last, but not least, I must thank my amazing daughters, Analiese and Helen. It is not always easy to grow up with a parent who is an anthropologist and journalist, and their childhood has taken some unexpected turns. But they have emerged with remarkable humor, resilience and budding anthro-vision. I hope they can use this to help their generation build a world that contains more empathy, open-minded curiosity, self-reflection, and wisdom. We need it.

NOTES

EPIGRAPH

1. Zora Neale Hurston, *Dust Tracks on a Road* (Philadelphia: J. B. Lippincott, 1942), p. 143.

PREFACE: THE OTHER "AI"
(or Anthropology Intelligence)

1. Ralph Linton, *The Study of Man* (New York: Appleton Century Company, 1936).
2. Gillian Tett, *Ambiguous Alliances; Marriage, Islam and Identity in a Soviet Tajik Village*, Cambridge University PhD, 1995.
3. Nassim Nicholas Taleb, *The Black Swan: Second Edition: The Impact of the Highly Improbable* (New York: Random House, 2010); John Kay and Mervyn King, *Radical Uncertainty: Decision-Making Beyond the Numbers* (New York; Norton, 2020), Margaret Heffernan, *Uncharted: How to Map the Future Together* (London: Simon & Schuster, 2020).
4. For a powerful treatise on why the word "exotic" can be so misleading (because we are all exotic to someone else) see Jeremy MacClancy, ed., *Exotic No More: Anthropology for the Contemporary World.* 2nd ed. (Chicago: University of Chicago Press, 2019).
5. H. M. Miner, "Body Ritual Among the Nacirema," *American Anthropologist* 58, no. 3 (June 1956): 503–7, doi:10.1525/aa.1956.58.3.02a00080.
6. "The Relation of Habitual Thought and Behavior to Language," written in 1939 and originally published in *Language, Culture and Personality: Essays in Memory of Edward Sapir*, edited by Leslie Spier (1941), then reprinted in John B. Carroll, ed., *Language, Thought and Reality: Selected Writings of Benjamin Lee Whorf* (1956). pp. 134–59. For another excellent illustration of these themes see Edmund T. Hall, *The Silent Language* (New York: Anchor Books, 1973, originally published in 1959).
7. This account is taken from Matthew Engelke, *Think Like an Anthropologist* (London: Pelican, 2018).

8. This quote is very widely attributed to Paul Broca and echoes the core of his intellectual arguments and academic approach. However, the precise source seems unclear.
9. For a fascinating explanation of how attitudes toward time can vary among Western professionals, see Frank A. Dubinskas, ed., *Making Time: Ethnographies of High-Technology Organizations* (Philadelpia: Temple University Press, 1988).
10. Victor Turner, *The Ritual Process; Structure and Anti-Structure* (Piscataway, NJ: Aldine Transaction, 1996; first published 1966). See also Victor Turner, *Forest of Symbols; Aspects of Ndembu Ritual* (Ithaca, NY: Cornell Paperbacks, 1970).
11. https://www.bbc.com/news/blogs-trending-38156985.
12. A similar point is made by the sociologist Arlie Russell Hochschild in her excellent book *Strangers in Their Own Land: Anger and Mourning on the American Right* (New York: The New Press, 2018).
13. Rebekah Park, David Zax, and Beth Goldberg, "Fighting Conspiracy Theories Online at Scale," case study, EPIC, 2020. See also Gillian Tett, "How Can Big Tech Best Tackle Conspiracy Theories?," *Financial Times*, November 4, 2020, https://www.ft.com/content/2ab6a100-3fb4-4fec-8130-292cab48eb83.
14. To see the parallels between modern conspiracy theories linked to groups such as the QAnon movement and traditional folklore in terms of shaping community, see James Deutch and Levi Bochantin, "The Folkloric Roots of the QAnon Conspiracy," *Folklife*, December 7, 2020, https://folklife.si.edu/magazine/folkloric-roots-of-qanon-conspiracy.
15. The seminal concept of "thick description," which has shaped so much of modern anthropology, is laid out in a chapter that bears this name in Clifford Geertz, *The Interpretation of Cultures* (New York: Basic Books, 2000; first published 1973), pp. 3–33.
16. See Ben Smith, "How Zeynep Tujecki Keeps Getting The Big Things Right," *New York Times*, August 23 2020, https://www.nytimes.com/2020/08/23/business/media/how-zeynep-tufekci-keeps-getting-the-big-things-right.html and "Jack Dorsey On Twitter's Mistakes." The Daily, *New York Times,* August 7, 2020.

ONE: CULTURE SHOCK
(or What Is Anthropology Anyway?)

1. Margaret Mead, *Sex and Temperament in Three Primitive Societies* (London & Henley: Routledge & Kegan Paul, 1977; first published 1935), p. ix.
2. A wonderful account of the challenge of trying to reconcile empirical and interpretative approaches and the suspicion of ethnography among scientists trained to focus on statistics can be found in T. M. Luhrmann, "On Finding Findings," *Journal of the Royal Anthropological Institute* 26 (2020), pp. 428–42.

3. For a good concise history of anthropology, see Matthew Engelke, *How to Think Like an Anthropologist* (London: Pelican, 2018), or Eriksen Thomas Hyland and Finn Sivert Nielsen, *A History of Anthropology* (London: Pluto, 2013). Also see Adam Kuper, *Anthropology and Anthropologists: The British School in the Twentieth Century* (New York: Routledge, 2015; originally published 1973).
4. Keith Hart, *Self in the World: Connecting Life's Extremes* (New York: Berghahn, 2021).
5. Marc Flandreau, *Anthropologists in the Stock Exchange: A Financial History of Victorian Science* (Chicago: Chicago University Press, 2016), p. 19.
6. Anthony Trollope, *The Way We Live Now* (1875).
7. Flandreau, *Anthropologists in the Stock Exchange*, p. 9.
8. Ibid., p. 49.
9. To see a full account of how the intellectual current around anthropology developed in the late nineteenth and early twentieth centuries, see the excellent work by Charles King, *Gods of the Upper Air: How a Circle of Renegade Anthropologists Reinvented Race, Sex and Gender in the Twentieth Century* (New York: Doubleday, 2019).
10. Ibid., pp. 29–31.
11. Franz Boas, *The Mind of Primitive Man* (New York: Macmillan, 1922; first published 1911), p. 103.
12. For a full account of this, see Isabel Wilkerson, *Caste: The Origins of Our Discontents* (New York: Random House, 2020).
13. Bronisław Malinowski, *Argonauts of the Western Pacific* (New York: Dutton, 1961; first published 1922), p. 25.
14. See "Nazis Burn Books Today; Anthropologist 'Not Interested,'" *Columbia Spectator* (May 10, 1933), http://spectatorarchive.library.columbia.edu/?a=d&d=cs19330510-01.2.6&.
15. In the mid-twentieth century a furious wave of criticism erupted inside the discipline after some anthropologists complained that the whole endeavor was rooted in white privilege and an "unequal power encounter." See Talal Asad, *Anthropology and the Colonial Encounter* (London: Humanities Press, 1995), or more recently Lee Baker, *Anthropology and Racial Culture* (Durham, NC: Duke University Press, 2010), or an article by Leniqueca A. Welcome that reflects the criticisms by some anthropologists today, "After the Ash and Rubble Are Cleared: An Anthropological Work for the Future," *Journal of the American Anthropological Association* (2020), http://www.americananthropologist.org.
16. See Adam Kuper, *Anthropology and Anthropologists: The British School in the Twentieth Century*, 4th ed. (Abingdon, UK: Routledge, 2015).
17. Caroline Humphrey, *Karl Marx Collective: Economy, Society and Religion in a Siberian Collective Farm* (Cambridge, UK: Cambridge University Press, 1983).

See also *Magical Drawings in the Religion of the Buryat*, PhD thesis, University of Cambridge, 1971.

18. Peter Hopkirk, *The Great Game: The Struggle for Empire in Central Asia* (New York: Kodansha International, 1992).
19. The expression "soft underbelly" was first used to describe Central Asia in a December 12, 1959, *New York Times*, article titled "Along the Soft Underbelly of the USSR," by C. L. Sulzberger. The concept cropped up repeatedly in foreign policy debates in the Cold War and continues to be used today. See, for example, Gavin Helf, *Looking for Trouble: Sources of Violent Conflict in Central Asia*, United States Institute of Peace, November 2020, https://www.usip.org/sites/default/files/2020-11/sr_489_looking_for_trouble_sources_of_violent_conflict_in_central_asia-sr.pdf.
20. Nancy Tapper, *Bartered Brides: Politics, Marriage and Gender in an Afghan Tribal Society* (Cambridge, UK: Cambridge University Press, 1991), p. xv.
21. Gregory J. Massell, *The Surrogate Proletariat: Moslem Women and Revolutionary Strategies in Soviet Central Asia 1919–1929* (Princeton, NJ: Princeton University Press, 2016; first published 1974).
22. Simon Roberts, *The Power of Not Thinking: How Our Bodies Learn and Why We Should Trust Them* (London: 535, an imprint of Blink Publishing, 2020).
23. Gillian Tett, *Ambiguous Alliances: Marriage and Identity in a Muslim Village in Soviet Tajikistan*, unpublished PhD thesis from the University of Cambridge, 1995, p. 109.
24. Ibid., p. 170.
25. Ibid., p. 142.
26. Joseph Henrich, *The Weirdest People in the World: How the West Became Psychologically Peculiar and Particularly Prosperous* (London: Allen Lane, 2020), p. 56.
27. Ibid., p. 193.
28. Pierre Bourdieu, *Outline of a Theory of Practice* (Cambridge, UK: Cambridge University Press, 1988: original French version 1972; original English translation 1977).
29. Grant McCracken, *The New Honor Code: A Simple Plan for Raising Our Standards and Restoring Our Good Names* (New York: Tiller Press, 2020).

TWO: CARGO CULTS

(or Why Did Globalization Surprise Intel and Nestlé?)

1. https://www.imdb.com/title/tt8482920/.
2. Amy Bennett, "Anthropologist Goes from Iguanas to Intel," *Computerworld*, September 15, 2005, https://www.computerworld.com/article/2808513/anthropologist-goes-from-iguanas-to-intel.html.

3. https://www.engadget.com/2016-08-16-the-next-wave-of-ai-is-rooted-in-human-culture-and-history.html.
4. http://www.nehrlich.com/blog/2012/09/19/the-anthropology-of-innovation-panel/.
5. Ulf Hannerz, *Cultural Complexity: Studies in the Social Organization of Meaning*. (New York: Columbia University Press, 1992).
6. David Howes, ed., *Cross-Cultural Consumption: Global Markets, Local Realities*. (Abingdon, UK: Routledge, 1996), pp. 1–15.
7. For a full description of cargo cults see https://www.anthroencyclopedia.com/entry/cargo-cults.
8. Clifford Geertz, *The Interpretation of Cultures*.
9. There is a ream of literature in anthropology around the idea that globalization fosters cultural distinction, as well as commonality; for one lucid example, see David Held and Henrietta L. Moore, eds., *Cultural Politics in a Global Age: Uncertainty, Solidarity and Innovation* (London: Oneworld, 2008).
10. Christian Madsbjerg, *Sensemaking: The Power of the Humanities in the Age of the Algorithm* (New York: Hachette, 2017), p. 118.
11. For an account of this see Tat Chan and Gordon Redding, *Bull Run: Merrill Lynch in Japan*. (Paris: INSEAD, 2003). Also Peter Espig, "The Bull and the Bear Market: Merrill Lynch's Entry into the Japanese Retail Securities Industry," *Chazen Web Journal of International Business*. (2003), https://www0.gsb.columbia.edu/mygsb/faculty/research/pubfiles/187/Merrill_Yamaichi.pdf.
12. David Howes, ed., *Cross-Cultural Consumption: Global Markets, Local Realities*, p. 1.
13. This history is all taken from the Nestlé archives and internal marketing literature.
14. This account is taken from a masterful analysis conducted by Philip Sugai in Japan, supplemented with author interviews with current and former Nestlé executives. See Philip Sugai, "Nestlé KITKAT in Japan: Sparking a Cultural Revolution," case studies A–D, Harvard Business Review Store, 2017.
15. Ibid.
16. https://soranews24.com/2017/08/22/now-you-can-buy-cough-drop-flavoured-kit-kats-in-japan/.
17. https://business360.fortefoundation.org/globetrotting-anthropologist-genevieve-bell-telling-stories-that-matter/.
18. https://www.bizjournals.com/sanjose/stories/2004/08/16/story5.html.
19. https://www.engadget.com/2004-08-24-intel-embraces-cultural-difference.html.
20. John Fortt, "What Margaret Mead Could Teach Techs," *CNN Money*, February 25, 2009, https://money.cnn.com/2009/02/25/technology/tech_anthropologists.fortune/index.htm.

21. Janet Rae-Dupree, "Anthropologist Helps Intel See the World Through Customers' Eyes," *Silicon Valley Business Journal*, August 15, 2004, https://www.bizjournals.com/sanjose/stories/2004/08/16/story5.html.
22. Michael Fitzgerald, "Intel's Hiring Spree," *MIT Technological Review*, February 14, 2006, https://www.technologyreview.com/2006/02/14/229681/intels-hiring-spree-2/.
23. Natasha Singer, "Intel's Sharp-Eyed Social Scientist," *New York Times*, February 15, 2014, https://www.nytimes.com/2014/02/16/technology/intels-sharp-eyed-social-scientist.html.
24. Genevieve Bell, "Viewpoint: Anthropology Meets Technology," *BBC News*, June 1, 2011, https://www.bbc.com/news/business-13611845.
25. Singer, "Intel's Sharp-Eyed Social Scientist."
26. Bell, "Viewpoint."
27. https://www.epicpeople.org/ai-among-us-agency-cameras-recognition-systems/.
28. https://www.epicpeople.org/ai-among-us-agency-cameras-recognition-systems/.
29. http://www.rhizome.com.cn/?lang=en.
30. https://www.ww01.net/en/archives/65671.
31. Kathi Kitner, "The Good Anthropologist: Questioning Ethics in the Workplace," in Rita Denny and Patricia Sunderland, eds., *Handbook of Anthropology in Business* (Abingdon, UK: Routledge, 2017), p. 309.
32. Shaheen Amirebrahimi, *The Rise of the User and the Fall of People: Ethnographic Cooptation and a New Language of Globalization*, EPIC, 2016. https://anthrosource.onlinelibrary.wiley.com/doi/epdf/10.1111/1559-8918.2016.01077
33. See, for example, Ortenca Aliaz and Richard Waters, "Third Point Tells Intel to Consider Shedding Chip Manufacturing," *Financial Times,* September 29, 2020; Richard Waters, "Intel Looks to New Chief's Technical Skills to Plot Rebound." *Financial Times*, January 14, 2021.
34. https://3ainstitute.org/about.

THREE: CONTAGION

(or Why Can't Medicine Alone Stop Pandemics?)

1. Rene Dubos, *Celebrations of Life* (New York: McGrawHill, 1981).
2. Interview with the author.
3. https://www.youtube.com/watch?v=NshGFgPv3As.
4. Engelke, *Think Like an Anthropologist*, p. 318. For the debate around Tebbit's comment on anthropology, see also https://www.jstor.org/stable/3033203?seq=1.
5. Paul Richards, *Ebola: How a People's Science Helped End an Epidemic* (London: ZED Books, 2016), p. 17.

6. https://www.thegazette.co.uk/awards-and-accreditation/content/103467.
7. https://www.hopkinsmedicine.org/ebola/about-the-ebola-virus.html.
8. This argument is laid out powerfully in the classic text Mary Douglas, *Purity and Danger* (New York: Routledge 2002; first published 1966), p. 80.
9. Mary Douglas and Aaron Wildavsky. *Risk and Culture; An Essay on the Selection of Technological and Environmental Dangers* (University of California Press, 1983), pp. 6–15.
10. Interview with the author.
11. Susan Erikson, "Faking Global Health," *Critical Public Health* 29, no. 4 (2019): 508–516, https://www.tandfonline.com/doi/full/10.1080/09581596.2019.1601159.
12. Michael Scherer, "Meet the Bots That Knew Ebola Was Coming," *Time*, August 6, 2014, https://time.com/3086550/ebola-outbreak-africa-world-health-organization/.
13. John Paul Titlow, "How This Algorithm Detected the Ebola Outbreak Before Humans Could," *Fast Company*, August 13, 2014, https://www.fastcompany.com/3034346/how-this-algorithm-detected-the-ebola-outbreak-before-humans-could.
14. Timothy Maher, "Caroline Buckee: How Cell Phones Can Become a Weapon Against Disease," "Innovators Under 35," in *MIT Technological Review*, https://www.technologyreview.com/innovator/caroline-buckee/.
15. https://www.ncbi.nlm.nih.gov/pmc/articles/PMC6175342/.
16. Ibid.
17. Adam Goguen and Catherine Bolten, "Ebola Through a Glass, Darkly: Ways of Knowing the State and Each Other," *Anthropological Quarterly* 90, no. 2 (2017): 429–56.
18. Richards, *Ebola*, p. 17.
19. Paul Farmer, *Fevers, Feuds, and Diamonds: Ebola and the Ravages of History* (New York: Farrar, Straus and Giroux, 2020), p. 21.
20. Ibid., p. 32.
21. Catherine Bolten and Susan Shepler, "Producing Ebola: Creating Knowledge In and About an Epidemic," *Anthropological Quarterly* 88, no. 3: 350–66.
22. Goguen and Belton, "Ebola Through a Glass Darkly."
23. This policy failure is laid out in chilling detail in Farmer, *Fevers, Feuds and Diamonds*.
24. For a discussion about whether or not anthropologists responded well to the challenges of Ebola, see Adia Benton, "Ebola at a Distance: A Pathographic Account of Anthropology's Relevance," *Anthropology Quarterly* 90, no. 2 (2017): 495–524, or Bolten and Shepler, "Producing Ebola." Also Farmer, *Fevers, Feuds and Diamonds*, p. 511.

25. Interview with the author.
26. http://www.ebola-anthropology.net/wp-content/uploads/2014/11/DFID-Brief-14oct14-burial-and-high-risk-cultural-practices-2.pdf.
27. Richards, *Ebola*, p. 133.
28. Julienne Ngoungdoung Anoko and Doug Henry, "Removing a Community Curse Resulting from the Burial of a Pregnant Woman with a Fetus in her Womb: An Anthropological Approach Conducted during the Ebola Virus Pandemic in Guinea," In David A. Schwartz, Julienne Ngoundoung Anoko, and Sharon A. Abramowitz, eds., *Pregnant in the Time of Ebola: Women and their Children in the 2013–2015 West African Epidemic* (New York: Springer, 2020), pp. 263–77.
29. Farmer, *Fevers, Feuds and Diamonds*, p. 521.
30. Christopher JM Whitty et al., "Infectious Disease: Tough Choice to Reduce Ebola Transmission," *Nature*, November 6, 2014.
31. Gillian Tett, "We Need More Than Big Data to Track the Virus," *Financial Times*, May 20, 2020, https://www.ft.com/content/042a1ca2-9997-11ea-8b5b-63f7c5c86bef.
32. Interview with the author.
33. Michael C. Ennis-McMillan and Kristin Hedges, "Pandemic Perspectives: Responding to COVID-19," *Open Anthropology* 8, No. 1 (April 2020), https://www.americananthro.org/StayInformed/OAArticleDetail.aspx?ItemNumber=25631,
34. See "Trump Says Coronavirus Worse 'Attack' Than Pearl Harbor, *BBC News*, May 7, 2020, https://www.bbc.com/news/world-us-canada-52568405, or Katie Rogers, Lara Jakes, and Ana Swanson, "Trump Defends Using 'Chinese Virus' Label, Ignoring Growing Critcism," *New York Times*, March 18, 2020, https://www.nytimes.com/2020/03/18/us/politics/china-virus.html.
35. https://oxfamblogs.org/fp2p/what-might-africa-teach-the-world-covid-19-and-ebola-virus-disease-compared/.
36. For details on mask culture see Christos Lynteris, "Why Do People Really Wear Face Masks During an Epidemic?," *New York Times*, February 13, 2020, https://www.nytimes.com/2020/02/13/opinion/coronavirus-face-mask-effective.html, also https://www.sapiens.org/culture/coronavirus-mask/, https://www.jstor.org/stable/23999578?seq=1#metadata_info_tab_contents, and Gideon Lasco, "The Social Meanings of Face Masks, Revisited," *Inquirer.Net*, July 30, 2020, https://opinion.inquirer.net/132238/the-social-meanings-of-face-masks-revisited.
37. https://hbr.org/2020/06/using-reverse-innovation-to-fight-covid-19.
38. For details on the Societal Experts Action Network (SEAN), see https://www.nationalacademies.org/our-work/societal-experts-action-network.

39. https://www.bi.team/blogs/facemasks-would-you-wear-one/.
40. See IFS annual lecture: Gus O'Donnell. "The Covid Tragedy; following the science or sciences?" 24 September, 2020, https://www.ifs.org.uk/uploads/IFS%20Annual%20Lecture%202020.pdf; Larry Elliott, "Covid Means UK Needs EU Deal to Avoid Calamity, Says Lord O'Donnell," *Guardian*, September 23, 2020, https://www.theguardian.com/politics/2020/sep/24/covid-means-uk-needs-eu-deal-to-avoid-calamity-says-lord-odonnell.
41. https://dominiccummings.files.wordpress.com/2013/11/20130825-some-thoughts-on-education-and-political-priorities-version-2-final.pdf.
42. Martha Lincoln, "Study of the Role of Hubris in Nations' COVID-19 Response," *Nature*, September 15, 2020, https://www.nature.com/articles/d41586-020-02596-8.
43. The question of how government officials and bureaucrats in the West are prisoners of their own culture is not often discussed. However, one excellent piece of analysis can be seen in a paper from the UK's Behavioral Insights Team, "Behavioral Government," July 11, 2018, https://www.bi.team/publications/behavioural-government/. For an angrier analysis, see David Graeber, *The Utopia of Rules: On Technology, Stupidity and the Secret Joys of Bureaucracy* (New York: Melville, 2016).

FOUR: FINANCIAL CRISIS
(or Why Do Bankers Misread Risks?)

1. Anaïs Nin, "Abstraction," in *The Novel of the Future* (New York: Collier Books, 1976; copyright 1968), p. 25.
2. Alan Beattie and James Politi, "'I Made A Mistake,' admits Greenspan," *Financial Times*, October 23, 2008. For a description of how Greenspan has rethought his economic approach to incorporate behavioral economics and uncertainty, see Alan Greenspan, *The Map and the Territory 2.0: Risk, Human Nature, and the Future of Forecasting* (New York: Penguin 2013).
3. Daniel Beunza, *Taking the Floor: Models, Morals, and Management in a Wall Street Trading Room* (Princeton, NJ: Princeton University Press, 2019).
4. Karen Ho, *Liquidated: An Ethnography of Wall Street* (Duke University Press, 2009).
5. Vincent Antonin Lépinay, *Codes of Finance: Engineering Derivatives in a Global Bank* (Princeton, NJ: Princeton University Press, 2011).
6. Laura Barton, "On the Money," *Guardian*, October 30, 2008, https://www.theguardian.com/business/2008/oct/31/creditcrunch-gillian-tett-financial-times.
7. Laura Nader, "Up the Anthropologist," memo to the US Department of Health, Education, and Welfare, found at https://eric.ed.gov/?id=ED065375.

8. Karen Ho, *Liquidated*, p. 19. A similar point about the problems of conducting anthropology among the power elite, but in a different context (nuclear energy) is found in Hugh Gusterson, "Studying Up Revisited," *POLAR: Political and Legal Anthropology Review* 20, no. 1, 114–19.
9. Paul Tucker, "A Perspective on Recent Monetary and Financial System Developments," *Bank of England Quarterly Bulletin*, 2007. https://papers.ssrn.com/sol3/papers.cfm?abstract_id=994890 For a full description of this period see Tett, Gillian, Chapter Four in *The Silo Effect* (New York: Simon & Schuster, 2016).
10. For more details see Gillian Tett, *Fool's Gold* (New York: Simon & Schuster, 2009).
11. Gillian Tett, "Innovative Ways to Repackage Debt and Spread Risk Have Brought Higher Returns But Have Yet to Be Tested Through a Full Credit Cycle," *Financial Times*, April 19, 2005; Gillian Tett, "Teething Problems or Genetic Flaw?," *Financial Times*, May 18, 2005; Gillian Tett, "Market Faith Goes Out the Window As the 'Model Monkeys' Lose Track of Reality," *Financial Times*, May 20, 2005; Gillian Tett, "Who Owns Your Loan?," *Financial Times*, July 28, 2005.
12. See: Gillian Tett, "Should Atlas Still Shrug?: The Threat That Lurks Behind the Growth of Complex Debt Deals," *Financial Times*, January 15, 2007; Gillian Tett, "The Unease Bubbling in Today's Brave New Financial World," *Financial Times*, January 19, 2007; Gillian Tett, "The Effect of Collateralised Debt Should Not Be Underplayed," *Financial Times*, May 18, 2007; Richard Beales, Saskia Scholte, and Gillian Tett, "Failing Grades? Why Regulators Fear Credit Rating Agencies May Be Out of Their Depth," *Financial Times*, May 17, 2007; Gillian Tett, "Financial Wizards Debt to Ratings Agencies' Magic," *Financial Times*, November 30, 2006.
13. To understand this concept of "habitus," it is worth reading Ho, *Liquidated*, or Pierre Bourdieu, *Outline of a Theory of Practice* (Cambridge, UK: University of Cambridge, 1977). However. since Bourdieu can be hard to read, it may be easier to absorb the key concepts via David Swartz, *Culture and Power: The Sociology of Pierre Bourdieu* (Chicago: University of Chicago Press, 1995).
14. Michael Lewis, *The Big Short: Inside the Doomsday Machine* (New York: W. W. Norton, 2011).
15. Gillian Tett, "In with the 'On' Crowd," *Financial Times*, May 26, 2013.
16. Bourdieu, *Outline of a Theory of Practice.*
17. Upton Sinclair, *I, Candidate for Governor: And How I Got Licked* (1935).
18. See James George Frazer, *The Golden Bough: A Study in Magic and Religion* (New York: Macmillan and Co., 1890), or Claude Lévi-Strauss, *Myth and Meaning* (Abingdon, UK: Routledge, 1978).

19. Hortense Powdermaker, *Hollywood: The Dream Factory* (Hollywood, CA: Martino Fine Books, 2013; first published 1950).
20. Gillian Tett, "Silos and Silences: Why So Few People Spotted the Problems in Complex Credit and What That Implies for the Future," *Banque de France Financial Stability Review* 14 (July 2010), p. 123, https://publications.banque-france.fr/sites/default/files/medias/documents/financial-stability-review-14_2010-07.pdf.
21. For a full account of this see Gillian Tett *Fool's Gold.*
22. Gillian Tett, "An Interview with Alan Greenspan," *Financial Times*, October 25, 2013, https://www.ft.com/content/25ebae9e-3c3a-11e3-b85f-00144feab7dc.
23. Richard Beales and Gillian Tett, "Greenspan Warns on Growth of Derivatives," *Financial Times*, May 6, 2005.
24. https://www.ft.com/content/25ebae9e-3c3a-11e3-b85f-00144feab7de.
25. Caitlin Zaloom, *Out of the Pits: Traders and Technology from Chicago to London* (Chicago: University of Chicago Press, 2006).
26. Ho, *Liquidated*, p. 12.
27. Donald Mackenzie, *An Engine Not a Camera: How Financial Models Shape Markets* (Cambridge, MA: MIT Press), pp. 2–7.
28. Annelise Riles, *Collateral Knowledge: Legal Reasoning in the Global Financial Markets* (Chicago: University of Chicago Press, 2011).
29. Melissa Fisher, *Wall Street Women* (Durham, NC: Duke University Press, 2012).
30. Daniel Scott Souleles, *Songs of Profit, Songs of Loss: Private Equity, Wealth and Inequality* (Lincoln, NE: University of Nebraksa Press, 2019).
31. Alexander Laumonier, https://sniperinmahwah.wordpress.com/.
32. Vincent Antonin Lépinay, *Codes of Finance: Engineering Derivatives in a Global Bank*, PhD thesis, Columbia University, 2011, p. 7, https://academiccommons.columbia.edu/doi/10.7916/D80R9WKD. See also Lépinay, *Codes of Finance.*
33. Keith Hart, "The Great Economic Revolutions Are Monetary in Nature: Mauss, Polanyi and the Breakdown of the Neoliberal World Economy, https://storicamente.org/har, 2009.
34. Douglas Holmes, *Economy of Words: Communicative Imperatives in Central Banks* (Chicago: University of Chicago Press, 2013). For similar themes see also David Tuckett, *Minding the Markets: An Emotional Finance View of Financial Instability* (London: Palgrave, 2011). Similar sentiments are expressed in Robert Shiller, *Narrative Economics: How Stories Go Viral and Drive Major Economic Events* (Princeton, NJ: Princeton University Press, 2019), and Richard Thaler, *Misbehaving: The Making of Behavioral Economics* (New York: W. W.

Norton, 2015). See also Margaret Heffernan, *Uncharted: How to Map the Future Together* (London: Simon & Schuster, 2020), and John Kay and Mervyn King, *Radical Uncertainty: Decision Making Beyond the Numbers* (London: W. W. Norton, 2020), for similar arguments.

FIVE: CORPORATE CONFLICT
(or Why Did General Motors' Meetings Misfire?)

1. George Orwell, "In Front of Your Nose," *Tribune*, March 22, 1946, https://www.orwellfoundation.com/the-orwell-foundation/orwell/essays-and-other-works/in-front-of-your-nose/.
2. Material for this exchange is taken from Briody's field notes, given to the author; see a partial synopsis of this in Elizabeth K. Briody, *Handling Decision Paralysis on Organizational Partnerships*, course reader (Detroit: Gale, 2010), from which details were supplemented by Briody.
3. https://www.fastcompany.com/27707/anthropologists-go-native-corporate-village.
4. W. Lloyd Warner, *A Black Civilization: A Study of an Australian Tribe*, revised ed. (New York: Harper, 1958, first published 1937).
5. https://blog.antropologia2-0.com/en/hawthrone-effect-first-contacts-between-anthropology-and-business/.
6. Elizabeth K. Briody, Robert T. Trotter II, Tracy L. Meerwarth, *Transforming Culture: Creating and Sustaining Effective Organizations* (New York: Palgrave Macmillan, 2010), p. 54.
7. Ibid., p. 52.
8. James C. Scott, *Weapons of the Weak: Everyday Forms of Peasant Resistance* (New Haven, CT: Yale University Press, 1985).
9. Full details of this scandal can be seen in the 2014 Valukas report on the safety problems at https://www.aieg.com/wp-content/uploads/2014/08/Valukas-report-on-gm-redacted2.pdf. See also the company's own statements and the speech of Mary Barra, which echoed many observations previously made by Briody et al. about corporate culture, at https://media.gm.com/media/us/en/gm/news.detail.html/content/Pages/news/us/en/2014/Jun/060514-ignition-report.html.
10. Elizabeth K. Briody, Robert T. Trotter II, Tracy L. Meerwarth, *Transforming Culture*, pp. 56–57.
11. Ibid., pp. 59–60.
12. Gary Ferraro and Elizabeth K. Briody, *The Cultural Dimension of Global Business*, 7th edition (Abingdon, UK: Routledge, 2016).
13. Frank Dubinskas, *Making Time*, p. 3.
14. Elizabeth K. Briody, S. Tamur Cavusgil, S. Tamur and Stewart R. Miller,

"Turning Three Sides into a Delta at General Motors: Enhancing Partnership Integration on Corporate Ventures," *Long Range Planning* 37 (2004), p. 427.

15. Gary Ferraro and Elizabeth K. Briody, *The Cultural Dimension of Global Business*, pp. 166–67.
16. Ibid., p. 174.

SIX: WEIRD WESTERNERS
(or Why Do We Really Buy Dog Food and Daycare?)

1. Meg Kinney and Hal Phillips, "Educating the Educators," presentation to EPIC, 2019, https://www.epicpeople.org/tag/parenting/.
2. Horace Miner, "Body Ritual Among the Nacirema," *American Anthropologist* 58, no. 3 (1956): 503–507.
3. Patricia L. Sunderland and Rita M. Deny, *Doing Anthropology in Consumer Research* (Walnut Creek, CA: Left Coast Press, 2007), p. 28.
4. Interview with the author.
5. Meg Kinney and Hal Phillips. *Educating the Educators.*
6. Rachel Botsman, "*Who Can You Trust? How Technology Brought Us Together and Why It Might Drive Us Apart*" (New York: *Public Affairs*, 2017).
7. Joseph Henrich, *The Weirdest People in the World: How the West Became Psychologically Peculiar and Particularly Prosperous* (London: Allen Lane, 2020).
8. Ibid, p. 55.
9. Ibid., p. 27.
10. Ibid., p. 34.
11. Ibid., p. 21.
12. Maryann McCabe, "Configuring Family, Kinship and Natural Cosmology," in Rita Denny and Patricia Sunderland, eds., *Handbook of Anthropology in Business* (Abingdon, UK: Routledge, 2013), p. 365.
13. Richards Meyers and Ernest Weston Jr., "What Rez Dogs Mean to the Lakota," *Sapiens*, December 2, 2020, https://www.sapiens.org/culture/rez-dogs/.
14. Maryann McCabe, "Configuring Family. Kinship and Natural Cosmology," p. 366.
15. Maryann McCabe and Timothy de Waal Malefyt, "Creativity and Cooking: Motherhood, Agency and Social Change in Everyday Life," *Journal of Consumer Culture* 15, no. 1 (2015): 48–65.
16. Maryann McCabe, "Ritual Embodiment and the Paradox of Doing the Laundry," *Journal of Business Anthropology* 7, no. 1 (Spring 2018): 8–31.
17. Ibid., p. 15.
18. Ibid., p. 17.
19. Kenneth Erickson, "Able to Fly: Temporarily, Visibility and the Disabled

Airline Passenger," Rita Denny and Patricia Sunderland, ed *Anthropology in Business* (Abingdon, UK: Routledge, 2013), p. 4

20. Nina Diamond et al., "Brand Fortitude in Moments of Consumption, Denny and Patricia Sunderland, eds., *Handbook of Anthropology in Business* (Abingdon, UK: Routledge, 2013), p. 619.
21. See Grant McCracken, "TV Got Better," *Medium*, 2021, https://grant27.medium.com/tv-got-better-how-we-got-from-bingeing-to-feasting-782a67ee0a1. Also Ian Crouch, "Come Binge with Me," *New Yorker*, December 13 2003, or https://www.prnewswire.com/news-releases/netflix-declares-binge-watching-is-the-new-normal-235713431.html.
22. To get a sense of how anthropology has influenced advertising and consumer research see also Timothy de Waal Malefyt and Maryann McCabe, eds., *Women, Consumption and Paradox* (Abingdon, UK: Routledge, 2020); Timothy de Waal Malefyt and Robert J. Morais, *Advertising and Anthropology: Ethnographic Practice and Cultural Perspectives* (Oxford, UK: Berg, 2012); Patricia Sunderland and Rita Denny, *Doing Anthropology in Consumer Research* (Walnut Creek, CA: Left Coast Press, 2007).
23. See Roberts, *The Power of Not Thinking*. Also: https://dscout.com/people-nerds/simon-roberts.
24. The work of the research platform overseen by Professor Bill Maurer, called the Institute for Money, Technology and Financial Inclusion, can be found here: https://www.imtfi.uci.edu/about.php. For additional background, see Bill Maurer, *How Would You Like To Pay? How Technology Is Changing the Future of Money* (Durham, NC: Duke University Press, 2015).
25. https://www.redassociates.com/new-about-red-.
26. ReD White Paper, *The Future of Money*, 2018.
27. Interview with the author.
28. Drawn from ReD presentations and interviews with the author.
29. Daniel Kahneman, *Thinking, Fast and Slow* (New York: Farrar, Straus and Giroux, 2011).
30. For information about how non-Western societies operate with parallel realms of exchange and different quasi monetary tokens, see Thomas Hylland Eriksen, *Small Places, Large Issues: An Introduction to Social and Cultural Anthropology*, 4th edition (London: Pluto Press, 2015), pp. 217–40. Also David Graeber, *Debt: The First 5,000 Years* (Brooklyn, NY: Melville, 2014; first published 2011), and Maurer, *How Would You Like to Pay?*
31. Interview with the author. See also https://www.worldfinance.com/wealth-management/pension-funds/how-anthropology-can-benefit-customer-service-in-the-pension-industry.
32. For a good illustration of the cultural paradox around Western concepts of

life insurance see Viviana A. Rotman Zeliser, Viviana, *Morals and Markets: The Development of Life Insurance in the United States* (New York: Columbia University Press, 2017).

SEVEN: "BIGLY"

(or What Did We Miss About Trump and Teenagers?)

1. Nicholas Carr, *The Shallows: What the Internet Is Doing to Our Brains* (New York: W. W. Norton, 2011), pp. ix–x.
2. See Tristan Harris's TED talk for a powerful example of this, https://www.youtube.com/watch?v=C74amJRp730.
3. For a full description of boyd's fieldwork see danah boyd, *It's Complicated: The Social Life of Networked Teens* (New Haven, CT: Yale University Press, 2014).
4. Daniel Souleles, "Don't Mix Paxil, Viagra, and Xanax: What Financiers' Jokes Say About Inequality," *Economic Anthropology* 4, no. 1 (January 11, 2017), https://anthrosource.onlinelibrary.wiley.com/doi/abs/10.1002/sea2.12076.
5. Salena Zito, "Taking Trump Seriously, Not Literally," *Atlantic*, September 23, 2016, https://www.theatlantic.com/politics/archive/2016/09/trump-makes-his-case-in-pittsburgh/501335/.
6. Naomi Klein, *No Is Not Enough: Defeating the New Shock Politics* (London: Allen Lane, 2017). See also Gillian Tett, "No Is Not Enough by Naomi Klein—Wrestling with Trump," review, *Financial Times*, June 16, 2017.
7. Roberts, *The Power of Not Thinking*.
8. Gillian Tett, "A Vision of Life Through a Dirty Lens," *Financial Times*, October 15, 2016.
9. See for example: Gillian Tett, "Making Slogans Great Again," September 30, 2016; Gillian Tett, "The Hack That Could Swing an Election," *Financial Times*, August 27, 2016; Gillian Tett, "What Brexit Can Teach America," August 6, 2016; Gillian Tett, "Female Voters and the Cringe Factor," *Financial Times*, July 30, 2016; Gillian Tett, "Is Trump a Winner?," *Financial Times*, January 30, 2016.
10. For an excellent description of Burrington's work, see https://www.youtube.com/watch?v=E5f7Jikg7ZU. Also Ingrid Burrington, *Networks of New York: An Illustrated Field Guide to Urban Internet Infrastructure* (New York: Melville House Printing, 2016).

EIGHT: CAMBRIDGE ANALYTICA

(or Why Do Economists Struggle in Cyberspace?)

1. This account is based on extensive author interviews with former Cambridge Analytica employees, managers, and shareholders between 2016 and the present day, including most of the people mentioned in this chapter.
2. It should be noted that I do not know whether the (subsequently controversial) Facebook data was used in the models I saw that day, since we never discussed it. Our conversation was about general data usage.
3. Christopher Wylie, *Mindf*ck: Inside Cambridge Analytica's Plot to Break the World* (London: Profile Books, 2019).
4. The criticism of Cambridge Analytica's behavior and the allegations about manipulative political campaigns and misinformation was laid out by its critics during extensive UK parliamentary hearings. It is also reflected in the report written by the House of Commons' Digital, Culture, Media and Sports Committee. See https://publications.parliament.uk/pa/cm201719/cmselect/cmcumeds/1791/1791.pdf, testimony from Chris Wylie, Britney Kaiser and others, https://www.parliament.uk/globalassets/documents/commons-committees/culture-media-and-sport/Brittany-Kaiser-Parliamentary-testimony-FINAL.pdf, and https://committees.parliament.uk/committee/378/digital-culture-media-and-sport-committee/news/103673/evidence-from-christopher-wylie-cambridge-analytica-whistleblower-published/. For an extensive rebuttal by Alexander Nix in the British parliament of his critics, see https://www.youtube.com/watch?v=SqKU0gqY7oo.
5. Interview with the author.
6. Adam Smith, *The Wealth of Nations*, Book 1, Chapter 4. See https://www.econlib.org/book-chapters/chapter-b-i-ch-4-of-the-origin-and-use-of-money/.
7. Kadija Ferryman, *Reframing Data as a Gift*, SSRN 22, July 2017, https://papers.ssrn.com/sol3/papers.cfm?abstract_id=3000631.
8. David Graeber, "On Marcel Mauss and the Politics of the Gift," https://excerpter.wordpress.com/2010/06/20/david-graeber-on-marcel-mauss-and-the-politics-of-the-gift/. See also David Graeber, *Debt*.
9. Stephen Gudeman, *Anthropology and Economy* (Cambridge, UK: Cambridge University Press, 2016). For another discussion of these themes see Chris Hann and Keith Hart, *Economic Anthropology* (Cambridge, UK: Polity, 2011), and Keith Hart, "The Great Revolutions Are Monetary in Nature," *Storiamente* (2008), https://storicamente.org/hart. Or look at Karl Polanyi, *The Great Transformation* (London: Farrar & Rinehart, 1945). Polanyi's work laid the foundation for much modern economic anthropology.
10. Some economists have also pointed this out in relation to the limitations around concepts such as gross domestic product. See, for example, Diane

Coyle, *GDP: A Brief but Affectionate History* (Princeton, NJ: Princeton University Press, 2014), or David Pilling, *The Growth Delusion: Wealth, Poverty, and the Well-Being of Nations* (New York: Tim Duggan, 2018).

11. https://archive.org/details/giftformsfunctio00maus.
12. Caitlin Zaloom, *Indebted: How Families Make College Work at Any Cost* (Princeton, NJ: Princeton University Press, 2019).
13. For a seminal discussion on barter, see Caroline Humphrey, "Barter and Economic Disintegration," *Man New Series* 20, no. 1 (March 1985): 48–72, https://doi.org/10.2307/2802221. Also Caroline Humphrey and Stephen Hugh-Jones, eds., *Barter, Exchange and Value: An Anthropological Approach* (Cambridge, UK: Cambridge University Press, 1992).
14. To see this exchange, watch https://youtu.be/IhvX9QCiZP0.
15. Interview with the author.
16. For a description of this see Vance Packard, *The Hidden Persuaders* (New York: Pocket Books, 1957 [original], reprinted by Ig Publishing, New York, 2007).
17. Cambridge Analytica drew up a legal letter dated July 29, 2015, while Wylie was officially living in Paris, that required Wylie and Euonia to sign a commitment promising "not to make use of the Listed Items or any of SCL's Confidential Information," i.e., the intellectual property that Wylie had created while at Cambridge Analytica, including the Facebook data set and models based on them. Wylie signed this. The relevant documents were supplied to the author.
18. The source is from a legal letter to the author, from Tamsin Allen, the lawyer acting for Wylie, on December 20, 2018. This acknowledges that Euonia pitched for work with the Trump organization but says "Mr. Wylie did not attend any meeting with Corey Lewandowski. The [Facebook] data was not pitched to the Trump Campaign. The pitch, organised by others within Eunoia, was to the Trump Organisation as this was before Trump had declared his candidacy for president. Mr. Wylie does not believe there was any breach of CA IP rights." Nix and other former Cambridge Analytica staff dispute this. For Wylie's version of events, see Chris Wylie, *Mindf*ck*, pp. 174–76.
19. Data on intangibles is drawn from research done by Aon and Ponemon Institute. See https://www.aon.com/getmedia/60fbb49a-c7a5-4027-ba98-0553b29dc89f/Ponemon-Report-V24.aspx.
20. For a description of the work that Project Alamo did in San Antonio, the role of the Facebook "embeds," and the comparison with the Clinton campaign, see Gillian Tett, "Can You Win an Election Without Digital Skullduggery?," *Financial Times*, January 10, 2020.
21. These activities are described extensively in the 2019 documentary film *The Great Hack* by Karim Amer and Jehanne Noujaim, https://www.youtube.com/watch?v=iX8GxLP1FHo.

22. Carole Cadwalladr and Emma Graham Harrison, "Revealed: 50 Million Facebook Profiles Harvested for Cambridge Analytica in Major Data Breach," *Guardian*, March 17, 2018.
23. See Rob Davies and Dominic Rush, "Facebook to Pay $5bn Fine as Regulator Settles Cambridge Analytica Complaint," *Guardian* July 24, 2019, and *BBC News* "Facebook 'to be Fined $5bn Over Cambridge Analytica Scandal,'" https://bylinetimes.com/2020/10/23/dark-ironies-the-financial-times-and-cambridge-analytica/. See also https://www.ftc.gov/news-events/press-releases/2019/07/ftc-imposes-5-billion-penalty-sweeping-new-privacy-restrictions and https://ico.org.uk/about-the-ico/news-and-events/news-and-blogs/2019/10/statement-on-an-agreement-reached-between-facebook-and-the-ico/.
24. Izabella Kaminska, "ICO's Final Report into Cambridge Analytica Invites Regulatory Questions," *FT Aphaville*, October 8, 2020, https://www.ft.com/content/43962679-b1f9-4818-b569-b028a58c8cd2. Also Izabella Kaminska, "Cambridge Analytica Probe Finds No Evidence It Misused Data to Influence Brexit," *Financial Times*, October 8, 2020.
25. https://www.imf.org/en/News/Seminars/Conferences/2018/04/06/6th-statistics-forum.
26. For more discussion on the pros and cons of GDP statistics, see Diane Coyle, *GDP*, or David Pilling, *The Growth Delusion*.
27. Gillian Tett, "Productivity Paradox Deepens Fed's Rate Rise Dilemma," *Financial Times*, August 20, 2015. See also Gillian Tett, "The US Needs More Productivity, Not Jobs," *Foreign Policy*, December 15, 2016.
28. Rani Molla, "How Much Would You Pay for Facebook Without Ads?," *Vox*, April 11, 2018, https://www.vox.com/2018/4/11/17225328/facebook-ads-free-paid-service-mark-zuckerberg.
29. http://www.pnas.org/content/116/15/7250.
30. David Byrn and Carol Corrado, *Accounting for Innovations in Consumer Digital Services: It Still Matters*, FEDS Working Paper No. 2019-049, https://papers.ssrn.com/sol3/papers.cfm?abstract_id=3417745.
31. See https://www.imf.org/external/mmedia/view.aspx?vid=5970065079001. See also minutes from session V11: Is All for Good in the Digital Age from the Sixth IMF Statistical Forum hosted at https://www.imf.org/en/News/Seminars/Conferences/2018/04/06/6th-statistics-forum.
32. See https://www.aon.com/getmedia/60fbb49a-c7a5-4027-ba98-0553b29dc89f/Ponemon-Report-V24.aspx.
33. https://ownyourdata.foundation/.
34. See a TED presentation by Jennifer Zhu Scott at https://www.ted.com/talks/jennifer_zhu_scott_why_you_should_get_paid_for_your_data?language=en.
35. Molla, "How Much Would You Pay?"

36. See the interview I conducted with Randall Stephenson at the Knight Bagehot Dinner in New York in 2015, https://www.youtube.com/watch?v=ZiiR_GfQspc.

NINE: WFH
(or Why Do We Need an Office?)

1. Daniel Beunza, *Taking the Floor: Models, Morals, and Management in a Wall Street Trading Room*. (Princeton, NJ: Princeton University Press, 2019), p. 26.
2. Interview with the author.
3. Resnick, P. On Consensus and Humming in the IETF. Internet Engineering Task Force (IETF) Request for Comments: 7282 June 2014, https://tools.ietf.org/html/rfc7282.
4. Niels ten Oever, "Please Hum Now: Decision Making at the IETF," https://hackcur.io/please-hum-now/.
5. To watch this debate (that took place in the IETF101-TLS-20180319-1740 meeting on March 19, 2018), see: https://rb.gy/oe6g8o.
6. The 134 sessions that took place at the EITF meetings in March 2018 can all be viewed on YouTube. See https://rb.gy/1n2dq7 and then follow subsequent connected links to watch them.
7. https://www.sec.gov/Archives/edgar/data/1321655/000119312520230013/d904406ds1.htm.
8. J. A. English-Lueck, *cultures@siliconvalley*, 2nd edition (Redwood City, CA: Stanford University Press, 2017), p. 76.
9. Margaret Szymanski and Jack Whalen, eds., *Making Work Visible: Ethnographically Grounded Case Studies of Work Practice* (Cambridge, UK: Cambridge University Press, 2011), p. xxi.
10. Douglas K. Smith and Robert C. Alexander, *Fumbling the Future: How Xerox Invented, Then Ignored the First Personal Compute*r (Lincoln, NE: toExcel, 1999). p. 14.
11. Szymanski and Whalen, eds., *Making Work Visible*, p. 2.
12. Scott Hartley, *The Fuzzy and the Techie: Why the Liberal Arts Will Rule the Digital World* (New York: Houghton Mifflin Harcourt, 2017).
13. Szymanski and Whalen, eds., *Making Work Visible* , p. xxii.
14. Julian Orr, *Talking About Machines: The Ethnography of a Modern Job* (Ithaca, NY: ILR/Cornell Press, 1996), p. 7.
15. Ibid., p. 18.
16. Ibid., p. 39–42.
17. Szymanski and Whalen, *Making Work Visible*, p. 28.
18. Orr, p. 45.
19. See Lucy Suchman, *Plans and Situated Actions: The Problem of Human*

Machine Communication (Cambridge University Press, 2007 (revised edition); first published 1987). Also see Szymanski and Whalen, *Making Work Visible*, pp. 21–33.

20. Suchman, *Plans*, pp. 121–64.
21. Ibid., pp. 130, 131.
22. Edwin Hutchins, *Cognition in the Wild* (Cambridge, MA: MIT Press, 1996). See also http://pages.ucsd.edu/~ehutchins/citw.html.
23. The 1985 memo which PARC published, based on Suchman's PhD dissertation, can be found at https://pdfs.semanticscholar.org/532a/52efca3bdb576d993c0dc53f075f172c1b07.pdf. For a full account of the research, see Suchman, *Plans and Situated Actions* .
24. http://pages.ucsd.edu/~ehutchins/citw.html.
25. See Karl E. Wieck. Sensemaking in Organizations (Thousand Oaks, CA: Sage Publications, 1995).
26. Szymanski and Whalen, *Making Work Visible*, p. xxiii.
27. Douglas K. Smith and Robert C. Alexander, *Fumbling the Future*, pp. 241–54.
28. For an example of how sense-making ideas crept into consumer research, see Christian Madsbjerg, *Sensemaking: The Power of the Humanities in the Age of the Algorithm* (New York: Hachette Books, 2017).
29. Patricia Ensworth, "Anthropologist as IT Trouble Shooter," in Rita Denny and Patricia Sunderland, eds., *Handbook of Anthropology in Business* (Abingdon, UK: Routledge, 2013), p 202–22.
30. Interview with the author.
31. Ensworth, p. 204.
32. For another studies showing why social patterns inside IT departments at global companies matter (in finance and elsewhere) see Sareeta Amrute, *Encoding Race, Encoding Class: Indian IT Workers in Berlin* (Durham, NC: Duke University Press, 2016); on the tribalism of Russian programmers, see Mario Biagioli and Vincent Antonin Lépinay, eds. *From Russia with Code: Programming Migrations in Post-Soviet Times* (Durham, NC: Duke University Press, 2019).
33. Ensworth, p. 219.
34. Beunza, *Taking the Floor*, pp. 21, 22.
35. Donald MacKenzie, *An Engine, Not a Camera: How Financial Models Shape Markets* (Cambridge, MA: MIT Press, 2008).
36. MacKenzie's important arguments here are also fleshed out in Donald MacKenzie and Taylor Spears, "'The Formula That Killed Wall Street': The Gaussian Copula and Modelling Practices in Investing Banking," *Social Studies of Science* 44, no. 3 (June 2014): pp. 393–417. See also Donald MacKenzie, *Material Markets: How Economic Agents Are Constructed* (London: Oxford University Press, 2009).

37. Douglas Holmes, *An Economy of Words: Communicative Imperatives in Central Banks* (University of Chicago Press, 2013). This argument is echoed in Annelise Riles, *Financial Citizenship: Experts, Publics and the Politics of Central Banking* (Cornell University Press, 2018), and variants of this point can also be seen in books such as Paul Tucker, *Unelected Power: the Quest for Legitimacy in Central Banking and the Regulatory State* (Princeton, NJ: Princeton University Press, 2018), and from a historical perspective in Liaquat Ahmed, *Lords of Finance: The Bankers Who Broke the World* (New York: Penguin, 2009).
38. To see the role of psychology and emotion in markets see David Tuckett, *Minding the Markets: An Emotional View of Financial Instability* (London: Palgrave Macmillan, 2011).
39. For an excellent discussion of this, see also Robert Schiller, *Narrative Economics: How Stories Go Viral and Drive Major Economic Events* (Princeton, NJ: Princeton University Press, 2019).
40. Ho, *Liquidated*, pp. 77–82.
41. Chloe Evans, "Ethnographic Research in Remote Spaces: Overcoming Practical Obstacles and Embracing Change," EPIC, September 25 2020, https://www.epicpeople.org/ethnographic-research-in-remote-spaces-overcoming-practical-obstacles-and-embracing-change/.
42. Stuart Henshall, "Recalibrating UX Labs in the Covid-19 Era," EPIC, September 25, 2020, https://www.epicpeople.org/recalibrating-ux-labs-in-the-covid-19-era/.
43. See proceedings: https://www.systemicrisk.ac.uk/events/market-stability-social-distancing-and-future-trading-floors-after-covid-19. Also Gillian Tett, "Bankers Crave Return of In-Person Trading Floors," *Financial Times*, September 2020, https://www.cass.city.ac.uk/news-and-events/news/2020/september/returning-to-the-office-how-to-stay-connected-and-socially-distant.
44. https://www.ietf.org/media/documents/survey-planning-possible-online-meetings-responses.pdf.
45. Hartley, *The Fuzzy And The Techie*.

TEN: MORAL MONEY
(or What Really Drives Sustainability?)

1. "Noam Chomsky on America's Economic Suicide," interview with Laura Flanders, *GRITtv*, May 4, 2012, www.alternet.org. See also https://chomsky.info/20120504/.
2. Anjli Raval, "New BP Boss Bernard Looney Pledges Net Zero Carbon Emissions by 2050," *Financial Times*, February 12, 2020; Lex, "BP" The Race to Zero," *Financial Times*, August 4, 2020; Gillian Tett, Billy Nauman, and

Anjli Raval, "Moral Money in Depth with Bernard Looney," *Financial Times*, May 13, 2020. For a good summary of the uncertainty about whether BP can hit its targets, see https://www.climateandcapitalmedia.com/does-bp-finally-get-it/.

3. Interview with the author.
4. Mike Isaac, "Mark Zuckerberg's Great American Road Trip," *New York Times*, May 25, 2017; Adam Lashinksy, "Mark Zuckerberg's Good Idea," *Fortune*, May 26, 2017; Reid J. Epstein and Deepa Seetharaman, "Mark Zuckerberg Hits the Road to Meet Regular Folks-with a Few Conditions," *Wall Street Journal*, July 12, 2017.
5. "Noam Chomsky on America's Economic Suicide."
6. Peter Kurie, *In Chocolate We Trust: The Hershey Company Town Unwrapped* (Philadelphia: University of Pennsylvania Press, 2018).
7. Gillian Tett, "Impact Investing for Good and Market Returns," *Financial Times*, December 14, 2017.
8. Gillian Tett, "Davos Man's Faith in Globalization Is Shaken," *Financial Times*, March 7, 2013; Gillian Tett, "Davos Man Has No Clothes," *Foreign Policy*, January 16, 2017.
9. The theory of VUCA is laid out in books such as *Strategic Leadership Primer* (Department of Command, Leadership and Management, United States Army War College, 1998), https://apps.dtic.mil/dtic/tr/fulltext/u2/a430467.pdf.
10. See https://www.edelman.com/research or Gillian Tett, "Should We Trust Our Fellow App Users More Than Politicians?," *Financial Times*, November 2017.
11. See, for example, Ronald Cohen, *Impact: Reshaping Capitalism to Drive Real Change* (London: Ebury Press, 2020).
12. "Moral Money" was a team effort. I dreamed it up with Andrew Edgecliffe-Johnson and built it with Billy Nauman, Patrick Temple-West, Kristen Talman, Tamami Shimizuishi, and Emiliya Mychasuk.
13. "Business Roundtable Redefines the Purpose of a Corporation to Promote 'An Economy That Serves All Americans,'" https://opportunity.businessroundtable.org/ourcommitment/.
14. Lucian Bebchuk and Roberto Tallarita, "Stakeholder Capitalism Seems Mostly for Show," *Wall Street Journal*, August 6, 2020.
15. To understand Bourdieu's concept of the doxa, look at Pierre Bourdieu, *Outline of a Theory of Practice* (Cambridge, UK: Cambridge University Press, 1987; first edition 1977), pp. 159–71.
16. *Exploring Sustainable Investing in a Changing World: Responsible Investing*, special report from BNY Mellon, September 2020.
17. Interview with Anne Finucane by Gillian Tett for Davos Goals House, January 2020, https://we.tl/t-CEaJjLDbNT.

18. Interview of Larry Fink by Gillian Tett for British American Business Taskforce, November 16, 2020, https://www.youtube.com/watch?v=PPjB1vwxjso.
19. "Businesses Plan Major Operational Changes as They Prioritize Resilience," *HSBC Navigator*, July 21, 2020, press release.
20. Nicholas Copeland and Christine Labuski, *The World of Walmart: Discounting the American Dream* (Abingdon, UK: Routledge, 2013), p. 3.
21. Ibid., p. 5.
22. Gillian Tett, Andrew Edgecliffe-Johnson, Kristen Talman, and Patrick Temple-West, "Walmart's Sustainability Chief: 'You Can't Separate Environmental, Social and Economic Success,'" *Financial Times*, July 17, 2020.
23. Knut Christian Myhre and Douglas R. Holmes, "Great Expectations: How the Norwegian Sovereign Wealth Fund Is Re-Purposing Corporations in a Time of Crisis," forthcoming research paper, 2020.
24. Knut Christian Myhre, "COVID-19, Dugnad and Productive Incompleteness: Volunteer Labor and Crisis Loans in Norway," *Social Anthropology/ Anthropologie Sociale* 28, no. 2 (2020): 326–27.

CONCLUSION: AMAZON TO AMAZON
(or What If We All Thought Like Anthropologists?)

1. See https://anatomyof.ai. Also Kate Crawford, *Atlas of AI: Power, Politics and the Planetary Costs of Artifical Intelligence* (New Haven, CT: Yale University Press, 2021).
2. https://www.moma.org/collection/works/401279.
3. https://read.dukeupress.edu/poetics-today/article-abstract/36/3/151/21143/Art-as-Device?redirectedFrom=fulltext
4. Mary L. Gray and Suri Siddharth, *Ghost Work: How to Stop Silicon Valley from Building a New Global Underclass* (Boston: Mariner, 2019).
5. https://www.thetimes.co.uk/article/amazon-admits-plan-for-workers-cage-was-bad-idea-dnndtvvxt and https://www.cbsnews.com/news/amazons-patent-for-caging-workers-was-a-bad-idea-exec-admits/.
6. Axel Leijonhufvud, *Life Among the Econ* (first published: September 1973), https://doi.org/10.1111/j.1465-7295.1973.tb01065.x.
7. For an example of how to rethink economics, see https://core-econ.org/the-economy, or for an example of the ANU project run by Bell, see https://3ainstitute.org/. See also projects at groups such as the Santa Institute, https://www.complexityexplorer.org/. See also the Building Forward report from the Bennett Institute, Cambridge University. https://www.bennettinstitute.cam.ac.uk.
8. Beunza, *Taking the Floor*.
9. This point is clearly laid out in Karen Ho, *Liquidated; An Ethnography of Wall Street*.

10. See J. A. English-Lueck, *cultures@siliconvalley.*
11. The dangers of failing to see how AI programs can embed and intensify bias and racism is laid out in Virginia Eubanks, *Automating Inequality: How High-Tech Tools Profile, Police and Punish the Poor* (London: St Martin's Press, 2018). See also Cathy O'Neill. *Weapons of Math Destruction: How Big Data Increased Inequality and Threatens Democracy* (New York: Crown, 2017), or Shoshana Zuboff, *The Age of Surveillance Capitalism: The Fight for a Human Future at the New Frontier of Power* (New York: Profile Books, 2019).
12. To understand this, see works like Annelise Riles, *Collateral Knowledge: Legal Reasoning in the Global Financial Markets* (Chicago: University of Chicago Press, 2011).
13. Tomas Hylland Erikson, *Small Places, Large Issues: An Introduction to Social and Cultural Anthropology* . Fouth Edition. (London: Pluto Press, 2015. First published 1995).
14. https://wiser.directory/organization/ziyodullo-shahidi-international-foundation/.
15. Ann Pendleton-Julian and John Seely Brown, *Design Unbound: Designing for Emergence in a White Water World* (Cambridge, MA: MIT Press, 2018).

POSTSCRIPT: A LETTER TO ANTHROPOLOGISTS

1. Ulf Hannerz, *Anthropology's World: Life in a Twenty-First Century Discipline* (London: Pluto Press, 2010).
2. Keith Hart, "Why Is Anthropology Not a Public Science?," http://thememorybank.co.uk/2013/11/14/why-is-anthropology-not-a-public-science/, 2013.
3. Paul Farmer, *Fevers, Feuds and Diamonds*, p. 511. Also Adia Benton, *Ebola at a Distance.*
4. https://www.anthropology-news.org/index.php/2020/10/26/raising-our-voices-in-2020/.
5. https://www.nationalacademies.org/our-work/societal-experts-action-network.

BIBLIOGRAPHY

The bibliography below is not intended to be a comprehensive list of my sources; the notes provide that. Instead it aims to answer a question that I am often asked by nonacademics: what can I read to find out about anthropology? I often direct people to the *Sapiens* website or the podcast *This Anthro Life* for a taste, and avoid citing academic papers, since these tend to be dense. Another brief, but brilliant introduction is Wade Davis's essay "Why Anthropology Matters" in *Scientific American* in February 2021. (https://www.scientificamerican.com/article/why-anthropology-matters/. The list below excludes some sources that academic anthropologists value. But for the layperson looking for books, consider these; they are merely a start.

TO GET A GENERAL SENSE OF CULTURAL/SOCIAL ANTHROPOLOGY FOR THE LAY PERSON TRY:

Matthew Engelke. *Think Like an Anthropologist* (London: Pelican, 2017).

Charles King. *Gods of the Upper Air: How a Circle of Renegade Anthropologists Reinvented Race, Sex and Gender in the Twentieth Century* (New York: Doubleday, 2019).

Thomas Hylland Eriksen. *Small Places, Large Issues; An Introduction to Social and Cultural Anthropology*, 4th edition (London: Pluto Press. 2015).

Jeremy MacClancy, ed. *Exotic No More; Anthropology for the Contemporary World.* 2nd edition (Chicago: University of Chicago Press. 2019).

Ulf Hannerz. *Anthropology's World. Life in a Twenty-First Century Discipline* (London: Pluto Press, 2010).

ON PHYSICAL ANTHROPOLOGY TRY:

Joseph Henrich. *The Weirdest People in the World: How the West Became Psychologically Peculiar and Particularly Prosperous* (London: Allen Lane, 2020).

Robin Dunbar. *Human Evolution* (London: Pelican, 2014).

Jared Diamond. *Guns, Germs and Steel: The Fate of Human Societies* (New York: W. W. Norton, 1999).

Jared Diamond. *Collapse: How Societies Choose to Fail or Succeed* (London: Penguin, 2011).

Yuval Noah Harari. *Sapiens: A Brief History of Humankind* (New York: Harper, 2011).

FOR GENERAL BOOKS ON CORPORATE ANTHROPOLOGY TRY:

Simon Roberts. *The Power of Not Thinking: How Our Bodies Learn and Why We Should Trust Them* (London: 535 Press, 2020).

Christian Madsbjerg. *Sensemaking: The Power of the Humanities in the Age of the Algorithm* (New York: Hachette, 2017.)

Christian Madsbjerg and Mikkel Rasmussen. *The Moment of Clarity: Using the Human Sciences to Solve Your Toughest Business Problems* (Boston: MA: Harvard Business Review Press, 2014).

Gary P. Ferraro and Elizabeth K. Briody. *The Cultural Dimension of Global Business* (Abingdon, UK: Routledge, 2012).

Mario Moussa, Derek Newberry, and Gregory Urban. *The Culture Puzzle: Harnessing the Forces That Drive Your Organization's Success* (Oakland, CA: Berrett-Koehle, 2021).

Rita Denny and Patricia Sunderland, ed. *Handbook of Anthropology in Business* (Abingdon, UK: Left Coast Press, 2014).

ON ANTHROPOLOGY AND FINANCE SEE:

Daniel Beunza. *Taking The Floor. Models, Morals and Management in a Wall Street Trading Room* (Princeton, NJ: Princeton University Press, 2019).

Karen Ho, *Liquidated; An Ethnography of Wall Street* (Durham, NC: Duke University Press, 2009).

Annelise Riles, *Collateral Knowledge: Legal Reasoning in the Global Financial Markets* (Chicago: University of Chicago Press, 2011).

Daniel Scott Souleles. *Songs of Profit, Songs of Loss: Private Equity, Wealth and Inequality* (Lincoln, NE: Nebraska University Press, 2019).

Viviana A Rotman Zeliser. *Morals and Markets: The Development of Life Insurance in the United States* (New York: Columbia University Press, 1979).

Caitlin Zaloom, *Out of the Pits: Traders and Technology from Chicago to London* (Chicago: University of Chicago Press, 2006).

David Tuckett. *Minding the Markets. An Emotional Finance View of Financial Instability* (New York: Palgrave MacMillan, 2011).

Melissa Fisher *Wall Street Women* (Durham, NC: Duke University Press, 2012).

Vincent Antonin Lepinay. *Codes of Finance; Engineering Derivatives in a Global Bank* (Princeton, NJ: Princeton University Press, 2011).

ON ANTHROPOLOGY AND ECONOMICS SEE:

Felix Martin. *Money: The Unauthorized Biography* (London: Bodley Head, 2013).

Chris Hann and Keith Hart, *Economic Anthropology: History, Ethnography, Critique* (Cambridge, UK: Polity, 2011).

Douglas R. Holmes. *Economy of Words: Communicative Imperatives in Central Banks* (Chicago: University of Chicago Press, 2014).

Michael Chibnik. *Anthropology, Economics, and Choice* (Austin, TX: University of Texas Press, 2011).

David Graeber. *Debt: The First 5,000 Years* (Brooklyn: Melville House, 2011).

Stephen Gudeman, *Anthropology and Economy* (Cambridge, UK: Cambridge University Press, 2016).

Nigel Dodd. *The Social Life of Money* (Princeton, NJ: Princeton University Press, 2014).

Caitlin Zaloom. *Indebted: How Families Make College Work at Any Cost* (Princeton, NJ: Princeton University Press, 2019).

ON ANTHROPOLOGY AND CONSUMER CULTURE SEE:

Patricia Sunderland and Rita Denny, ed. *Doing Anthropology in Consumer Research* (Abingdon, UK: Left Coast Press, 2007).

Timothy de Waal Malefyt and Robert J. Morais, *Advertising and Anthropology: Ethnographic Practice and Cultural Perspectives* (Abingdon, UK: Berg, 2012.)

Timothy de Waal Malefyt and Maryann McCabe, ed. *Women, Consumption and Paradox* (Abingdon, UK: Routledge, 2020).

David Howes, ed. *Cross-Cultural Consumption: Global Markets, Local Realities* (Abingdon, UK: Routledge, 1996).

Clifford Geertz. *The Interpretation of Cultures* (New York: Basic Books, 1973).

Grant McCracken. *Culture and Consumption*, 2nd ed. (Bloomington, IN: Indiana University Press, 2005),

Grant McCracken. *Culturematic: How Reality TV, John Cheever, a Pie Lab, Julia Child, Fantasy Football, Burning Man, the Ford Fiesta Movement, Rube Goldberg, NFL Films, Wordle, Two and a Half Men, a 10,000-Year Symphony, and ROFLCon Memes Will Help You Create and Execute Breakthrough Ideas* (Boston, MA: Harvard Business Review Press, 2012).

ON COVID-19, EBOLA, AND MEDICAL ANTHROPOLOGY SEE:

Paul Farmer. *Fevers, Feuds, and Diamonds: Ebola and the Ravages of History* (New York: Farrar Straus and Giroux, 2020).

Paul Richards. *Ebola; How a People's Science Helped End an Epidemic* (London: Zed Books, 2016).

Susan Shepler and Catherine Bolten. "Producing Ebola: Creating Knowledge In and About an Epidemic." *Anthropological Quarterly* 90, no. 2 (February 2017): 355–74. (Project: Special Issue of *Anthropological Quarterly* on Production of Knowledge About Ebola.)

Mary Douglas and Aaron Wildavsky. *Risk and Culture: An Essay on the Selection of Technological and Environmental Dangers* (Oakland, CA: University of California Press, 1983).

Mary Douglas. *Purity and Danger: An Analysis of the Concepts of Pollution and Taboo* (Abingdon, UK: Routledge, 1984).

ON ANTHROPOLOGY AND TECH SEE:

Mary L. Gray and Siddharth Suri. *Ghost Work; How to Stop Silicon Valley from Building a Global Underclass* (New York: Houghton Mifflin Harcourt, 2019).

danah boyd. *It's Complicated: The Social Lives of Networked Teens* (New Haven, CT: Yale University Press, 2015).

Virginia Eubanks. *Automating Inequality: How High-Tech Tools Profile, Police, and Punish the Poor* (London: Picador, 2019).

Sareeta Amrute. *Encoding Race, Encoding Class: Indian IT Workers in Berlin* (Durham, NC: Duke University Press, 2016).

J. A. English-Lueck. *Cultures@SiliconValley;* 2nd ed. (Oakland, CA: Stanford University Press, 2017).

Julian Orr. *Talking About Machines: An Ethnography of a Modern Job* (Ithaca, NY: ILR Press, 1996).

Lucy Suchman. *Human-Machine Reconfigurations: Plans and Situated Actions*, revised edition. (New York: Cambridge University Press, 2007).

Edwin Hutchins. *Cognition in the Wild* (Cambridge, MA: Bradford Books, 1996).

INDEX

ABOUT THE AUTHOR

GILLIAN TETT chairs the editorial board, US, for the *Financial Times* and writes columns for the world's leading newspaper covering finance, business, and the political economy. She has been named British Journalist of the Year, Columnist of the Year, and Business Journalist of the Year in the UK and won two Society for Advancing Business Editing and Writing awards in the US. She speaks regularly at conferences around the world on finance and global markets and has a PhD in social anthropology from Cambridge University. Tett is the author of *Saving the Sun: How Wall Street Mavericks Shook Up Japan's Financial World and Made Billions*, *Fool's Gold: The Inside Story of J.P. Morgan and How Wall St. Greed Corrupted Its Bold Dream and Created a Financial Catastrophe*, and *The Silo Effect: The Peril of Expertise and the Promise of Breaking Down Barriers.*